✄ MELTING-POT MODERNISM

MELTING-POT
MODERNISM

SARAH WILSON

CORNELL UNIVERSITY PRESS
Ithaca and London

First published 2010 by Cornell University Press

Printed in the United States of America

Library of Congress Cataloging-in-Publication Data

Wilson, Sarah, 1973–
    Melting-pot modernism / Sarah Wilson.
        p. cm.
    Includes bibliographical references and index.
    ISBN 978-0-8014-4816-4 (cloth : alk. paper)
  1. American literature—20th century—History and
criticism.   2. Assimilation (Sociology) in literature.
3. Acculturation in literature.   4. Emigration and
immigration in literature.   5. Modernism (Literature)—
United States.   6. Americanization—History—
20th century.   I. Title.
    PS228.A82W55   2010
    810.9'3552—dc22   2010003024

Cornell University Press strives to use environmentally
responsible suppliers and materials to the fullest extent
possible in the publishing of its books. Such materials
include vegetable-based, low-VOC inks and acid-free
papers that are recycled, totally chlorine-free, or partly
composed of nonwood fibers. For further information,
visit our website at www.cornellpress.cornell.edu.

Cloth printing   10 9 8 7 6 5 4 3 2 1

For Mark

❧ CONTENTS

❧ Acknowledgments

I have been working on this book for so long, I can hardly number the people who have helped me with it. Still: for guidance and inspiration from the very beginning, I'd like to thank Robert Ferguson, Ann Douglas, Bob O'Meally, Elizabeth Blackmar, Ross Posnock, Josh Goren, Ilyon Woo, and Lori Harrison-Kahan. I've been lucky to find excellent readers in Toronto and beyond: for patience and great ideas, thanks to Alan Ackerman, Andrea Most, and Jonathan Warren; Nancy Bentley, Mary Chapman, Rosanne Currarino, Dana Dragunoiu, Mary Esteve, Jonathan Freedman, Darren Gobert, Eric Haralson, Jean Lutes, and Alice Maurice. And for much-needed advice, thanks to Priscilla Wald, Michael Elliott, Michael Cobb, Paul Downes, Melba Cuddy-Keane, Deak Nabers, and Walter Benn Michaels. I am also very grateful for the heroic efforts of Peter Potter and Candace Akins at Cornell University Press. Many thanks to my family for their support, particularly to Julie (and Bruno) for giving me the time to revise the manuscript last winter. Finally, my greatest (and luckiest) debt is recognized in the dedication.

❧ MELTING-POT MODERNISM

Introduction
"A Form which Makes the Intelligible Answer Recede"

DAVID

{ *Prophetically exalted by the spectacle [of New York City].* }
It is the fires of God round His Crucible.
{ *He drops [Vera's] hand and points downward.* }
There she lies, the great Melting-Pot—listen! Can't
you hear the roaring and the bubbling? There gapes
her mouth
{ *He points east.* }
—the harbor where a thousand mammoth feeders
come from the ends of the world to pour in their
human freight. Ah, what a stirring and seething! Celt
and Latin, Slav and Teuton, Greek and Syrian,—black
and yellow—

VERA

{ *Softly, nestling to him.* }
Jew and Gentile—

DAVID

Yes, East and West, and North and South, the palm
and the pine, the pole and the equator, the crescent
and the cross—how the great Alchemist melts and
fuses them with his purging flame!

—Israel Zangwill, *The Melting-Pot* (1914)

It is a drama that goes on, without a pause, day by day
and year by year, this visible act of ingurgitation on the
part of our body politic and social, and constituting
really an appeal to amazement beyond that of any
sword-swallowing or fire-swallowing of the circus. . . .
I think indeed that the simplest account of the action
of Ellis Island on the spirit of any sensitive citizen who
may have happened to "look in" is that he comes
back from his visit not at all the same person that he
went. He has eaten of the tree of knowledge, and the
taste will be for ever in his mouth. He had thought
he knew before, thought he had the sense of the
degree in which it is his American fate to share the
sanctity of his American consciousness, the intimacy
of his American patriotism, with the inconceivable

1

alien; but the truth had never come home to him with
any such force. In the lurid light projected upon it by
those courts of dismay it shakes him—or I like at least
to imagine it shakes him—to the depths of his being;
I like to think of him, I positively *have* to think of him,
as going about ever afterwards with a new look, for
those who can see it, in his face, the outward sign of
a new chill in his heart.

—Henry James, *The American Scene* (1907)

Immigration both transfixed and transformed
the United States at the turn of the twentieth century and during the several
decades that followed. In 1905, as Henry James chronicled his return to the
United States, the number of immigrants exceeded one million per year for
the first time in the nation's history; between 1891 and 1920, over 18 million
foreign-born migrants entered the United States.[1] The effects of this massive
immigration were observed, recorded, and widely discussed, in the United
States and elsewhere: a governmental commission assigned to investigate
the immigration "problem" published more than forty volumes of findings
on the question, for instance.[2] According to Mary Antin, a Russian Jewish
immigrant, the question of immigration was so pressing by the turn of the
twentieth century that "we [Americans] called an army of experts in con-
sultation, and the din of their elaborate discussions has filled our ears ever
since.... [We] have suffered ourselves to be guided by the conflicting reports
of commissions and committees, anthropologists, economists, and statisticians,
policy-mongers, calamity-howlers, and self-announced prophets."[3] Rather
than mastering the problem, this cacophony of expertise instead mimicked
the multiplicity of voices that immigration released into the United States.
Melting-Pot Modernism examines a series of innovative literary texts and techniques that intervened in this cacophony. As I will show, a version of assimilation imagined as cultural fusion fired the imaginations of a select group of
writers and intellectuals at the turn of the century. This version of assimilation, profoundly informed by literary modes of thought, manifests itself in the
early stirrings of U.S. modernism. Drawing on this literary turn, *Melting-Pot
Modernism* proposes to put a freshly literary mode of analysis in the service
of cultural history.

Melting Pots

Not every turn-of-the-century response to immigration recognized the need
for a new approach to the topic: responses differed widely, ranging across

a variety of spectrums. Nativist arguments, for example, largely opposed immigration, on the basis of native-born superiority. (These arguments, best chronicled by the historian John Higham in *Strangers in the Land,* lie beyond my purview here.) Those who speculated about immigrant *assimilation,* or the incorporation of immigrants into the United States, adopted a range of contrasting views. Vida Scudder's *A Listener in Babel* (1903), a little-known novel of the immigration crisis, stages this conversation instructively. Scudder's protagonist, new to settlement house work, listens to her peers discuss possible responses to immigration: one proposes indoctrinating immigrants through the school system (exemplifying the Anglo-conformity or *Americanization* position); another proposes reconceiving of the United States as a collection of culturally different communities united by political bonds (the *cultural pluralism* position); the third articulates a position best described as a *melting-pot* position: "if we ignore the wealth of traditions which our emigrants bring us, we ignore still more their creative powers.... Wouldn't [Anglo-American] civilization profit from the gifts of other races, less competent in action, it may be, but with more aptitude for emotion and dream?"[4] For Scudder's proponent of melting-pot assimilation, immigration becomes an occasion to foreground the value of creativity and imagination; it makes possible a figurative exchange of "gifts." According to the set of ideas drawn upon by this interlocutor, the melting pot represents a process through whose action both individuals and cultures would be made flexible, multiple, and continually changing.

More famously, Israel Zangwill's play *The Melting-Pot* popularized a process that, he specified, differed from "simple surrender to the dominant type, as is popularly supposed." Instead, in a turn of phrase that leans heavily on the hyphen, Zangwill asserted that the melting pot signifies "an all-around give-and-take."[5] In 1913 the influential sociologist Robert E. Park defined assimilation along similar lines, as "a process that goes on in society by which individuals spontaneously acquire one another's language, characteristic attitudes, habits, and modes of behavior."[6] This book extends Zangwill's and Park's theories to recognize the melting pot as a modern episteme, one that in its moment provided a signal location for theorizing novelty, change, and difference. This cluster of ideas represents an important antecedent to contemporary theories of both the self and the text. That is, I agree with James Livingston that "the increasingly 'postmodern' sensibility of our time is in fact predicated on the rediscovery of turn-of-the-century intellectual and cultural agendas," but (unlike Livingston) I see those agendas as emerging principally from the radical changes entailed by immigration and migration.[7]

Melting-pot ideas emphasized assimilation as a broad-ranging process of intellectual integration of difference—one undergone by both immigrants and native-born, and signifying first of all in aesthetic and philosophical terms. Walter Lippmann understood immigration in these terms when, in his major articulation of Progressive-era anxiety, *Drift and Mastery* (1914), he asserted that "All of us are immigrants spiritually."[8] Analyzing the "spiritual" dimension in which Lippmann saw immigration penetrating American society, this book follows Werner Sollors and Philip Gleason in understanding the melting-pot idea as first and foremost a discursive phenomenon.[9] For better and for worse, Progressive-era melting-pot thinking emerged from literary idioms, and then turned back to them to solve its political and philosophical problems. To avoid the ideological pitfalls of ideas of both static difference and totalizing homogenization, melting-pot thinkers turned for a model to the oscillation between similarity and difference that they saw in literature and art, and imagined a similar oscillation structuring the process of assimilation.[10] Literary artists of the era similarly conceived of the aesthetic as a means of evading pat identifications. Because literary uses of language promote both salutary and disturbing slippages of meaning—and melting-pot ideas exploited these slippages particularly cannily—a full intellectual history requires special attention to the operations of language. Reading the literary and philosophical resonances of melting-pot versions of assimilation, *Melting-Pot Modernism* fills the need for a history attuned to the literary and imaginative dimensions of immigration and assimilation.

For Henry James, in the absence of an "intelligible answer" to the question posed by immigration, the "form" of the question took on increased significance.[11] This shifting of attention is typical of the literary engagements I consider here. Absent a straightforward answer, James approaches the question through synecdoche, shifting the analysis to a feature of the question. This literary approach does not promise speedier resolution, but it does expand the ways in which the question might be approached, multiplying the productive avenues of inquiry. *Melting-Pot Modernism* takes this shift seriously, considering literary maneuvers in their own terms, in order to gauge their particular (and too-often overlooked) effects. James's description of the scene of immigration, quoted above, sees the form of the question as homologous with the form of the self: shaken "to the depths of his being," the native-born observer registers those depths in a "new look." This look registers "in his face"—not "on" his face, as we might imagine a shaved beard, or even a fleeting expression, but "in," as if features have been subtly rearranged: the form of the face seems changed. The "outward sign" telegraphs the inward state, and it is there to be read by those who know how, just as it is in James's formally complex novels. This study relies on such homologies—and metonymies, and metaphors—not only because they constitute the dominant idiom of the melting pot but also because they provide an opportunity for critical connection-making that is as flexible and expansive as the social connection-making envisioned by melting-pot thinkers.

As in the Jamesian reflections above, the literary framing of assimilation by melting-pot thinkers resulted in ideas of *form* playing a central role in many melting-pot theories. As Lewis Hine's famous photograph of an Italian immigrant on New York's Lower East Side (fig. 1) suggests, immigration and assimilation posed significant interpretive challenges at the level of outward signs: here, an immigrant woman walks with an enormous bundle of garments balanced on her head. Her silhouette recalls the familiar ones of early twentieth-century American women, but, on the top, yields a confusing mess and partially obscured face. Unlike the conventional before-and-after photos that dramatized immigrant assimilation as a transition from "foreign" dress to American fashions, this photo exposes an in-between moment, in which associations (here, literally, garments, outfits) pile up on the foregrounded immigrant form. The baggage of immigration, along with the rag-picking and push-carting of new-world employment, transformed human figures, producing challenging, sometimes uncomfortable shapes. Hine's photograph dramatizes the "bundles" that figured so prominently in contemporaneous descriptions of immigrant silhouettes, scripting a new kind of urban encounter with unfamiliar forms.

At even closer inspection, immigration produced an almost chaotic fluidity of form: in Abraham Cahan's *Yekl* (1896), Jake (Yekl) observes his newly landed wife, Gitl, shifting shapes, the signs of her race, ethnicity, and gender grown suddenly discordant. Like Hine's photo, Cahan's scene emphasizes the role of perspective in effecting this transformation, thereby issuing a warning against confusing perceptual effects with literal change. *Melting-Pot Modernism* balances the ambitious claims of melting-pot theorists (that immigration and assimilation effected fundamental formal change) against warnings, such as these, that such transformations may be little more than perceptual tricks. I rely here on Matthew Jacobson's work, which has shown the immigration debates of the nineteenth and twentieth centuries to be engines of racial division and consolidation. (Jacobson's *Whiteness of a Different Color* shows that post-1840 immigration debates solidified apparently fluid "races" into the hegemonic white "race" later implied by ethnicity; his *Barbarian Virtues* further demonstrates the imaginative intertwining of disdain and desire in responses to U.S. immigration and imperialism at the turn of the century.) Gary Gerstle's *American Crucible* more particularly shows U.S. rhetorics of

Figure 1. Lewis Hine, *Italian Immigrant, East Side, New York City,* 1910. Courtesy of the Library of Congress.

inclusion (such as melting-pot discourse) to be premised upon, reliant on, and enabling of enduring American racial exclusions.[12] *Melting-Pot Modernism* departs from these important accounts of the discursive struggles over immigration by attending more closely to the texture of discourse (especially melting-pot rhetoric), in order to reveal its full complexity. In this I follow James Livingston, who associates such "forensic complexity" with a release from the "tragic renditions of the past which now regulate modern American historiography."[13]

As the melting-pot position articulated in Scudder's *A Listener in Babel* demonstrates, melting-pot ideas were hardly uncompromised by racism and cultural condescension: one can argue for the value of different cultural gifts while still believing that certain "races" are "less competent in action" or have "more aptitude for emotion and dream." These kinds of stereotypical perspectives are more common than not in melting-pot writing, and they are the perspectives that most easily serve in familiar critiques of the melting pot. While such critiques find their mark, they do not constitute the final word on the subject; they merely suggest the degree to which melting-pot thinking participated in the prejudices of its age, an age superbly documented by historians. Rather than focusing on these now well-recognized stereotypical perceptions, this book chooses instead to isolate and interrogate the aspects of melting-pot thinking whose ideological limitations are less patent. My aim here is in part to avoid duplicating the field-defining work of Jacobson and others; however, I also believe that because these traces of turn-of-the-century stereotyping are not unique to the melting pot, they constitute an imperfect basis for the analysis and critique of this idea. By attending to the more nuanced logics shared by a range of melting-pot perspectives, I aim to give a truer account of the ideological variability of the melting pot, as well as to produce a basis for criticism that moves beyond presentist judgment. That those who fashioned and employed the melting-pot model often fell short of their own articulated aspirations will, of course, be of concern to me. However, I see analyzing these aspirations as articulated and circulated as more valuable, especially in light of continuing contemporary aspirations to fashion difference-friendly discourses.[14]

Understanding the aspirations of those who employed the melting-pot model means, for the most part, understanding the social, political, and philosophical environment of turn-of-the-century U.S. Progressivism. Like their European counterparts, U.S. Progressives were a generation of social reformers who subscribed to a wide range of different beliefs. (Like the historian Philip Ethington, I consider Progressivism a "discursive environment... neither a discrete set of new policy goals, nor the expression of the interests of a particular social group... [but] a reorganization of the public sphere that enabled the pursuit of interests by groups and their leaders."[15]) The Progressive era (ca. 1889–1917) was "an era of shifting, ideologically fluid, issue-focused coalitions, all competing for the reshaping of American society," characterized by intervention into political, industrial, economic, educational, and social spheres.[16] Progressive writing reveals many of these reformers to be driven by anxiety that existing social, intellectual, and institutional forms were too rigid to accommodate the social changes they were witnessing.[17] A "chameleonic" discourse of social democracy, one that esteemed change and changeability in its conception of social, political, and economic forms, emerged as the broader context in which a similarly change-oriented response to immigration might be formulated.[18] This book brings the Progressive genealogy of modernism to light, and thereby expands our conceptions of what constitutes both Progressive and modernist literature.

Melting-pot discourse bears out the contradictory, contesting nature of Progressivism. *Melting-Pot Modernism* opens with epigraphs from Israel Zangwill and Henry James not only because these epigraphs signal the importance of immigration at the turn of the century but also because they indicate an important failure to agree on what, exactly, the melting pot entailed. Zangwill (and, in the sequence quoted above, his representative of melting-pot thinking, David Quixano) articulated a full and fierce embrace of cultural fusion, one that cast the cultural losses to the "purging flame" as an advance from conflict to harmony. James, whose reactions to immigration were considerably more ambivalent, saw "complete" assimilation as impossible; for him, the melting pot registers as an advance from harmony to more interesting conflict. Despite their utter disagreement, these are both melting-pot perspectives, to my mind, because they engage so seriously with assimilation—that is, with the radical change on all cultural fronts that characterized an age of immigration—and never conclusively write it off. In fact, the portrait of the melting pot that I will elaborate in *Melting-Pot Modernism* understands both the shared area of inquiry and the explicit lack of consensus between these figures to be characteristic of melting-pot thinking. It is my aim here to resist resolving these contradictions and inconsistencies into a neat picture; I insist on literary modes of expression in part because they do such a good job of resisting resolution. This literary non-resolution, like the melting pot, keeps juxtapositions of perspective in the foreground, even as it frustrates our urge to synthesize and conclude.

Modernism

All this is to say that this book is not a history of immigration, but a history of how a particular group of people *talked* about immigration, and the surprising literary origins and legacies of such talk. Reading early transitional U.S. modernist prose in its Progressive-era context, *Melting-Pot Modernism* makes a new connection between the ideological ferment of melting-pot discourse and the literary experimentation of high modernism. Daniel Joseph Singal argues that American modernism was constituted by a focus on "pluralistic integration" (which he associates with William James, John Dewey, and Franz Boas).[19] In a parallel gesture, Werner Sollors connects ethnic literature with quasi-modernist formal experimentalism.[20] *Melting-Pot Modernism* completes this circuit by illuminating the link connecting Singal and Sollors's positions. (Not surprisingly, there is no critical consensus on the question of modernism's relation to assimilation: Peter Nicholls's leading question, "Is it too much to say that [the] grounding of the aesthetic in an objectification of the other would constitute *the* recurring problem of the later modernisms?" suggests, *contra* Singal and in keeping with Walter Benn Michaels's argument in *Our America,* that modernist aesthetics in fact align more easily with nativism than with assimilation.[21]) As Progressive-era melting-pot discourse intertwined form with reform, an unlikely generation of literary modernists came to maturity. Reading formally experimental works by Henry James, James Weldon Johnson, Willa Cather, and Gertrude Stein *as* (and with) elaborations and interrogations of melting-pot thinking, I show American literary modernism and Progressive-era assimilation to be fundamentally intertwined.[22]

The full story of the polyglot ideological arena of the early twentieth century, or the modernism that evolved in it, has not been told, even by path-breaking studies such as Michaels's *Our America* (which uncovers the symmetrical logics of modernist pluralism and nativism) or Michael North's *The Dialect of Modernism* (which indicts the racial cross-identifications that fueled modernism). Melting-pot thinking did sample from pluralistic idioms and racial masks—but it mixed them with a multitude of other discourses. As a result, the melting pot comes closer to evoking the full ideological range and complexity of its era than do many other single ideological formations. *Melting-Pot Modernism,* in this sense, pursues an integrationist project akin to Ross Posnock's *Color and Culture,* but sketches the broader conversation (about theories of cultural sharing) into which Posnock's African American cosmopolitans fit. For my purposes, the figure of the melting pot intimates both the wide scope of this particular political discourse and the more general breadth of discursiveness, especially as evidenced by modernist literature. For this reason, I give closer attention to the texture of discourse than does even a literary history like *Terrible Honesty,* Ann Douglas's evocation of the cultural intersections and exchanges that constituted 1920s U.S. culture.[23] Literary uses of language advanced a range of melting-pot objectives that we risk missing without close reading.

As I will show, the early modernist prose of the United States centered on the challenge of *assimilating*—of enacting a suggestion of melting-pot dynamism within the actual form of expression. This prose takes up the task of transmuting the theatrical and autobiographical inclinations of melting-pot thinking into forms less transparently "natural" to them, understanding prose as the adopted and adapted country of melting-pot discourse. (Indeed, the free indirect discourse used by so many of these writers accomplishes something unavailable to traditional theatrical and autobiographical expression: it evokes a self beyond the immediately known self, some continuity and unity that is not transcendent, but rather, contingent.) Melting-pot modernist texts, in other words, produce polyglot formal effects akin to those produced by immigration in the turn-of-the-century United States: they do not so much aim to describe the melting pot as to inscribe its effects on their own forms. This process differs from the one narrated by Priscilla Wald in *Constituting Americans,* for melting-pot forms do not so much expose dissonance from an official national narrative as model a self constituted through resolutely unofficial pastiche.[24] The formal experiments I analyze do not instruct about difference; they embody difference. Because of the distinct reading experience they produce, formally experimental texts are indispensable to any intellectual history of the efforts to come to terms with difference in the United States.

By tracing formal experimentalism back to the turn of the century, and then pursuing the intellectual ferment of Progressivism through three decades of modernist experimentation by James, Johnson, Cather, and Stein, *Melting-Pot Modernism* recognizes the resonance of the idea of "form" in both traditional and non-traditional ways. Melting-pot modernists engaged with the multivalent and often unclear uses of the word "form" in melting-pot discourse, and crafted a program of literary-formal experimentalism that draws primarily on Aristotelian conceptions of form (as that which is essential, non-accidental, and dynamic). In this sense, "form" represents the arrangements by which we mark differences in the otherwise indistinguishable base stuff, or matter, common to all. In the unconventional structures of their works, as well as their generic and tonal fusions and syntactical peculiarities, these older American modernists drew attention to the flexibility and changeability of literary "arrangement."[25]

By recognizing and exploring this convergence of aesthetic experimentalism and social engagement, I aim, in Sara Blair's words, to "reconsider the political aspirations of modernist texts long canonized as hermetic literary machines, indifferent to social experience," by recovering "the fierce contests over the social meaning of the literary that themselves... constitute the real politics of Modernism—understood not only as engagement in particular movements but as a set of ongoing activities."[26] Thus when Henry James celebrates the novel's ability as "the most independent, most elastic, most prodigious of literary forms," he speaks a cognate language to that of Progressive reformer Jane Addams, who described the settlement Hull-House as an attempt "to focus and *give form*" to the social life of her immigrant neighborhood. (Addams insisted that the "one thing to be dreaded in the Settlement is that it lose its flexibility, its power of quick adaptation, its readiness to change its methods as its environment might demand."[27])

Gertrude Stein suggested as early as 1926 that such visions of form (or, in her terms, "composition") signified historically: "composition is the difference which makes each and all of them then different from other generations."[28] Melting-pot literary experimentalism does indeed emerge from a specific historical, even generational, experience. According to Horace Kallen, the idea of the melting pot was the central mythology of the generation before his own: "That the image of these United States as a 'melting-pot' might be a delusion and its imputed harmony with democracy a snare was not an idea which, prior to the Great War, seemed even possible to Americans."[29] (Kallen's own estrangement from both the melting pot and the pre-war years is patent here: his predecessors may not have conceived of delusions and snares, but he does.) The war often serves as a dividing line in considerations of Progressivism and modernism—usually with the effect of sealing them off from each other, each on a different side of the fundamental rupture. Older participants in the age, however, were not so lucky. Dewey, Addams, Stein, Cather, Johnson, even the aged James, were profoundly shaken by the war, and found themselves alternately defending, refashioning, and interrogating the ideas they had smuggled over a now heavily fortified historical border. They suddenly found themselves in the position of emigrants from a past age, bearing archaic cultural baggage.

In 1914, Ezra Pound (a contemporary of Kallen's, if also his ideological adversary) wrote to Harriet Monroe: "Personally I favour the assassination of all Americans over fifty, with the sole exception of Henry James."[30] Pound (born in 1885, so twenty-nine at the time) excelled at the theorization of modernism, and the violent rupture with the past that he advocates here is not unfamiliar. We must recognize, however, that the generation of Americans over fifty as Pound wrote represented the Progressive era of U.S. culture: Jane Addams, born in 1860, was fifty-four in 1914; the philosopher and educator John Dewey, born in 1859, was fifty-five; Ida B. Wells, the muckraking African American journalist and reformer, born in 1862, was fifty-two. The Progressive-era modernists considered in *Melting-Pot Modernism* teeter dangerously on Pound's generational boundary line: the always-exceptional Henry James was well over fifty at seventy-one in 1914 (b. April 15, 1843); James Weldon Johnson was forty-three (b. June 17, 1871), while Willa Cather and Gertrude Stein were both forty (b. December 7, 1873 and February 3, 1874). These writers, all born before the collapse of Reconstruction, came to intellectual maturity at least ten years before most of their modernist peers, at the very moment when Progressivism and the melting pot spoke most deeply to the imaginations of Americans. Their ages required them to navigate the border Kallen saw separating the prewar from the postwar (and separating enchantment by the melting pot from its revelation as a delusion), importing their Progressive-era preoccupations with them.

Responsive to the volatility of the times, Gertrude Stein observed that "any two years can make a generation," and that the only thing that makes a difference (or, in her words, "is any different") is "the historical fact that you are older or younger."[31] The melting-pot modernists all felt the difference produced by their proximity to Pound's generational dividing line. Johnson acted as the father figure of the modernist Harlem Renaissance. Cather wrote that the "world broke in two in 1922 or thereabouts," and that her writing would "have little interest for those under forty years of age."[32] Stein became a figure at which younger modernists, most notoriously Hemingway, tilted.[33] Together with James, these writers became "old" modernists, an ambivalent and contradictory position in a movement characterized by its pursuit of newness. In their own idiosyncratic ways, all the writers considered here looked back to their generation's nexus of ideas about immigration and assimilation. Yet over their careers and through their writings in multiple genres, these figures helped to make the melting pot new again, just as the melting pot helped to make their work new.

My discussion of this alternately collaborative and contesting literary dynamic will proceed as follows. Chapter One, "The Melting Pot: 'Assimilation to One Another,'" surveys the richness of contemporaneous discourse about the melting pot and introduces many of the questions explored more extensively in later chapters. My intention in this chapter is to balance the idiosyncratic nature of melting-pot ideas with a sense of the general disposition (and the areas of dispute) shared by most, if not all, melting-pot theories. I focus on identifying the shared patterns of melting-pot modern*ism* rather than on categorizing melting-pot modern*ists*. Rather than classifying thinkers or artists pro and con, I go along with the unclear allegiances of discourse, revealing the ways that melting-pot assumptions insinuated themselves into unexpected places.

Chapter Two uses Henry James's late writings to frame melting-pot modernism as a moment of formal speculation about the nature of selfhood. James also explicitly extends the formal flexibility theorized by melting-pot thinkers to the aesthetic realm; through his prefaces, the chapter shows, he constructs a theory of fiction that embeds melting-pot thinking in the foundations of American literary modernism, and thus constitutes the frame for considering the melting-pot modernists at issue in the following chapters. Chapter Three elaborates the problems of melting-pot subjectivity in coming to terms with the racial inequality and violence of the Progressive era: its central questions are ones of power and equity. Exploring James Weldon Johnson's insistence on putting questions of justice at the center of the communal bonds imagined by melting-pot assimilationists, the chapter considers whether Johnson's integrationism succeeded in imagining a way, in Eric Sundquist's terms, "that racial history may be at once memorialized and redeemed...[and] the values of hybridity...be measured stylistically and tonally as well as demographically."[34] Chapter Four turns to Willa Cather's novels to explore the logical, ethical, and aesthetic problems posed by melting-pot ideas of the past, especially as they emerge in discussions of inheritance, cultural "gifts," and cultural loss. Finally, Chapter Five reads Gertrude Stein's explorations of the logic of possessive individualism that infused melting-pot figures of circulating selves, cultures, and forms. In Stein's shift from fascination to frustration with market-based formulations of individual agency, the chapter finds hints of the ways mangled melting-pot thinking survived into the late twentieth century.

As a whole, *Melting-Pot Modernism* follows Progressive-influenced literary output over three decades, tracing the affinities and clashes of early modernists with melting-pot thinkers from Zangwill to Zitkala-Sa to Edward Bok to Jane Addams. This book emphasizes the literary and philosophical resonance of the melting pot, for the self-conscious turn to literary logics and devices animates this version of assimilation (and has too long escaped notice). Melting-pot literature for the most part has little interest in adversarial positions; instead, it uses semantic complication to penetrate more deeply into political and ethical conundrums. Accordingly, my analysis privileges probing that semantic complication. For although the melting pot failed to definitively answer the questions of its age, its literature still provides surprisingly nuanced models of the overlapping affiliations that can be brokered through language.

✍ CHAPTER 1

The Melting Pot

"Assimilation to One Another"

In 1915, the pragmatist philosopher John Dewey wrote to Horace Kallen that, although he "never did care for the melting pot metaphor," he did feel that "genuine assimilation to one another not to Anglo-Saxondom—seems to be essential to an American."[1] Dewey's ambivalence here is instructive. Despite his (and Kallen's) distaste for the metaphor, he uses the term "melting pot" to evoke "genuine assimilation," an assimilation distinctly "to one another" and "not to Anglo-Saxondom." This understanding of the term did not go without saying in the volatile teens: Dewey had to spell it out. Kallen had just published his famous critique of the melting pot, "Democracy *Versus* the Melting-Pot"; Dewey, for his part, was using the word "assimilation" to articulate a vision of social being resistant to *both* the repressive Americanization campaigns of the mid-teens *and* Kallen's vision of the separate "substance and form" of the "nationalities" making up the United States.[2] As I show in this chapter, Dewey's ambivalent attachment to the terms "assimilation" and "melting pot" was very much of his era—as, indeed, was his sense that the processes these terms denoted still required definition.

The melting pot does not seem so indefinite today; rather, it seems a closed story, an unfashionable concept, a version of repressive assimilation in the service of cultural homogenization.[3] In accepting this narrative, we have lost sight of both the reasons that compelled smart and sensitive thinkers like Dewey to argue in favor of the melting pot, and the equally important and complicated problems that Dewey and other melting-pot proponents identified (and sometimes missed) in the model. This chapter refuses the closed story and, instead, tracks the melting pot in all of its original elasticity and contradiction. The cluster of ideas that John Dewey defended as "genuine assimilation to one another" are as relevant and contentious today as they were in the teens; they have a great deal to teach us about the blind spots of more recent thinking about identity and social change. When contemporary literature depicts ethnicity in the United States as a complicated, never-pure state; when it approaches the self as a construction, put together from bits and pieces and exquisitely sensitive to environment; when it represents culture as mobile and malleable, it bespeaks an occluded but indubitable melting-pot lineage. Further, as scholars and critics increasingly seek to think across boundaries (of nationality, race, class, and geography, to name just a few) we would do well to reflect on the successes and failures of a much earlier attempt to think across boundaries. For all of these reasons, it is time for a nuanced and updated understanding of the melting pot.

Our current association of assimilation with cultural uniformity was secured by the ethnic revivals of the sixties; Nathan Glazer and Daniel P. Moynihan's *Beyond the Melting Pot* (1963) was most influential in casting the melting pot as a repressive (and ultimately unsuccessful) paradigm of assimilation.[4] But Horace Kallen was there as early as 1915, associating the melting pot with "the complete cutting-off of the ancestral memories of the American populations, the enforced, exclusive use of the English language and English and American history in the schools and in the daily life" (*CD*, 112). Clearly this repressive melting pot is no fantasy—indeed, it has a long and influential history. The famous World War I "melting-pot" graduation ceremony at the Ford Motor Company English School, for example, required immigrants to act out their abandonment of distinct ethnic origins for an undifferentiated "Americanness." In this drama workers wearing various national costumes processed from a steamship into the "Ford English School Melting Pot" and emerged all identically attired in "American clothes" and waving American flags.[5] Theodore Roosevelt, similarly, saw no inconsistency in enthusiastically supporting Israel Zangwill's play *The Melting-Pot* and equally enthusiastically denouncing "hyphenated" identities. Kallen's critique of this Americanizing use of the melting pot finds its mark. However, the ideology of Ford and Roosevelt represents only a partial portrait of the melting pot—the "Anglo-Saxondom" that John Dewey rejected for assimilation "to one another."

Despite their very different agendas, Ford and Kallen shared a totalizing vision of the melting pot, which has in turn set the terms of our contemporary understandings of it as a force of homogenization. This totalizing vision, however, misses the ways in which the melting-pot trope served equally as a force of mediation and moderation; it misses the way that, for a number of Progressive-era thinkers, the melting pot represented an indispensable means of imagining *alternatives* to the extremes of Anglo-conformity and cultural pluralism. There are two main reasons why, despite this alternative tradition, the "homogenization" narrative of the melting pot still enjoys undisputed critical dominance. First, as Kallen and Ford's unlikely alignment suggests, the Deweyan view of the melting pot was only ever a minority perspective. Ideas of "assimilation to one another" were not the most widely held ideas of their day, or even of the American Progressive movement.[6] (The ideas of Kallen and Ford, as well as many other popular Progressive-era responses to immigration, have received excellent treatments at the hands of other scholars, and so cannot be my central focus here.) Second, as opposed to the clearly defined vision offered by Kallen and Ford, the alternative melting pot consists of a diffuse and contradictory discursive tendency. The "genuine" assimilation that Dewey ambivalently associated with the melting pot was not even a proper "theory," so much as a congeries of ideas centered on a vivid figure and operating through literary means. These ideas were neither as popular nor as well defined as the familiar melting-pot narrative, but what they lacked in coherence they have made up in longevity. To fully understand the intellectual conflict over cultural mixture in the twentieth century—at its very beginnings, at its end, and even beyond—we must reopen Dewey and Kallen's debate. To that end, the following pages illuminate the long-misunderstood language of cultural sharing and changeability that Dewey associated with the melting pot.

Like Dewey himself, this melting pot stands at the intersection of two related intellectual movements, pragmatism and Progressivism. The idea bears the traces of both movements in its language and its arguments; indeed, melting-pot debates often served as conduits for ideas to pass from one movement to the other. Like both pragmatism and Progressivism, the melting-pot figure lent itself to unorthodox uses: Henry Pratt Fairchild, the notorious anti-immigrant sociologist and eugenicist, noted, "The figure was a clever one—picturesque, expressive, familiar, just the sort of thing to catch the popular fancy and lend itself to a thousand uses."[7] It was most popular at the beginning of the twentieth century, before the surge of anti-immigrant U.S. nationalism associated with the Great War. In this period of immigration and internal migrations, the mobility of the key concepts of assimilation and the melting pot mirrored that of many American populations. The nature of these processes was so contested that it is not unusual for "assimilation" or "the melting pot" to be used completely differently by different speakers (or even by the same speaker, sometimes).[8] When Henry Ford deployed the figure of the melting pot, for example, he used it very differently from Israel Zangwill, the playwright who popularized it. As Ralph Ellison writes in his essay "The Little Man at Chehaw Station":

> lest we ourselves forget, the melting-pot concept was never so simplistic or abstract as current arguments would have it.... Their [Americans of an earlier day] outlook was pragmatic, their way with culture vernacular, an eclectic mixing of modes... they improvised their culture as they did their politics and institutions—touch and go, by ear and by eye—fitting new form to new function, new function to old form.[9]

The improvisatory approach to culture that Ellison celebrates produces a tremendous rhetorical, formal, and intellectual jumble on the question of assimilation. This chapter traces the jumble, but it does not pretend to assimilate the many versions of melting-pot thinking to one reductive scheme. Writers who borrowed logics, tropes, and even phrases from one another were rarely in total agreement about the melting pot. Indeed, the melting pot interests me for precisely this reason: in Ellison's terms, it was a pragmatic, vernacular, improvisatory, eclectic, mixed discourse, one constituted more through disagreement than through consensus. Approached as such—that is, if we allow it the flexibility of its own contradictions and conflicts—it represents a signal instance of a *non*-homogenizing discourse. It thus represents a valuable model for contemporary thinkers concerned with building flexibility into theoretical discourses.

This Deweyan strain of melting-pot thinking did not always succeed at producing material political changes; rather, in line with Herbert Croly's prescription for American Progressivism, it attempted to issue "a deliberate, persistent, and... radical challenge to popular political prejudices and errors."[10] As one compelling alternative to the most outrageous prejudices of its day, the idea of the melting pot structured the social imaginations of a number of early twentieth-century U.S. intellectuals (and the literary imaginations of their peers). Thinkers like the activist Israel Zangwill, the sociologist Robert Park, the reformer Jane Addams, the philosopher John Dewey, the anthropologist Franz Boas, and the public intellectual W. E. B. Du Bois all imagined new forms of cultural fusion as part of the necessary transformation of a misguided society.[11] Their broader progressive politics were organized by an accretive, synthetic logic that the melting pot encapsulates perfectly. By moving beyond materialism, the melting-pot idea telegraphs the ambitions of Progressive-era imaginations; these complicated ambitions continued to resonate through the social, philosophical, and literary currents of the twentieth-century United States.[12]

This chapter pursues the Deweyan version of the melting pot through the following steps: I begin by contextualizing assimilation with reference to Boasian anthropology and Robert Park's Chicago sociology. From the extended sociological attention given to defining melting-pot assimilation, I draw the sketchy and often inconsistent parameters of the figure. This definitional exercise requires explicit analysis of the ways sociologists relied on figuration and literary discourses to elaborate (and sometimes obscure) the idea of melting-pot assimilation. Indeed, I will show that tropology infuses melting-pot thinking well beyond the limited arena of sociological speculation: a literary insistence on discourse as *process*, as means of action rather than as passive reflection, unites melting-pot modes of thought. But melting-pot discourse also tends to discount the real-world obstacles to changes that work in the literary realm. As I suggest in what follows, the tropological approach used by many melting-pot thinkers risks overestimating the agency available to actual melting-pot subjects. To the end of illuminating this problematic theoretical tendency, this chapter turns to the vexed issue of race in the melting pot, particularly the way certain thinkers imagined defusing, avoiding, and even counteracting racial prejudice through melting-pot means. That these means were primarily literary and imaginative, I conclude, constitutes both the strength and the weakness of melting-pot thinking.

Indeed, the centrality of literary logics to the ideas of malleable selfhood and cultural cross-fertilization that melting-pot thinkers developed cannot be overemphasized. The melting pot offers a powerful example of the kind of nuance that literary logics can lend to the articulation of social and political relations. Through the use of connective literary devices, such as metaphor, metonymy, and homology, melting-pot thinkers forged discursive relations when material relations were in question. Figuration accommodated the most mundane concerns and the most abstruse speculations—indeed, it joined them, modeling the ways in which materiality and possibility might be brought to inform one another. Recognizing both the capacities and limits of literary logics, as I will do here, represents a crucial step to properly reintegrating literary modes of representation, and the complication they so ably convey, into the social and political debates of our own time.

Defining Progressive-Era Assimilation

Given Dewey and Kallen's disagreement over the nature of the melting pot, we might begin by stepping back and considering the term "assimilation,"

which Dewey seems to consider less problematic. According to the sociological thinking that began to coalesce around the topic at the turn of the
twentieth century, "assimilation" generally did not imply miscegenation; it
implied a process more like acculturation. Even the eugenicist Henry Pratt
Fairchild distinguished between amalgamation (a physical and biological
process, pertaining to "race") and assimilation (a societal process, pertaining to "nationality").[13] The separation of these two spheres was difficult
to maintain in early twentieth-century practice, however. Julius Drachsler's
immigrant-sympathetic *Democracy and Assimilation: The Blending of Immigrant
Heritages in America* (1920) is exemplary in this respect: it studies intermarriage as an indispensable index of ethnic fusion, arguing that "the economic
and the cultural" interweavings produced by marriage out of one's immediate sphere should not be underestimated. Drachsler directly considers, and
ultimately dismisses, the significance of "biologic" fusion (indeed, he suggests that it can serve as a dangerous distraction from "the ideal of intellectual and emotional harmony among the masses of diverse elements").[14]
However, his central chapters on intermarriage suggest just how tangled the
economic-cultural and biological strands could become: how is one strand
to be separated from the other when considering a child of intermarriage?
Assimilation, in other words, might signal a shifting of attention away from
the biological realm, but no clear and systematic purging of biology from
one's arguments.

Even as thinkers struggled to understand an "assimilation" separate from
"amalgamation," this version of assimilation elaborated an embryonic notion
of culture. In melting-pot era discussions of assimilation, culture as represented by the turn-of-the-century anthropology of Franz Boas (culture as the
manners, mores, and beliefs of a particular people) intersected with an earlier
model of culture (culture as, in the words of Matthew Arnold, a process
"which consists in becoming something rather than in having something").[15]
Boas's own official contribution to the debate on American immigration
both insists on the culturally embedded nature of the melting-pot subject
and shows how these culturalist ideas remained imbricated with biological
thinking. In a 1911 study conducted for the Dillingham Immigration Commission, Boas gathered and compared physical measurements of the children of immigrants; his results showed that the offspring of immigrants were
physically more similar to one another, and to other native-born children,
than they were to their foreign-born parents. Though Boas stopped short of
fully articulating the culturalist implications of his anti-hereditarian findings,
his report clearly resisted the nativist bent of the Immigration Commission.
By recognizing immigrant bodies as, above all, changeable, Boas understood

himself as confirming the "plasticity of human type." He did go so far as to suggest that such plasticity was not exclusively physical: "It follows... that if the bodily form undergoes far-reaching changes under a new environment, concomitant changes of the mind may be expected."[16] Others were less hesitant than the careful scientist: melting-pot writers from John Dewey to Mary Antin, Edward Steiner, and Elias Tobenkin elaborated culturalist versions of Boas's idea of "plasticity of type," often even casting them as emancipations from, rather than extensions of, biological thinking.

To some extent, such philosophical picking and choosing was not only fundamental to melting-pot theories of being but also friendly to Boas's own understanding of the operations of culture. Many of Boas's writings understood the distinct ideas and practices of his subjects (what became referred to as "culture") as produced not only by the particular needs of groups but also by their historical experiences of mobility and contact. According to the Boasian principle of "diffusion," tools, methods, beliefs, and artistic forms could be passed from people to people and from context to context. Some of Boas's most provocative work in this area involved tracking shared myths and phonemes in order to demonstrate "the complexity of their origin."[17] Like the bodies of immigrants' children, then, cultures—the stories subjects told, the beliefs they held, the practices they valued—were conceived of as porous and changeable, acutely responsive to environment. "Culture" was particulate as well as particular: its elements were related, but not bound into a necessary and unchanging whole. Instead, culture operated on the basis of an ongoing principle of particulate diffusion.[18]

Though it was influential in certain circles, Boas's thinking about culture was not common knowledge at the beginning of the twentieth century. (Indeed, even for anthropologists his theories were sometimes difficult to access, as they remained embedded in minutely particular discussions of such things as bead-working practices). However, Boas seriously engaged with the Dillingham Commission's investigation of immigration, and in 1908 Jeremiah Jenks confirmed that Boas's proposed study greatly interested the commission. The press also gave play to the findings outlined in Boas's preliminary report to the commission, with both the *New York Times* and the *Boston Evening Transcript* attempting to argue back against Boas's conclusions.[19] Boas's ideas also registered in a variety of other Progressive contexts: he gave a rousing defense of African cultural achievements at Atlanta University in 1905, and impressed W. E. B. Du Bois by the cogency of his analysis of race and culture. John Dewey referred to Boas in *Experience and Nature* (1925), and Boas's *The Mind of Primitive Man* shows up in both Julius Drachsler's *Democracy and Assimilation* and Grace Abbott's *The Immigrant and the Community*

(1917). Boasian thinking was not as fundamental to Progressivism as was Robert Park's Chicago sociology, but diffusionism resonated with many melting-pot thinkers.

John Dewey deployed his own version of Boasian diffusionism in the immigration debates, pointing out that contemporary attacks on "the hyphen" (of which Theodore Roosevelt's was the most famous) were misbegotten because they were founded on "false terms"; that is, "they seem to assume something which is already in existence called America to which the other factor may be externally hitched on."[20] That stable and solid thing, according to Dewey, was a delusion. The American, Dewey asserted, "is not American plus Pole or German. But the American is himself Pole-German-English-French-Spanish-Italian-Greek-Irish-Scandinavian-Bohemian-Jew and so on."[21] While "so on" on the one hand silently signals Dewey's unwillingness to name non-European participants in the melting pot, it also represents an unpredictability that cannot exclude those who remain unspoken here.[22] It is crucially different from mere silent omission, for it operates as a linguistic marker for that which cannot be foreseen, that which refuses to be named, and even that which is deliberately excluded. According to the logic of the melting pot, the American might simply be expressed as this "so on."

By emphasizing the discursive instability of national identity, Dewey did his best to generalize and extend a discursive instability more frequently (and often uncomfortably) associated with "assimilation." As the sociologist Sarah E. Simons noted in "Social Assimilation," a ground-breaking series of articles that ran in the *American Journal of Sociology* through 1901 and 1902, fixing the identity of even the term "assimilation" then seemed a near-impossible task. "Assimilation" had only recently irrupted into American critical discourse, Simons recounted, and by virtue of its novelty, the term remained unstable. When the term is used, she complained,

> no clearly defined, stable idea seems to exist, even in the mind of the author. Thus Giddings at one time identifies assimilation with "reciprocal accommodation." In another place he defines it as the "process of growing alike," and once again he tells us it is the method by which foreigners in United States society become American.[23]

Simons's articles duly attempt to locate her own scholarly endeavor within a field explored by her sociological forerunners, Franklin Giddings and Edward Alsworth Ross. However, this produces more confusion than critical foundation, for the canonical sociological theory of the late nineteenth century treats assimilation as both result and process. Simons attempts to keep these poles separate, but the intertwining she diagnoses is instructive. The term "assimilation" was afflicted with the very fluidity it aimed to describe. "Result" could not be separated from "process" in this arena.

Simons's own definition of assimilation cannily privileges the fluidity that challenged her search for definition. She favors process:

> [Assimilation] may, perhaps, be defined as that process of adjustment or accommodation which occurs between the members of two different races, if their contact is prolonged and if the necessary psychic conditions are present. The result is group-homogeneity to a greater or less degree. Figuratively speaking, it is the process by which the aggregation of peoples is changed from a mere mechanical mixture into a chemical compound. (791–92)

In part, Simons privileges process because end results are even more unclear where assimilation is concerned. For a definition, she employs an extraordinary number of qualifications: may, perhaps, or, if, if, to a greater or less degree, figuratively speaking. Her qualification of the result of group-homogeneity—that it occurs *"to a greater or less degree"*—particularly conveys her uncertainty. What are degrees of homogeneity? Homogeneity is a total conception—it does not function in partial doses. Even the figure of the chemical compound, to which Simons resorts, is an imperfect one for a discussion of homogeneity. To consider a compound a "homogenization" of its constituent parts is to miss the significance of the chemical bonds formed between its distinct elements, and of the mutual transformation of constituent parts. Simons's expert sociological tone makes a peculiar match with the hedging evident both above and elsewhere, in sentences such as "assimilation has a dual character—is more or less reciprocal in its action—a process of give and take to a greater or lesser degree" (803). And yet this cohabitation of contradictory discourses if anything makes Simons's writing more representative of melting-pot writing, especially as it evinces all of the possibilities and problems associated with inconsistency. Like many melting-pot writers, Simons attempts to maintain simultaneous theoretical allegiances, with troubling effects on her logic. Her willingness to be inconsistent leaves the process about which she writes unclear: she dodges the task of definition by raising the question of resemblance or similarity. In other words, assimilation requires Simons to find a third term, one between (and possibly mediating between) pure difference and pure sameness. Indeed, the root of the word assimilation lies in "similarity."

However, Sarah Simons's work on assimilation shows that theoretical discomfort about homogeneity did not preclude arguments relying on the logic of identity. For example, in "Social Assimilation" Simons rules out any possibility of Chinese assimilation to western cultures, explaining:

> The ideals of the Chinese are diametrically opposed to those of the western man; there are no common culture bonds between the two races; there is no possibility of agreement as to a view-point for matters essential to a common life. Hence, since all this precludes the formation of fellowship feelings, there can be no assimilation. (799)

The uncertainty that Simons evinces in the theoretical realm of definition here fades into the certitude of sociological description. While Park might more diplomatically describe this situation in terms of "dissimilar apperception masses," Simons categorically distinguishes "western man," from "the Chinese," and equates the impossibility of "fellowship" (likeness, alignment) with the impossibility of "agreement" (identity). Simons shows that we cannot expect perfect coherence (or identity) of sociological theory and sociological practice, in other words. Though they attend closely to melting-pot topics, and represent a rich vein of melting-pot writing, sociological materials are no more likely to produce perfect internal agreement, or consistency, than are autobiographical or fictional texts. Here and elsewhere in *Melting-Pot Modernism,* I use sociological observation with the understanding that the philosophies elaborated by these kinds of documents are often compromised and contradictory. This side of melting-pot thinking—the inconsistencies anathema to conventional social theory tolerated through a kind of literary logic—represents both the unusual potential and the vulnerability of these ideas. My own literary analysis follows from the logics I see at work here: I track patterns with the understanding that they are rarely perfect or exhaustive. Instead, I take the tropes and devices of the melting pot as representative of a fundamental will to extend, to encompass, and to include in ways only imaginable through literary means.

Assimilation and Figuration

The critical phrase of Sarah Simons's definitional project is one that does not so much define assimilation, but rather points to the difficulty of definition and proposes an alternative strategy: "figuratively speaking." Indeed, as the figurative term "melting pot" suggests, both early sociology and melting-pot discourse relied on literary devices to clarify their ideas in the absence of perfect definitions. Early sociologists made extensive use of figuration, particularly tropes such as simile, metaphor, and symbol.[24] Simons, above, likens the social process of assimilation to one of chemical fusion; through figuration her language performs the action that it describes, transforming the mixture of sociological terms into an intellectual compound with mass and solidity. *Old World Traits Transplanted* (1921), a study of immigrant "Americanization" credited to Park and co-authors, but largely written by W. I. Thomas, compares assimilation to skin grafting, "where the new tissue is not applied to the whole surface, but spots are grafted, and from these the connecting tissues ramify," and to ecological balance: as in "a geographical region sufficiently marked in its features to put a characteristic imprint on its flora and fauna...the human inhabitants of a country develop a body of characteristic values."[25] These tropes both clarify and confuse the concept of assimilation. The figure is elaborated, but its limits are never demarcated; the point at which the similarity ends and the idea of the skin graft is no longer useful to us remains unmarked. We cannot gauge the extent and the reliability of the likeness. In a discursive field so rich in similes, the different figures together make up a body of knowledge about the concept, but they do not map perfectly onto each other. That is, they share a likeness, but again, the extent of that likeness is not clear. Paradoxically, the messy points of missed contact, overlap, and contradiction create the "unified" field of meaning to which the figures contribute.

As political philosophers and sociologists framed it, assimilation entailed a process of drawing similarity that paralleled those involved in simile, metaphor, and symbol. In that sense, literary figuration illuminates not only *what* assimilation is but also *how* it works; metaphors provide demonstrations of how the process of assimilation might operate. This messy intellectual nexus resists the kinds of one-to-one equations that the late twentieth century came to expect from a definition of assimilation. The power of both metaphor and assimilation instead rests on active faith, that imaginative "will to believe" that proved so philosophically interesting to William James. In a lecture published in the *Atlantic Monthly* in 1880, James argued that metaphor was a form of thought for the "highest order of minds," using proto-melting-pot language (and figuration) to express his esteem:

> Instead of thoughts of concrete things patiently following one another in a beaten track of habitual suggestion, we have the most abrupt cross-cuts and transitions from one idea to another, the most rarefied abstractions and discriminations, the most unheard-of combinations of elements, the subtlest associations of analogy; in a word, we seem suddenly introduced into a seething caldron of ideas, where everything is fizzing and bobbing about in a state of bewildering activity, where partnerships can be joined or loosened in an instant.[26]

For James, here, language does not simply reveal an associative turn of mind, but performs association; he is not talking about the kind of neutral description that we might imagine the sociologists striving for. Literary expression is important to him because it cuts new channels, linking previously unlike terms, releasing one from familiar associations, and suggesting new possibilities. Whether used in literary texts or imagined as linking individual participants in the melting pot, figuration calls upon faith to actively enact a relationship, to yoke two terms together in the absence of a precise definition of that relationship. At the same time, as James's references to discriminations and loosened partnerships make clear, figurative thinking presumes a certain degree of faith*less*ness, a continued tension or difference that keeps the constitutive terms of the figure separate. Because early American sociologists recognized these capacities in literary discourse, they left a body of work that demands literary interpretation, and that suggests the importance of literary expression and analysis in arenas not traditionally considered their purview.

Framing the self, the other, the community, and relations between them through this literary lens, melting-pot thinkers privileged the discursive arena's ability to give shape to, rather than merely reflect, the material world. To some extent, this emphasis on the discursive realm produced a shift of attention away from material conditions (which, in the context of the immigration debates, meant race and biology). This does not mean, however, that bodies become irrelevant in melting-pot thinking: Sarah Simons, for example, has no problem arguing that "the process of assimilation is of a psychological rather than a biological nature," and then again, that "a population having the blood of both elements in its veins is more readily influenced by the dominant element than before the mixture of race occurred" (801, 817). In the Progressive era, blood-oriented racist laws and putatively "natural" prejudices regulated consent and contract, the melting pot's most privileged rhetorical bindings. Language was marked and policed by biological thinking (anti-immigrant feeling often expressed itself in language regulation in the early twentieth century), and, in its turn, framed and produced biological thinking. Anzia Yezierska's *Bread Givers* (1925) suggests as much when a scene of ethnicized language pronunciation ("sing-gg") culminates with the tips of a teacher's corrective fingers held against the throat, where the blood pulses, unmentioned but unavoidable. In short, the discursive realm was implicated in biologically based ideologies, even when the evidence it offered seemed indifferent or contradictory to those ideologies. Nonetheless, to many melting-pot thinkers literary discourse seemed to promise the best means of being faithless to biology and materiality. Indeed, despite Jane Addams's insistence that "action is indeed the sole medium of expression for ethics," many melting-pot thinkers worked on transforming ethics via the discursive realm rather than taking to the barricades.[27] Likely they did so in part because the discursive realm was less brutal, dispiriting, and exhausting than the material one. But they also did so because they refused to believe that discursive changes had no implications for the material world. Because so many melting-pot thinkers refined their progressive politics discursively, their literary strategies require a closer analysis than they have received until now.

Even Boas, the diligent scientist, participated to some extent in the melting-pot literary turn. His study of immigrant children's bodies for the Dillingham Commission was unusual for him: more typically Boasian studies of cultural diffusion use language groups or narrative clusters as evidence, tracing the shifts and transformations of phonemes and folklore in the way that the Dillingham Commission study traced the changing bodies of immigrants' children. And Horace Kallen, the young critic of the melting pot, also saw that literary logics were indispensable to theorists of cultural merging; he noted that "no word, not even the nakedest symbol of the mathematician nor the emptiest gurgle of the popular song-writer, stands purely for one thing or the other; each is hyphenated, and in each a meaning and a mood interpenetrate."[28] A sweatshop worker in Abraham Cahan's *Yekl* (1896) puts it more pithily, vouching for the vitalizing syncretism of language in the melting pot: "America for a country and *dod'll do* [that'll do] for a language!"[29] Second languages, translation, and multi- and interlingual play secured the Progressive-era linkage of immigration and literary self-consciousness. Words themselves provided abstract exemplars of the flux, impurity, and combination and recombination that melting-pot thinkers envisioned as the conditions of selfhood in the twentieth-century United States. Even without explicit recourse to tropes such as simile, metaphor, and symbol, then, writers might understand the syncretic nature of language to infuse (and indeed, constitute) their representations of cultural mixture.

In this sense, melting-pot ideas of assimilation assumed literary approaches that extended well beyond the abundant use of figuration. The sociological methodology that Robert Park promoted in this period turned to language and, specifically, to narrative—namely, autobiography, fiction, correspondence, and journalism—to supplement the data of surveys and statistics.[30] Despite also insisting on quantitative research, Chicago sociology imagined itself into being through a paradigmatic employment of melting-pot discursivity: W. I. Thomas and Florian Znaniecki's *The Polish Peasant in Europe and America* (1918) devoted much of its first and all of its second volume to immigrant correspondence recounting the experience of displacement. *Old World Traits Transplanted* includes 168 "illustrative documents," usually first-person accounts by immigrants; rather than deferring to an omniscient sociological narration, the text stages a jostling of immigrant attitudes, wishes, and experiences. In the apparatus to the text these documents are described as "concrete means" of evoking "the variety of attitudes and values which exist in the world and may be brought to America as immigrant heritages"; they explicitly "are not an attempt to characterize the groups in question, though they necessarily do this to some extent," the text notes (*OWT*, 4). Conceding that the materials may, indeed, "characterize the groups in question," the apparatus grants the texts an ungovernable agency, but emphasizes their capacities as evidence of the particularity of assimilation; the statement itself dramatizes the melting-pot idea of inclusion without ideological consensus. Classic Chicago sociology privileges these diverse voices and narrative strategies over tables and graphs, at least in terms of allocation of space and attention. According to this approach, assimilation is represented best through a flexible, but manifestly literary, form.

For sociologists, literary idioms also provided useful means for insisting on a readerly approach to immigration. Literary reading provided a model for founding conceptual, public syntheses in specific narratives.[31] By synthesizing the particularities provided by literature, the sociologists reasoned, each reader becomes a more sophisticated theorist (and herself performs an individualized version of assimilation).[32] Neither synthesis nor understanding could occur in isolation, and literature was understood to puncture social isolation: *Old World Traits Transplanted* declares that the "function of literature, including poetry, romance, and the newspaper, is to enable all to share vicariously in the life of each" (271). Because literature assists in the recognition of particularity, the reasoning goes, it also enables syntheses and combinations of particularity, especially through encouraging both aliens and native-born to imagine likeness. The settlement founder Lillian Wald drives home the political importance of the particularity that sociologists located in literature when she observes that "few, if any, of the men and women who have had extended opportunity for social contact with the foreigner favor a further restriction of immigration."[33] Exposure to particularity, Wald suggests, generates empathy and common cause, if not full identification. This reasoning does not rely upon sameness to generate shared significance. Instead, it calls upon the faith-driven thinking of metaphor to find relatedness between two only tenuously connected fields.

According to these thinkers, writing serves these purposes so effectively because it does not only advance, but also emerges from, syncretic processes that are of a piece with melting-pot assimilation. Cahan's "*dod'll do*" is a linguistic shorthand for what Elizabeth Stern associated with writing more generally. Stern's immigrant autobiography depicts her apprenticing as a writer by writing letters for her immigrant community, which "inextricably twined" the lives of those around her "into our life": "For it was as if all the life of Soho streamed through our little kitchen, through mother's life and mine, by way of those letters which I wrote for our neighbours."[34] Stern learns her craft by assuming different voices; understanding herself as a writer means understanding herself as immersed in a stream of identities. According to this model, literary representation both requires, and extends, the capacity to loosen one's narrow definition of self. From the more theoretical explorations of figuration to the practical reflections of the settlement worker, these discussions use the confusions of literary discourse as a means of conceptual sharing.

Means without Ends

By offering parables and metaphors in place of a traditional definition of the melting pot, my discussion has privileged the process of definition over its end. Melting-pot thinking also esteemed figuration for its capacity to emphasize process over ends, and to derive new insight and pleasure from the *means* of expression. Henry Adams saw this shift of focus as typical of the industrial era: the dynamo, or means, dominates over the Virgin, or cultural end.[35] While melting-pot thinkers reached no clear consensus on the question, the most acute among them realized that privileging means and process meant relinquishing the notion of a fixed end to the process of assimilation, for means are ever-active. Certainly, Robert Park and his associates in the new sociology were putting this conclusion forward in the teens and twenties. Park's *Old World Traits Transplanted* and *The Immigrant Press and Its Control* appeared in a series of "Americanization Studies" edited by Allen T. Burns; each volume of the series begins with a publisher's note that reframes Americanization in melting-pot, not coercive, terms:

> [Americanization is] the union of native and foreign born in all the most fundamental relationships and activities of our national life. For Americanization is the uniting of new with native-born Americans in fuller common understanding and appreciation to secure by means of individual and collective self-direction the highest welfare of all. Such Americanization should perpetuate no unchangeable political, domestic, and economic régime delivered once for all to the fathers, but a growing and broadening national life, inclusive of the best wherever found. With all our rich heritages, Americanism will develop best through

a mutual giving and taking of contributions from both newer and older Americans in the interest of the commonweal. (*OWT,* n. pg.)

This paragraph insistently denies the fixed end (or régime): it finds no required content (political, domestic, or economic). Rather, it focuses on an ongoing means, or process. (Horace Kallen considered this founding assumption ironic, in light of the book's conclusions about the inevitability of assimilation.)[36] Park's enormously influential *Introduction to the Science of Sociology* (1921) defines assimilation similarly, as "a process of interpenetration and fusion in which persons and groups acquire the memories, sentiments, and attitudes of other persons or groups, and, by sharing their experience and history, are incorporated with them in a common cultural life."[37] Like John Dewey, Park rejects the idea of a unitary American culture into which one assimilates. In this view melting-pot culture is constantly reconstituted: its fund of practices and beliefs is continually expanded through the process of assimilation.

Park's terms "interpenetration and fusion" evoke the power of a very particular version of the melting-pot metaphor. In Israel Zangwill's famous play *The Melting-Pot,* David Quixano rhapsodizes about the "melting" and "fusion" occurring in the pot. (Theodore Roosevelt famously praised Zangwill's play, at least in part for its dramatization of ancient animosities jettisoned in favor of new-world alliances. However, Zangwill's play is not as hyphen-unfriendly as Roosevelt's support might suggest.) In the afterword to his play Zangwill distinguished the melting pot from "assimilation or simple surrender to the dominant type, as is popularly supposed."[38] Instead, he asserted in 1914, the melting pot signifies a vernacular, hyphenated "all-around give-and-take" (203). By 1921, Park's *Introduction to the Science of Sociology* cited Zangwill's play, indicating that as far as the new sociology was concerned, assimilation should be understood according to this model.

Zangwill's and Park's melting pots are very different from that of the Ford English School. That is not to say that they entirely repudiate the idiom of the Ford English School; simply that, like Mary Antin, who represented her cultural inheritance as a "garment," and thus alienable, Zangwill's and Park's assimilation operates as if teachers, audience, and graduates had all entered the pot together and left wearing some unpredictable combination of "American" clothes and each other's ethnic attire (and, indeed, modified versions of each).[39] In the "melting" brought about by this assimilation, the pot does not reduce all to some undifferentiated fluid. Rather, in a quasi-culinary take on the alchemical metaphor, the heat of the process assists in the mixing of properties as if they were flavors: the metaphor itself shifts just as it imagines identities doing. The cultural "contents" of assimilation, in other words, were made fluid at least in part by the unpredictable processes of the metaphors through which they were conceptualized.

Though Jane Addams's settlement house Hull-House represents a more material take on these metaphorical processes, she imagined the settlement as a flexible and adaptive means for the continuous search to "give form" to assimilation.[40] Addams wrote about the settlement house as Henry James would later write about his novels; indeed, her best criticism considers the settlement house, rather than works of art or literature. Yet the terms she sets out have clear implications for the kinds of anthologies that Chicago sociologists were compiling, and for the literary-formal experiments that would emerge from melting-pot philosophies. Like these others, Addams privileged form as a process that constituted and reformed cultural "contents."

According to Addams, the settlement could ease the transition of immigrants into American society by mixing immigrants with native-born and by incorporating their various cultural heritages into the mixture. She framed the cultural gifts of settlement visitors as contributions to Hull-House's common fund of knowledge, from which ghetto residents and settlement workers profited equally. Settlement workers were expected to share the manners and language of their native culture, and immigrants, in return, shared their own cultural gifts (languages, stories, music, and other artisanal traditions). Addams compared experience at the settlement to travel and higher education, in terms of its cosmopolitan effects: Hull-House could make one "a citizen of the world" with a "growing understanding of all kinds of people with their varying experiences" (*HH*, 359). By framing the settlement analogically, Addams urges us to consider it not only as a place of practical works but also as a place that *does work* at an analogical, literary level. Indeed, Addams's *Twenty Years at Hull-House* emphasizes that the discursive regime of Hull-House constituted a significant part of its material impact on the neighborhood.

Hull-House both shaped and was given shape by what Addams described as a nascent "social morality." Introducing the series of lectures published as *Democracy and Social Ethics* (1902), she argued that men and women of the Progressive era were becoming increasingly aware of a need to move beyond the narrow confines of the individual identity:

> We may indeed imagine many of them saying: "Cast our experiences in a larger mold if our lives are to be animated by the larger social aims. We have met the obligations of our family life, not because we had made resolutions to that end, but spontaneously, because of a common

fund of memories and affections, from which the obligation naturally develops, and we see no other way in which to prepare ourselves for the larger social duties.".... We are learning that a standard of social ethics is not attained by travelling a sequestered byway, but by mixing on the thronged and common road where all must turn out for one another.[41]

In the "larger mold" (or form) to which Addams appeals to exceed the bounds of the individual self, the "common fund of memories and affections" that the subject draws from is extended beyond the single family into a broader social world. Feeling and acting on social ethics entails a "spontaneous" response to "mixing," a mixing that is intriguingly described as a process of "all turn[ing] out for one another." This figure suggests participation and presence (turning out *onto* the road), but also the willingness to step aside (turning out *from* the road), feeling the immediacy of another's trajectory above one's own. "Turning out" also connotes a process of becoming—that is, it is in the space of mobility and mixture that the self "turns out," and "is turned out," through contact with diverse others. Turning also emphasizes process over the "end" made unavailable by circularity.

In *Twenty Years at Hull-House*, Addams emphasizes the moral and intellectual challenge represented by "the labyrinth of differing ethical teachings and religious creeds which the many immigrant colonies of our neighborhood presented." She finds a model for meeting this challenge in "those groups of homesick immigrants huddled together in strange tenement houses,"

among whom I seemed to detect the beginnings of a secular religion or at least of a wide humanitarianism evolved out of the various exigencies of the situation; somewhat as a household of children, whose mother is dead, out of their sudden necessity perform unaccustomed offices for each other and awkwardly exchange consolations, as children in happier households never dream of doing. (*HH*, 39–40)

For Addams the immigrant scene demands adaptation from both individuals and ideologies. According to Addams's analogy (which resonates with her own early loss of her mother), the exigencies of the scene spur these figures to take on new roles in addition to the old. As opposed to children living in comfortable familiarity, those called upon to assimilate to a new order develop improvisatory relationships and new selves. This melting-pot social ethics is based in individual assumptions of new roles and activities. That is, in anticipation of critics of the institutional component of settlement work—such as Elizabeth Stern, who explicitly dismissed settlements because

"Races do not become friends by the will of others, but by their own, and not through groups, but through individuals in each group"—Addams traces the agency and achievements of settlements through individual forms.[42] In Addams's vision of the settlement, "exchange" is keyed to performance: workers and residents, native-born and immigrant, develop a cosmopolitan range of roles within their own individual selves precisely because they are called upon to perform in that range. In other words, because Addams's social ethics looks to couch changeability and communal exchange within individual forms, it turns to theatricality as a favored means.

Performing the Melting-Pot Self

Constantine Panunzio's autobiography, *The Soul of an Immigrant* (1921), similarly founds assimilation in a theatrical experience. At the Maine Wesleyan Seminary, Panunzio won the role of Shylock in a senior production of *The Merchant of Venice*. Having entered the school late and focused single-mindedly his studies, he found himself "in the senior class by adoption, but not by inheritance"; some students protested against a "foreigner" being cast in the senior play.[43] According to Panunzio, he earned his peers' appreciation by learning not only his own lines but also those of all other parts in the play. He transformed his fellows' "spirit" by "often putting into the mouths of other players the words of their parts, saying good-naturedly: 'Speak the speech I pray you as I pronounce it to you'" (*SI*, 170). Panunzio becomes a kind of nexus of roles (among them Hamlet, himself a theatrical nexus), yet, as he reports, reviews of the play praised the authenticity of his Shylock. Cast as the outsider figure, the forced convert, he understands that figure's centrality to both the individual performance and the broader experience of acting. This theatrical experience, in its turn, illuminates the process of assimilation: his success in the play brings his "first desire to remain in America and become a part of her" (*SI*, 171). The word "part," here, plays multiple roles, just as Panunzio and the children described by Jane Addams do.

While Addams and Panunzio represent relatively straightforward celebrations of melting-pot theatricality, Abraham Cahan's novel *Yekl* (1896) nuances and complicates these ideas. Cahan's Jake (Yekl) expresses his ardent assimilationism through theatrical displays of his reinvented self—and yet this hyperbolic and unconflicted theatricality is a closer cousin to coercive Americanization than it is to Jane Addams's melting-pot theatricality. Cahan's novel instead evokes the unpredictable nature of the melting-pot self through Jake's newly landed, greenhorn wife, Gitl. When Jake rediscovers Gitl in an Ellis Island holding shed, she seems not the familiar woman he expected, but something altogether different: "the nine or ten days spent at sea had covered her face with a deep bronze, which combined with her prominent cheek bones, inky little eyes, and, above all, the smooth black wig, to lend her resemblance to a squaw" (*Y*, 72). Jake insists that she take off the wig, and she substitutes a kerchief for it, but he then thinks that the kerchief "made her look like an Italian woman of Mulberry Street on Sunday" (*Y*, 78). This is not theatricality, traditionally conceived (although Gitl later takes up this headwear theme when she assumes theatrical poses before the mirror, trying on an American-style hat). Gitl is not consciously assuming the roles of "squaw" and "Italian" for her audience; instead, these roles seem to be playing over her, like the play of light on a scene. Even from Jake's recently Americanized perspective, Gitl represents an unnerving fluidity. She has entered into a state of sudden and surprising flux for which even theatricality is an imperfect metaphor.

Despite its imperfections, theatricality was attractive to melting-pot thinkers because it figured the possibility of multiple roles for an individual self. Melting-pot thinkers could not envision cultural or racial groups, or even families, assimilating as undifferentiated blocks, but they could imagine individuals assimilating. Indeed, Robert Park credited individualism itself with enabling the cultural instrumentalism of the melting pot: "The individualism which is characteristic of Western cultural societies, and which is largely the result of increased communication, means the tendency to construct a scheme of life and relationships based on the intelligent use of all values that can be found anywhere in the world, disregarding to some extent allegiance to persons and localities" (*OWT*, 41). Park suggested that by virtue of turn-of-the-century immigration, "all values that can be found anywhere in the world" were increasingly available to a range of Americans. In the immigrant-rich early twentieth-century United States, assimilation made possible a new, more multiple, more *constructed* self, in Park's words.[44] Gitl at Ellis Island is not construct*ing;* indeed, we have no access to her interiority, no sense of her agency. She is, however, freshly revealed as construct*ed,* and suddenly the range of roles through which she might be constructed seems vastly expanded.

When Park characterizes the construction of selves and culture as *intelligent,* conscious, he makes particular reference to native-born participants in the melting pot. In a theorization consistent with Gitl's early mutability in Cahan's *Yekl,* but not with either the later Gitl or Constantine Panunzio, Park emphasized the unconscious dimensions of assimilation in the immigrant. To his mind, by virtue of emerging from quasi-feudal social contexts, immigrants were less "individualized" than contemporary Americans and thus less likely to engage in self-conscious self-construction.[45] The artful and multivocal immigrant autobiographies of the period amply demonstrate his error, sometimes even arguing directly back to his theory. Mary Antin's famous autobiography *The Promised Land* (1912), for example, asserts her *I* as "a new being, something that had not been before" (1). Horace Kallen's critique of the melting pot goes so far as to complain that "the Riises and Steiners and Antins together with Edward Bok and their numerous other recent imitators mostly female and Jewish, protest too much; they are too self-conscious and self-centered."[46] What Kallen implies is the hysterical and excessive nature of melting-pot selfhood may explain Robert Park's sense that immigrants failed to reproduce traditional American individualism. Elizabeth Stern's autobiography *My Mother and I* (1917) opens by making the excessiveness of the melting-pot self manifest: "In myself I see one hundred thousand young men and women with dark eyes aflame with enthusiasm, or blue eyes alight with hope."[47] While the individual remains central to these formulations of selfhood, the unitary status of individuality is clearly under assault. The sense of the self as a collection of roles allows these writers to chart a course between the inadequate self-consciousness alleged by Park and the excessive self-consciousness alleged by Kallen.

Mary Antin, for example, introduces her autobiography by declaring her- self "absolutely other" than the person whose story she tells, and yet calling the story "my life's story" (*PL,* 1). The roles only multiply from there. In order to describe her trip from the old world to the new, Antin reprints, and comments upon, a letter written by her younger self: the spatial crossing that brings the new self into being registers in a formal multiplication of voices. Antin explicitly traces this unconventionally multiple self to the experience of assimilation; she playfully collapses boundaries between roles: "Should I be sitting here, chattering of my infantile adventures, if I did not know that I was speaking for thousands? Should you be sitting there, attending to my chatter, while the world's work waits, if you did not know that I spoke also for you? I might say 'you' or 'he' instead of 'I' " (*PL,* 72). Antin erects a rhetorical hall of mirrors, in which self and other are endlessly refracted. "Should I be sitting here" maps uncannily onto "Should you be sitting there," while the multiplied, echoing "w" of "while the world's work waits" defuses the dualism of "you" and "I," anticipating the more pluralistic " 'you' or 'he' instead of 'I.' " By destabilizing the very pronoun that structures the autobiographical form, *The Promised Land* begins reforming self, other, and representation in line with the melting pot's ethos of multiple roles.

The melting pot thus spurs exactly the literary figurations of multiplicity (ambivalent, divided, dissonant, contradictory selves) that are so often read as signaling *resistance* to assimilation. Rather than focusing on the interactions of established cultural groups, in the sense of Horace Kallen's cultural pluralism, melting-pot thinkers imagined a pluralism achieved through multiple and shifting identities *within the self.* Cahan, Stern, and Antin represent these unconventionally multiple voices and positions by drawing on theatricality to dramatize states of internal flux. "I could speak in the third person," Antin claims in her autobiography, "and not feel that I was masquerading"—that is, what most would experience as masquerade she experiences as the normal conditions of selfhood (*PL,* 1). Both Cahan's novel and Antin's autobiography accommodate a shifting changeability of role that is more often considered to be the purview of actors—and they were not alone. Lillian Wald wrote of New York's Lower East Side that "The drama is taken seriously in our neighborhood" (*HS,* 270).[48] Settlements often had burgeoning drama programs, but Cahan's and Antin's work suggests that the drama was taken seriously as a trope as well as an art form.

In the context of these recurring allusions to roles and performances, it is not surprising that a play named and popularized this vision of assimilation: the success of the melting-pot metaphor can be traced to Israel Zangwill's famous *Melting-Pot,* which was first performed in 1908. In Act II, assimilation is comically performed by the Quixano family's maid, Kathleen; her anti-Semitism of Act I has given way to assertions that "Bekaz we're Hebrews" the family must wear the false noses she has bought in Hester Street for "our carnival," Purim (*MP,* 72). In this act, the grotesque false noses come to represent the Jewish cultural heritage that the elderly and traditional Frau Quixano fears will be abandoned by the male Quixanos (Mendel and especially young David). Strikingly, Zangwill's Purim masquerade sequences seize upon a stereotypical marker of racialized Jewishness (and a consumer product sold in Hester Street) in order to signify the theatricalization of culture. In *The Melting-Pot,* as Kathleen forgets she's wearing her nose, drops it and crawls beneath the furniture hunting for it, and as David puts his on to please his grandmother, this erstwhile signifier of an essentialized racial Jewishness becomes shifting and parodic, just another mask to be assumed.

Zangwill's masquerade sequences suggest a relation to the past that is at once easier and more complicated than Jane Addams's well-meaning arguments for the preservation of ethnic heritages would have it. "Loss" and "retention" cannot adequately describe the dynamics enabled by this theatricality. As the scientific racist Charles Davenport observed, the melting pot was entirely incompatible with the eugenic idea "that characters are inherited as units and do not readily break up."[49] In Zangwill's *Melting-Pot,* culture is broken up and made available to ever-changing performances mounted by self-conscious characters. Even after David decides to defy his family out of love for the gentile Vera, he can still, ambivalently, assume the fake nose and play a familiar tune on the violin for his grandmother. Rejecting and then embracing his "inheritance," David's gestures echo Kathleen's from earlier in the play. By staging David's performance as derivative, second-order, Zangwill's play suggests that David's bond with the fake nose and with Purim is no more authentic than Kathleen's. *The Melting-Pot* values the Jewish past of tradition and ritual, but it ultimately casts Kathleen as an equally appropriate (if comedic) inheritor of that past. Zangwill's scripting of assimilation makes sense only if we understand cultural inheritance itself as a role that is both divisible and transferable.[50]

In Zangwill's play, melting-pot theatricality provides an occasion to become individually self-determining, or at least for David and Kathleen to repudiate certain hateful roles (David the ancient and not-so-ancient enmities of Kishinev, Kathleen her own recent anti-Semitism). This contribution to the fierce debate over agency in assimilation suggests just how the theatrical metaphor might overstate the role of individual agency in the melting pot. David, in particular, represents Zangwill's fullest elaboration of a melting-pot fantasy of individual self-consciousness and assimilative agency. This fantasy was not Zangwill's alone: it was widespread enough to provoke Julius Drachsler to warn against the dangers of fixating on purposefulness in assimilation. In *Democracy and Assimilation* (1920), Drachsler rebukes contemporary thinkers for using purposive verbs like "'select' or 'extract' or 'distil'" with reference to assimilation. Putting aside the matter of self-determination, Drachsler points out that imagined control over the nature and course of assimilation was only a few short steps from misbegotten attempts at social engineering: "the attempt at conscious direction or at the molding of a culture or civilization is not only a contradiction in basic concepts but a hopeless if not a perilous adventure" (*DA*, 185). As Drachsler's intervention suggests, extreme visions of role-playing self-determination like Zangwill's end up obscuring the social context and social consequences of assimilation. Imagining that one can "mold" the self, forge a new role, comes dangerously close to embarking on the "perilous adventures," like eugenics, that attracted a very different set of Progressives.

A metaphor used by Chicago sociology speaks eloquently of the material context that is minimized in Zangwill's version of radical self-fashioning.[51] *Old World Traits Transplanted* compares assimilation to a skin graft, "where the new tissue is not applied to the whole surface, but spots are grafted, and from these the connecting tissues ramify" (280).[52] This figure makes the physicality of performance vivid. The figure of the skin graft reminds us of the potent significance of bodies (skins) in role-playing. Unlike David Quixano's fake nose, the skin graft is not so easily assumed and discarded. This metaphor draws attention to a primary site for the fixation of anxiety about race, and yet it also draws attention to the possibility of construction—literal biological collage, diffusion and redistribution—at this very site. It goes one step further to suggest that constructed features can come to seem and feel, indeed *be,* "natural," and that constructedness does not mean that change won't feel like an assault.

Robert Park's thinking represents the opposite extreme from Zangwill's on the question of agency; according to him, the unconscious played the primary role in the process of assimilation.[53] Park's sociology aligns here with Henry James's emphasis on the passive creativity and collaboration of the assimilative spectator, which I will discuss in Chapter Two. However, for those who did not fully identify with the dominant Anglo-American culture, such as Zangwill, Antin, and James Weldon Johnson, claiming agency in melting-pot assimilation was critical. As we learn from Abraham Cahan's Gitl watching herself in the mirror in *Yekl,* and from Johnson's ex-colored man scrutinizing his youthful reflection in the mirror, these characters experience cultural merging through carefully considered decisions of how to play a part and to enter an economy of theatricalized identity-barter. This is not to say that the process of assimilation is driven by a solitary agent: the assimilative performances cataloged above are certainly communally produced. They are shaped by social pressures and social contacts, by the eyes of onlookers and the props afforded by consumer culture. However, the melting pot's many masquerades illustrate the centrality of the individual to this version of assimilation; as a result of that centrality, the question of assimilative agency remained contentious among early twentieth-century writers.[54] To what extent must identity and difference be understood as produced by individual performances, if melting-pot assimilation is to take place? Who and what scripts this performance, and who may perform?

Race in the Melting Pot

That is, if Gitl can briefly perform the part of the American Indian, can the American Indian also perform Gitl's part? Could cultures be taken on across the racial boundaries associated with physical bodies, especially skin colors, in the United States? Even if the physicality implied by race at the turn of the century were not at issue, how was the melting pot to address what W. E. B. Du Bois termed a "kinship" with its "essence" in a "social history of slavery . . . discrimination and insult"?[55] Israel Zangwill imagined an interracial melting pot: he insisted in his afterword to *The Melting-Pot* that the melting pot must be extended beyond the confines of the mainly European immigration of the early twentieth century. Zangwill's afterword emphasizes David Quixano's famous description of the "Melting Pot," in which he "expressly throws both 'black and yellow' into the crucible" (*MP,* 204). Like others of his generation (such as the writer Charles Chesnutt), Zangwill dreamed of a miscegenated future; for the present, however, he turned to culture, reasoning that it more easily flouts the color line. Citing ragtime as evidence of "spiritual miscegenation," he emphasized that the "action of the crucible is thus not exclusively physical" (*MP,* 207). In other words, according to Zangwill's idea of the melting pot, each time that Kathleen assumes the fake nose—or dances to ragtime—she makes the argument of race, of merged identities derived exclusively from biological mixture, less compelling. Fresh off the boat and still new to U.S. racial discourse, Abraham Cahan's David Levinsky argumentatively performs a version of this cross-racial role-shifting by meeting an onlooker's appraisal of his "greenness" (he still ritually washes before eating) with the retort, "Suppose I am [green].... Do the yellow ones or black ones all eat without washing?"[56] Mingling the language of immigrant "ripening" with that of American racialization, Levinsky embeds changes of state in the language of the "natural." Like push-cart bananas, he implies, the immigrant may go from green to yellow or black. Black and yellow are in this pot, but to what effect?

Though Zangwill's Kathleen may be able to assume and discard racial and ethnic masks, her abilities do not necessarily correlate with equal flexibility on the part of the racially marked. In fact, as Matthew Jacobson, David Roediger, and Noel Ignatiev have argued, Kathleen's flexibility is bought at precisely the price of that of the racially marked.[57] The asymmetries of power that constitute the spaces of assimilative performance are evident in Charles Chesnutt's *The Marrow of Tradition* (1901), when the scoundrel Tom Delamere assumes blackface: first for entertainment, in a cakewalk, and then later as cover for violent misdeeds. Each time, Tom assumes the identity of his family's trusted servant, Sandy Campbell—and each time, Sandy pays, first by communal disgrace and later by a near-lynching. In these sequences, the white native-born man is bound by neither scruples nor race: the "availability" of the black role works only to his benefit. Sandy experiences the opposite of such flexibility: he is jailed for the murder performed in his guise. Chesnutt's novel shows that the color line acts as a powerful constraint on the assumption of multiple identities. As scholars of blackface have suggested, such performances may in fact emphasize the boundedness of populations not admitted into the performance.[58]

Put most simply, the pervasive racism of the Progressive-era United States still structures the melting pot, compromising its ability to produce "equal" sharings: Sandy's freedom to put on the nose and perform Jewish culture at will, even for a short while, is questionable. Self-consciousness may sometimes enable artful constructions of multiple selves in defiance of resistant observers, but the racially ascriptive gaze (and more active policing of the color line) still exercises significant power, as we will see from the work of James Weldon Johnson (Chapter Three). Along with the ascription of racial identity went a circumscription of the "fund" from which one might draw roles. William James linked this circumscription to imperialist violence, and traced both to racist failures of the imagination: the United States went to war against the Philippines because "we" regarded Filipinos "as if they were a painted picture, an amount of mere matter in our way," without any "inwardness."[59] Racial ciphers could not be imagined as equal partners in the reformulation of "inwardness." Robert Park pursued a similar argument in 1914:

> the chief obstacle to the assimilation of the Negro and the Oriental are [sic] not mental but physical traits.... The fact that the Japanese bears in his features a distinctive racial hallmark, that he wears, so to speak, a racial uniform, classifies him. He cannot become a mere individual, indistinguishable in the cosmopolitan mass of the population.... The Japanese, like the Negro is condemned to remain among us an abstraction, a symbol.[60]

According to Park's argument here (his views on the subject changed over time), Sandy is fixed in his skin color, his self-transformative range less than that of the "mere individual."[61] African Americans were in the distinct position of having been constructed by racialist rhetoric for several generations; the slippage and fluidity of symbolic roles played by recent immigrants seemed less available to them. The "uniform" that Sandy wears for Park is thus quite different from the "garments" that recently arrived immigrants experimentally exchange.[62]

The mid-century sociologist E. Franklin Frazier understood this iteration of Park's thought as representing a "static phase of race relations," one that implicitly acquiesced to the "fatalism" of his sociological predecessor William Graham Sumner; Frazier charged later generations of sociologists with taking up the more "dynamic" understandings implicit in Park's later writings.[63] Indeed, Park does not fully explain why the literary writing that served to particularize immigrants in his sociological publications cannot perform that same task for African Americans and Asian Americans. Reading practices are central to Park's thinking; when, in *The American Scene,* Henry James details the shocking novelty of the Rutgers Street ghetto, he produces an account of reordering the self through the kinds of reading processes that Park also theorized. In this model, readers are continually engaged in the naturalization, through abstraction, of new and challenging forms of selfhood. In Park's explanation of race prejudice, pre-existing abstraction complicates reading by endangering the reader's construction of particularity-based metaphorical links between self and other: racial abstraction produces illegible objects, unavailable for metaphorical connection. In other words, while the melting pot works through a process of abstracted *relations,* the figures between whom these relations obtain must recognize each other as individuals for the consent-based system of exchange-through-reading, exchange-via-metaphor, to work.

Nonetheless, as scholars of whiteness have demonstrated, the Quixanos' maid Kathleen would have been portrayed in terms not unlike Sandy through much of the nineteenth century.[64] The "squaw" and Italian woman whom Gitl evokes in Cahan's *Yekl* were understood as having similarly nonwhite racial status. Sandy is not necessarily or naturally barred from exploring metaphorical links between his own state and these two cultural positions. In fact, Sandy's historic exclusion—the effects of slavery and enduring racial prejudice in the United States, which produce the African American and the "ethnic" immigrant as two incommensurable positions—was alternately asserted and refused as a limit for self-reinvention and cultural fusion at the beginning of the century. In very different registers, both racial leaders like W. E. B. Du Bois (in the 1897 text *The Conservation of Races*) and racist leaders like Benjamin "Pitchfork" Tillman argued against the desirability of considering African Americans assimilable. On the other hand, even these arguments suggest that the question was open for debate—and, as can be seen in the very different positions taken by Charles Chesnutt, the later Du Bois, and James Weldon Johnson, very little was taken for granted at the beginning of the twentieth century. Forms of ethnic and racial categorization were in crisis, and scientific knowledge and political thought were changing rapidly, unmoored from traditional bases of authority, resulting in a wide range of positions on the nature of racial difference.[65] This crisis produces both a sense of possibility and a peculiar blindness to racial exclusion at the optimistic extreme of melting-pot thinking.

Chesnutt's Sandy intuits and explores the meaning of this racial slippage, asking of the man he has just seen perform him: "ef I wuz in yo' place, and you wuz in my place, an' we wuz bofe in de same place, whar would I be?"[66] Sandy's words anticipate Mary Antin's later autobiographical contortions: personal pronouns ("I," "you," "we,") repeatedly collapse into each other, both under-lining Sandy's individuality (through the "I") and asserting his commensura-bility with the other (in the "we"). The comedy of Sandy's question lies in the abstraction of the pronouns, which both confuses the positions that the pronouns intimate and articulates a very particular analysis of the context upon which they depend for meaning. Abstraction, here, *contra* Park, enables slippage and maneuverability. Placement is of critical importance in Sandy's question; in other words, relative positionings, and not putative "essential" or interior differences, are at issue in this encounter. Historical placement divides the African American from the immigrant; but, as Paul Gilroy has suggested, the trans-ethnic experience of modernity as a form of alienation finds its prototype in the African experience in slavery. That is, the immi-grant's modern, even modernist, experience of self-fragmentation is founded in a modern black experience of alienation—one that, Gilroy also notes, has been figured through cross-cultural tropes such as that of diaspora.[67] With its emphasis on positionality, Chesnutt's scene suggests that black participation in the melting pot is not reducible to a simple analogy of blacks to immi-grants, but must be understood in terms of the overlapping, intersecting his-torical experiences of alienation and modernity. Likeness, here, is not identity, but it is not incommensurability, either.

For James Weldon Johnson, who toyed with "The Chameleon" as a potential title for *The Autobiography of an Ex-Coloured Man,* the theatrical changeability at issue in theories of the melting pot represented the central means of negotiating melting-pot inclusion for blacks. As he declared in a speech given at the State Industrial School for Negroes in Savannah, Georgia, on September 16, 1915:

We can shape and mould ourselves absolutely to conditions. Wherever we may be, we are able to make the language, the customs, the laws, the religion, and the mode of thought of the people among whom we live our own. I have seen the colored West Indian gentleman in London, and he is more English than a Lord. I have seen the Haitian gentle-man in Paris, and he is more Frenchy than a marquis. I believe we could make good chinamen, with the exception of the pigtail—and some of us could do even that. This inherent power of adaptability is one of our greatest assets. It serves to blunt the arrows of persecution and to temper the blows of oppression that would otherwise crush us. ... Neither is our power of adaptability mere outward conformity or monkeyish imitation; it is the power to make ourselves an integral part of the whole.[68]

Careful and considered, black performance is the means by which "we are able to make...our own," or establish a new kind of self-possession. As a means of "blunt[ing] the arrows of persecution and temper[ing] the blows of oppression that would otherwise crush us," black chameleonism saves the self by re-figuring it. Exteriority and interiority are indissoluble here: adaptability to circumstances and responsiveness to shifting relations signal neither mere superficial conformity nor uncritical imitation. Rather, they are "inherent," Johnson argues, suddenly making the discourse of inherent racial differences itself chameleonic, exploring an inherence that is nothing but changeability, but that still offers evidence of a contested interiority. Johnson poses these (immigrant) performances—of Englishness, Frenchness, even Chineseness—as precisely the means by which to throw Park's "racial uniform" into question and "to make ourselves an integral part of the whole."

Johnson's use of the multiply allegianced black performer draws on an important early-twentieth-century trope, one most memorably refined by W. E. B. Du Bois. Du Bois's opinions are far too varied for him to be considered exclusively, or even primarily, a melting-pot thinker; however, his idea of "double-consciousness" proved irresistible to a range of melting-pot writers.[69] In *The Souls of Black Folk* Du Bois theorized an African American who "ever feels his two-ness,—an American, a Negro; two souls, two thoughts, two unreconciled strivings; two warring ideals in one dark body."[70] Difference, here, is not parceled out to different bodies, but contained in one individual form. True to the melting pot's unpredictable irruption of new identities, double-consciousness suggests a kind of individualized version of Abraham Cahan's "human hodgepodge with its component parts changed but not yet fused into one homogeneous whole" (*Y,* 30). Combined in the way that different races and ethnicities were in the melting pot, the two impulses in Du Bois's figure are never reconciled, fused, concluded; neither, however, can they be cleanly separated. With double-consciousness Du Bois theorized a self perpetually engaged in the messy process of encounter and mediation, a self theatricalized but by no means improbably self-determining, or even internally consistent. For Du Bois this doubleness is most acutely registered at the level of nationality—the racialized agent is both in and not of, of and not in, the national community. This eccentric position produces imperfect integration, registered psychically, at the level of the individual, as the fragmentation of the self. It should not be surprising, then, that Du Bois's famous words were so thoroughly assimilated by the theorists of assimilation. When Mary Antin announces that she can "speak in the third person" of her pre-immigration self, she articulates a melting-pot double-consciousness (*PL,* 1).

In highly figurative language, *The Souls of Black Folk* associates double-consciousness with a form of insight Du Bois terms "second-sight" (*SBF,* 9). Melting-pot writers seconded this reading: Antin, for example, claimed that impressions produce "double associations" in immigrants who are continually mediating between cultures (*PL,* 3). Du Bois's African American approaches his own ambivalent performances of self as both performer and audience. His "second" sight entails the perspective of the audience ("the eyes of others") added to that of the performer, but it is also secondary in the sense that David Quixano's repudiation and embrace of Jewishness is: it is self-consciously derivative, social, and shared, *not* primary, original, or authentic. According to Du Bois, such an existence yields the African American "no true self-consciousness, but only lets himself see himself through the revelation of the other world" (*SBF,* 9). The circumscribed performances possible in a hostile society deny the subject "true" self-consciousness, but as compensation offer him a self refracted through revelatory glimpses of "the other world." Du Bois's actor is like Constantine Panunzio in the sense of having an expanded and enhanced awareness of the other roles in the drama, without necessarily having full or perfect access to them. With a self both constituted and destabilized through incorporation of "the other world," Du Bois's African American understands "true self-consciousness" to be a fantasy; the self is a cipher, figure, metaphor.[71] The psychic and discursive syncretisms driving this ironic wariness of "truth" in *The Souls of Black Folk* represent important contributions to melting-pot thinking.[72]

The affinities between Du Bois's theory of double-consciousness and early twentieth-century melting-pot theories of selfhood are not simply rhetorical. Du Bois's model focuses explicitly on non-repressive assimilation, or "merging"; it deploys the language of assimilation in the context of a melting-pot yearning parallel to that of David Quixano. Du Bois's African American feels a "longing" to:

> merge his double self into a better and truer self. In this merging he wishes neither of the older selves to be lost. He would not Africanize America, for America has too much to teach the world and Africa. He would not bleach his Negro soul in a flood of white American-ism, for he knows that Negro blood has a message for the world. He simply wishes to make it possible for a man to be both a Negro and an American. (*SBF,* 9)

Du Bois's "Negro" imagines a merging that will not be so complete as to produce the wholesale conversions of "Africanization" and "bleaching." In melting-pot terms, he longs for a form to accommodate his own multiplicity. Du Bois's version of the assimilative self is never fully integrated; his important contribution lies in his commitment to imagining imperfect integration. This "merging" would produce fuller insight into to a shared fund of twentieth-century cultural identities. It would offer a route to adaptive multiplicity, to a doubleness that is not pathological. Of course, as Du Bois's other essays in *The Souls of Black Folk* suggest, and as James Weldon Johnson's work confirms, Progressive-era social programs failed to bring about the imagined merging. Kallen, once again, justly argued against melting-pot optimism that "All is not . . . fact, because it is hope."[73] And yet at the turn of the twentieth century, neither Du Bois nor Johnson was willing to abandon hope for fact. Both issued their challenges to the imagination, calling on wishes and longings; taking their critiques of asymmetrical power in the United States seriously means turning to the literary imagination for evidence.

"Calling It by Name"

As the settlement worker Lillian Wald noted, "gathering up the story of the immigrant, I sometimes wonder if he, like the fairies, does not hold up a magic mirror wherein our social ethics are reflected, rather than his own visage" (*HS,* 304). Wald's references to "fairies" and "magic" convey the elements of imagination and fantasy that infused most melting-pot discussions of assimilation. To Wald the fantasy, or its abstraction, "social ethics," in fact pre-empts the witnessing of the individual immigrant, his specific materiality, "his own visage." Though this dynamic is collaborative (the immigrant self-consciously holds up the mirror, helping to shape the social worker's imaginings), the abstraction of ethics signals what can be lost in even the most sensitive process of cultural merging. Despite (indeed, through) the seductive "magic" of the imaginative "mirror," the particularity of the immigrant's visage is obscured. Such losses wend through melting-pot literature: in Zangwill's *Melting-Pot,* a cultural merging with Kathleen appears to Mrs. Quixano as the undoing of a distinct tradition of Jewish ritual. Mrs. Quixano's culture survives for her only in its coherence; diffusion entails a loss beyond recuperation.[74] As I discuss in Chapter Four, figures like Mrs. Quixano guard a sacredness that melting-pot thinking cannot, by its nature, respect. The imaginative element of melting-pot assimilation inexorably compromises its objects, always abstracting them from their original contexts. Thus the "magic mirror" represented by the melting pot may promise the freedom of the literary imagination, but it just as surely promises a high cost for that freedom.

This is not to say that melting-pot thinkers simply agreed to sacrifice the sacred (in the sense of the kinds of historical particulars that Mrs. Quixano values). Jane Addams and John Dewey, for example, attempted to protect historical differences through education: according to them, schooling made unique histories of both achievement and disadvantage meaningful for a wider range of actors. Dewey's educational writings suggest how delicate was the balance between cultural blending and cultural protectionism in melting-pot theory. He insists on teaching "the great past contributions of every strain in our composite make-up" in the public schools; in terms that frame sacrifice as inevitable, he welcomes "hyphenism,"

> in the sense of extracting from each people its special good, so that it shall surrender into a common fund of wisdom and experience what it especially has to contribute. All of these surrenders and contributions taken together create the national spirit of America. The dangerous thing is for each factor to isolate itself, to try to live off its past, and then to attempt to impose itself upon other elements, or, at least, to keep itself intact and thus refuse what other cultures have to offer.[75]

Dewey's word "contribution" takes the histories and languages of melting-pot participants seriously. However, the word "surrender," to Dewey's credit, does not minimize the losses entailed in even the most benignly formulated versions of assimilation. Such a phrase—or the idea of "extraction" of a "special good"—adumbrates the industrial-era power differentials of the assimilation process. Dewey imagines cultural "goods" passing beyond exclusive control; his proposed educational project disrupts the proprietary relation to culture. Casting refusals of such a system as "dangerous" isolationism, forms of monopolism, Dewey frames his melting-pot faith in the language of a modified free-market economy. Dewey's progressivism here consists *not* in a claim that cultural sharing ought not to entail losses, but rather in the view that such losses ought to be equally shared. To resist such losses, according to his logic, is to participate in a cultural version of the accumulation economy he critiqued in his era.

Dewey's language evokes the conceptual trade-offs of the melting-pot model, but in its emphasis on provocative figuration it falls short of demonstrating the full range of real-world compromises tolerated by melting-pot ideologies. (The compromises that constituted Jane Addams's support of Theodore Roosevelt and the Progressive Party of 1912, for example, evince the practical vulnerabilities of an ideology of slippage and compromise.) For Horace Kallen, it was precisely the metaphorical tenor of melting-pot discourse that made it dangerously cavalier about cultural loss. Pointing, like Wald, to the threat of abstraction, Kallen argued that the children of immigrants threw off the social traditions of their ancestors for little more than figuration, no more than the "externals" of a life: "as the public school imparts it, or as the social settlement imparts it, it is not really a *life;* it is an abstraction, an arrangement of words."[76] Kallen's critique is acute, even if the bloodless life that he foresaw for assimilating immigrants was not logically necessary; the ideas of the melting pot are indeed premised upon a faith in "abstraction" and the "arrangement of words." Practically, social and economic mobility remained tethered to Anglo-conformity for most children of the settlement and public school, and Kallen predicted that fierce cultural attachments would be sacrificed for this mobility. To Kallen's mind, while abstraction was fine for imagining the political organization of a nation, it could not serve as an imaginative center for either an individual or a true community.

Marcus Ravage, an immigrant autobiographer, implicitly responded to Kallen's horror of empty homogeneity by demonstrating the ways in which melting-pot metaphoricity infused abstraction with affective range. Ravage appealed to the image of the immigrant in the minds of the native-born to conjure up the redemptive capacities of figuration. According to Ravage, the imagined immigrant is made up of "bundles—funny, picturesque bundles of every shape and size and color. The alien himself, in his incredible garb, as he walks off the gang-plank, appears like some sort of an odd, moving bundle. And always he carries more bundles."[77] Like the bundle obscuring the immigrant's face in Lewis Hine's photo (fig. 1), these bundles act as engines of abstraction, making the figure of the immigrant particularly communicative in terms of form. The word itself as Ravage uses it represents a parallel engine of abstraction, for although "bundles" is the basis for Ravage's figure, both literally and in its role in the sentence, it is a full, even cluttered vehicle. One *is* bundles and one *has* bundles, and sometimes these states are themselves bundled together. The bundles are at once general and specific, evocative of the unusual collection that is, materially, immigrant life but also, culturally, immigrant experience; they represent the views of the native-born that cluster about the figure of the immigrant, and the masses of immigrant beliefs; in their abundance and the abundance of their signification, they represent the continual multiplication and overflowing that paradoxically frustrate the urge to "bundle." The bundle functions abstractly, but it also makes reference to the material conditions of displacement: upheaval, disorganization, impoverishment, but also a commitment to transporting certain critical items. Ravage's figure perfectly evokes the extent to which melting-pot figuration could guard against Kallen's bloodless abstraction: by underlining the *multiplicity* of readings, specific investments, and routes to participation in assimilation, melting-pot thinkers attempted to control the forces of abstraction in their figures.

Jane Addams's contribution to this debate was a school that attempted to institutionalize a balance between abstraction and protections for the particularity of cultural "memory." *The Second Twenty Years at Hull-House* (1930) describes how the settlement encouraged forms of play and arts that assisted in the expression of diverse cultural histories: in a pottery class "trying historic subjects," it was not unusual to see that "the Scandinavian boy made a Viking bowl, the Mexican an Indian hut, the Greek the capital of a Corinthian column, the Italian the dome of St. Peter's." Addams's pluralistic fable exceeds a simplistically proprietary vision of culture by appealing to language: "The variety was interesting," she continues, "but not nearly so significant as the fact that each boy recognized what the other boy had made and called it by name."[78] While each boy employs his "own" form, then, he instructs his fellows in it, so that they become familiar with a whole range of cultural forms. Calling the other boys' forms "by name," the boys claim them as their own, as part of their culture and language. While these boys do not share cultural backgrounds, they share a common vocabulary and a curiosity about the ideas and traditions that each of them brings to the table.

In *Democracy and Education* (1916), John Dewey used the idea of "like-mindedness" to evoke what Addams cast as calling things "by name." For Dewey, like-mindedness was the aim and means of a melting-pot pedagogy. It requires neither conformity nor agreement; rather, it represents a kind of shared vocabulary, in experiential terms:

> Suppose that conditions were so arranged that one person automatically caught a ball and then threw it to another person who caught and automatically returned it; and that each so acted without knowing where the ball came from or went to. Clearly, such action would be without point or meaning. It might be physically controlled, but it would not be socially directed. But suppose that each becomes aware of what the other is doing, and becomes interested in the other's action and thereby interested in what he is doing himself as connected with the action of the other. The behavior of each would then be...socially intelligent.[79]

In Dewey's metaphor, as in so many melting-pot metaphors, cultural content is troped by a transferable object (here a ball, elsewhere a garment). Like-mindedness, on the other hand, is a frame, or a form, in which to interpret the ball, or cultural content: here, it entails a shared knowledge of the game. Players need not have a uniform outlook or technique; they should, however, be "aware" and "interested," "socially intelligent" about the broader context in which their individual contact with the ball occurs. For Jane Addams, the calling of others' forms by name indicates just such an awareness of the larger imaginative game. Both of these theorizations of broad-mindedness attempt to preserve what they can of traditional artistic and intellectual patterns: not through nationalistic protectionism, but through a kind of cosmopolitanism.

If Addams has her way, her students' sculpted forms will be assimilated by one another as named forms; an attempt will be made to protect the integrity of the pasts they represent by respecting their specificity. However, Mary Antin's autobiography insists that the past is a constructed thing, and there can be no guaranteeing its integrity. Antin makes much over a question of memory and naming, describing a scene of "deep-red dahlias" that she was later told "were not dahlias at all, but poppies" (*PL,* 66). Antin insists on her dahlias, however, claiming that her memory is lost if she attempts to imagine the flowers as *"poppies."* As Antin's discussion suggests, the naming of the flower-form neither preserves it intact, nor guards it against manipulation. As in Jane Addams's scene of named pottery forms, the name is learned and later redeployed, but the form itself cannot be held constant. The amorphous forms that concern these writers shift with the future uses that the scene of name-sharing both anticipates and actively creates. That is, if the logic of the melting pot were put into practice, the pottery class would begin sampling and citing from the archive of forms made available to them. This later generation of sculptures would both evoke and exceed the names of its predecessors.

Addams's cosmopolitanism was embedded in her settlement. Her form was largely one of material social action. When it came to expressing cultural intermixture and learning, she distinguished language—"calling it by name"—from the material, creative activity of the children's sculpting hands. Language and literary form did occupy a special position in Addams's philosophy: she explicitly connected novels with assimilation, because "they in a measure satisfy an unformulated belief that to see farther, to know all sorts of men, in an indefinite way, is a preparation for better social adjustment."[80] However, because for Addams writing serves as access-point for a shared reality, it must provide a faithful representation of "all sorts of men." This language must be reliable enough to serve as a shared vocabulary—to be trusted to encapsulate, translate, and generally make sense of the messy imperfections produced by clumsy little hands. But, as the example of Marcus Ravage's bundles suggests, melting-pot language is more often faithless than faithful, itself the messily imperfect vessel. Addams's theory of cosmopolitan naming, in other words, still required translation into the more fluid idiom of the melting pot.

The work of Henry James, James Weldon Johnson, Willa Cather, and Gertrude Stein reveals Addams's separation of "naming" and formal crafting to be utterly false. For these proto-modernists, literary form became an indispensable mode of meeting the intellectual challenges posed by Progressive-era ideas of the melting pot. The problem of loss—as well as questions of sharing, merging, changeability, individuality, agency, cultural possession, and inequality—registers differently across their works, sometimes even contradictorily. Their Deweyan "like-mindedness," like that of many melting-pot thinkers, is constituted more by responsiveness to a set of questions than by any kind of ideological conformity. They share more than this thematic link, however: for these melting-pot modernists, literary form became (in Dewey's terms) the shared knowledge of the game, the frame, as well as the ball passed from player to player. These writers put questions of literary form in the position of cultural and intellectual prominence that they retain today. The problems and promises of the melting-pot idea are still traceable in their literary innovations. Even more important, vestigial melting-pot premises still infuse modernist and even post-modernist literary innovations, in ways that we would do well to be alert to. Addams, Dewey, Robert Park, Marcus Ravage, and Mary Antin could not agree on how to approach the losses entailed in melting-pot modes of thought: melting-pot modernists did no better at achieving resolution. The formal experimentalism that has become a literary hallmark of the twentieth century, then, still carries significant cultural baggage.

We can best understand the formal experimentalism of melting-pot modernists in Frances Ferguson's terms, as "the emergence of the question of individuation, in contradistinction to the notion of form as given."[81] Formal experimentation as we see it in these proto-modernist texts conceives of a text as individual, or logically parallel to the individual; in the context of melting-pot thinking, the text-as-individual produces a distinctive relation between reader and text. "To know all sorts of men," in Jane Addams's words, is quite different in a post-realist context, when one knows "all sorts of men" by knowing all sorts of texts *as one would know men,* not by reading texts as vehicles for the knowing of men: that is, when the text itself is conceived along the lines of a person, rather than when the text claims to document persons.[82] As we will see, Henry James theorized this shift most fully. But along with him, James Weldon Johnson, Willa Cather, and Gertrude Stein produced the effect of the text signifying as person in part through infusing life writing with fiction and drama, and fiction with life writing and drama.[83] They troubled the boundaries between fiction and life writing, evoking the melting-pot traffic between forms of selfhood and forms of literary expression. As well as suggesting that fiction is the only thing "essential" to the form of the self, melting-pot modernists endowed the text with kinds of agency usually reserved for persons. These experimental approaches foreground the messy constructedness of the melting-pot person, be it textual, figural, or literal.

While the melting-pot modernists considered in the next chapters do not perfectly follow the literary theories of Robert Park and Jane Addams, then, they do act on the logical extension of those theories when they imagine literary artifacts on the model of persons. By encoding the melting pot's contradictory model of selfhood in their texts, melting-pot modernists emphasized a textual idea of personhood that was very much of their moment, and that logically informed their developing ideas about the animate nature of texts. As Dorothy Hale argues, the consequences of this analogy between persons and texts now extend well beyond literary-critical practices to inform social theory: to this I might add that, given the foundations of Jamesian "social formalism" in the social theory of the melting pot, its late twentieth-century instantiation seems less an evolution than a peculiarly alienated return to the origin.[84] As the melting-pot works of Henry James that I discuss in the next chapter suggest, this vision of text and person is the beginning, not the end, of a continuing process of literary and cultural interpretation. In other words, the melting-pot historical context for literary modernism also represents the historical context for many current presumptions about the nature of texts and their relation to the world. In turn, these understandings of texts extend into social theory, requiring closer reading strategies from cultural historians and social theorists as well as literary critics.

✍ CHAPTER 2

Henry James in the "Intellectual *Pot-au-feu*"

Henry James seems an unlikely melting-pot modernist. Born in 1843 and expatriated in 1866, he did not fully experience the waves of immigration that gave rise to melting-pot discourse at the turn of the twentieth century. Though *The American Scene* (1907), which recounts his travels through the United States in 1904–1905, represents one of the most perceptive accounts of the transformations the nation was undergoing at the turn of the century, it alone cannot justify James's inclusion as a melting-pot modernist. For this reason James is in fact an ideal figure with which to begin this study; his example illuminates melting-pot modernism *not* as a canon of exclusively immigration-focused texts but as a moment of far-reaching speculation about the nature, form, and expression of selfhood. James's early twentieth-century writings stage an early and influential exploration of the expressive problems and possibilities associated with the melting-pot idea. As I will show, James's late works articulate a version of melting-pot formal experimentalism that applies equally to the self and to the text—indeed, that makes important and lasting connections between the forms of self and text. This dimension of Jamesian thinking shaped both literary modernism and twentieth-century literary criticism—a formidable melting-pot legacy.

Writing about his visit to the United States, James revealed the social vision implicit in his commitment to formal experimentalism: "one must

follow up the formidable process—*that* is of the essence," he assured a correspondent.[1] Neither the United States nor its inhabitants were in fixed or final
form, he saw; taking his cue from his brother William's popular philosophy,
he deemed changeability to be essential. Faced with the relentless outward
changeability of the early twentieth-century United States, James did not
seek changeless inner truths, but recognized change of form, "formidable
process," as speaking "of the essence." The pages that follow will demonstrate
the fundamental intertwining of ideas of form and selfhood brought about
by a sensitive response to the phenomena of early twentieth-century U.S.
immigration. In effect, I argue, the context of immigration both sharpens
James's sense of "nonidentity" (in Ross Posnock's influential term) and shows
this "nonidentity" to have very specific literary-formal implications.[2] The
revisionist pragmatism of what Posnock and David McWhirter have identified as James's "fourth phase" has a very specific melting-pot context: that
context explains both the experimentalism and the formal self-consciousness
that James bequeaths to literary modernism.[3]

In his works of the early twentieth century, James lavished his considerable
attention on the surprising fluidity of ostensibly fixed forms. After returning to his native country in 1904, only to experience himself as alien to its
changeable and often unfathomable culture, he wrote of the implications
of this experienced fluidity for both subjectivity and aesthetic practice with
new precision. His narrative of this journey, *The American Scene,* casts the
United States as an amorphous and superabundant reproach to the catalog
of insufficiencies with which he described it in his youthful essay *Hawthorne*
(1879). The travelogue itself ironically assumes the form of a voyage always
incomplete and thus subject to change. After his American trip, James's
projects demonstrate the intertwined fluidities of person and text even more
clearly. The New York Edition of his works foregrounds his fluid authorial
persona while freeing many of his most popular works from their previous
textual incarnations, providing editorial puzzles for generations to come. His
unfinished autobiography, *A Small Boy and Others, Notes of a Son and Brother,*
and *The Middle Years,* so diffuses his own image and that of his family that it
constitutes a radical revision of the autobiographical form. For many years
this phase of James's career was seen as one of shoring up, of solidification of
his role as the "Master"; more recently, scholars have recognized the phase
as one of destabilization. That the destabilizations of self were so fundamentally tied to a modernist formal experimentalism, however, only becomes
clear in the context of James's melting-pot experiences. Despite William
James's attempts to warn him off the 1904–1905 trip, Henry insisted on a
U.S. visit in part because he envisioned it as an opportunity to be shocked

and overwhelmed; he needed the early twentieth-century United States, he explained, for a "renovation of one's too monotonised grab-bag."[4] James's late-career destabilizations show his willingness to consider both self and art as "grab-bags" and as constantly under renovation.

James had early imagined that a capacity for cultural sharing would prove to be Americans' distinctive cultural and aesthetic achievement: in a letter of 1867 he praised the ability of the American "race" to "deal freely with forms of civilization not our own... [to] pick and choose and assimilate and in short (aesthetically, etc.) claim our property wherever we find it," pronouncing, "I think it not unlikely that American writers may yet indicate that a vast intellectual fusion and synthesis of the various National tendencies of the world is the condition of more important achievements than any we have seen."[5] By the beginning of the twentieth century, both his wide reading and his correspondence had exposed James to new American ideas about the "vast intellectual fusion and synthesis of the various National tendencies" of the melting-pot era. His brother and frequent correspondent, William, had started the series of works leading to his conceptualization of pluralism. (William had also pressed a copy of W. E. B. Du Bois's *Souls of Black Folk* on his younger brother.) Henry James had been in close contact with Stephen and Cora Crane, gaining access to Crane's extensive journalistic experience in the immigrant-dense cities of the American northeast. James's friendship with Edith Wharton exposed him to yet another perspective on the changing face of the urban United States. Old friends such as Henry Adams and Henry Cabot Lodge understood the nation to be at a historical crisis, largely due to its changing population. James had sternly repudiated Theodore Roosevelt's response to the crisis, warning of the "violent" "simplifications" by which Roosevelt responded to "an age when so much of the ingenuity of the world goes to multiplying contact and communication, to reducing separation and distance, to promoting, in short, an inter-penetration that would have been the wonder of our fathers."[6] James's longtime friend and literary ally William Dean Howells had become deeply interested in questions of immigration and social synthesis after moving to New York. Through these contacts and others, James became increasingly aware of the melting pot as a signal force of modernity.

In the early Progressive era, even the less coercive discussions of assimilation (such as in Jacob Riis's *How the Other Half Lives,* 1890) focused straightforwardly on enabling the social, political, and economic integration of foreign-born populations. James's melting-pot innovations are less concerned with the idea of a crucible for the "other half." Instead, James's late writings find immigration bringing home formal challenges to the dominant institutions and identities of the turn-of-the-century United States: that is, he is ceaselessly faced by the necessity of a melting-pot crucible for "this half" (indeed, one through which this division into halves no longer makes sense). As James wrote, having arrived in the United States, "I have been bethinking myself much of my necessary kind of form and tone and feeling, how it *must* be absolutely personal to myself and proper to my situation."[7] James's melting-pot formalism must be personal because he discovers the action of the melting pot to be personal. As James's writings reveal, the melting pot works upon both the personal self and the very concept of self; through the action of the melting pot, others and otherness appear as new versions of the self. Unlike certain members of his class, James refused to insulate himself from the melting-pot moment. As a result, in late James, the melting-pot subject *is,* quite naturally, an aging, genteel member of the United States' northeastern elite. By undermining the stability of the privileged cultural positions of his era, James emphasizes the thoroughgoing nature of the melting pot.

James's return to the United States in 1904–1905 marked a transition in his literary output: it followed his completion of the three novels of his major phase, *The Ambassadors, The Wings of the Dove,* and *The Golden Bowl.* However, it preceded (and, given the name of the project, can be said to have prompted) the major revision of his work and articulation of his aesthetic principles in the New York Edition. This chapter traces the troubling of selfhood from *The American Scene* to the critical prefaces of the New York Edition and the late autobiographies, showing that James's melting-pot experience was indispensable to his inter-articulations of selfhood and literary form.

New York, the city of James's birth, the irresistible center around which the many parts of *The American Scene* gravitate, the presiding genius of the late-career revision, and the ever-eloquent setting of much of the autobiographies, provides both starting-place and connective thread for this discussion. By the early twentieth century, James's New York (whether it be the visited New York of 1904 or the remembered New York of his childhood) is characterized by surfeit, and the sensitive intelligence is often strained to its limits by the responsibility of responding to and representing the scene. As a result, *The American Scene* becomes largely a narrative of *himself,* faced with what he termed "our huge national *pot au feu,*" "the fusion, as of elements in solution in a vast hot pot," "the cauldron of the 'American' character."[8] As I will show, the self that understands itself (and selfhood more generally) to be implicated in this immigrant-infused cauldron goes on to write the major statements of modernist formal practice, framing them as a late burst of autobiographical creativity. He thereby elaborates the contours of melting-pot modernism.

Excesses of the American Scene

When James returned to the United States in 1904, he believed himself to have "had time to become almost as 'fresh' as an inquiring stranger... [but not] enough to cease to be, or at least to feel, as acute as an initiated native" (*AS*, 3). *The American Scene,* published in 1907, details James's analysis of American culture from this starting-point of doubleness. As a result of his internal incoherence, the James of *The American Scene* forms fleeting, qualified, and unpredictable alliances with a wide variety of different interlocutors. This combination of internal incoherence and wide-ranging but ambivalent alliances complicates traditional versions of selfhood, blurring the boundaries between self and other. James's consciousness enacts multiple allegiances, none of them ever entire or "natural." As scholars since Ross Posnock have noted, *The American Scene* resolutely denaturalizes the literary presentation of selfhood: the text's central consciousness positions itself eccentrically and assimilatively as both participant and observer, both performer and audience, both detective and victim, both artist and reader. To these readings I wish to add the important point that James's denaturalizations draw on, and add to, a similar and robustly immigrant-focused discourse. (Mary Antin's immigrant autobiography *The Promised Land,* of 1912, is only the most well-known immigrant account centered on such eccentric assimilative positionings, in which "one body served more than one spiritual organization."[9]) Exulting in this kind of instability, in *The American Scene* James refers to himself in the third person (sometimes as the "restless analyst," sometimes as a less clearly marked agent) as often as he does in the first person. ("I could speak in the third person," announces Mary Antin's autobiographical persona (*PL*, 1); in 1921, Edward Bok's *Americanization of Edward Bok* literally does so.)

Like theorists of the melting pot, James had long enjoyed playing with the implications of "form." In his hands, form was at once the outward shape of an individual or thing, and the act of giving or taking shape; at once a series of social gestures and performances (like "culture," in this sense), and the structural arrangement of a literary expression. Early in *The American Scene,* James connects his adoption of strategies of self-diffusion with the importance that form takes on in the turn-of-the-century United States. Reflecting on a visit to William James's family compound at Chocorua, New Hampshire, soon after his arrival, he blames the empty ugliness of rural New England society on its "so complete abolition of *forms,*" italicizing the word to emphasize its importance (*AS*, 22). James reads the absence of forms in the interactions of locals; form as it figures here is not only plural, but socially constituted. He finds promise for New Hampshire in imagining a drama of formal evolution that is still to come: "could forms only *be*, as a recognized accessory to manners, introduced and developed, the ugliness might begin scarcely to know itself" (*AS*, 22). Forms and alienation travel easily together, and entail a productive confusion about the self and what it means (scarcely knowing oneself). The stifling proprieties of the area have devolved into an awful self-certainty, a fixation upon what is "not owed by the parties themselves, but owed *to* them, not to be rendered, but to be received" (*AS*, 23). Whether these dues are to be called standards, or manners, James resists calling them forms. For him forms arise through generosity, a turning outward of the self as opposed to a grasping inward for the self. Such a process entails turning away from the sterility of one's current practices, to "aesthetic enrichment" through the environment beyond the self (*AS*, 23). From this encounter with the other, with the "charming secrets" of the scene beyond the self, James predicts the "production and imposition of forms" (*AS*, 23). For this reason, it is fitting that an account James envisioned as "The Return of the Native" was eventually titled *The American Scene;* the change of title indicates a focus shifted outward from the personal journey, toward the production of forms enabled by a sensitive response to one's surroundings.[10]

In *The American Scene* the Jamesian narrator is fluid and inconsistent, never guilty of the self-certainty he identified in New Hampshire. However, this approach always threatens to become inadequate to the task of relating scenes (both in the sense of connecting them and in the sense of recounting them); the central consciousness's outward turn may enable the production of forms, but often it also obscures the continuities constitutive of both narrative and selfhood. (If the "restless analyst" is not to be recognized from scene to scene, then how are the scenes connected?) As first published in *Harper's Magazine* and the *North American Review,* James's impressions were a series of regional snapshots. Without book publication, they might have testified to the pluralist regionalism of the turn-of-the-century United States. However, *The American Scene* compulsively asserts relatedness, as if to exceed the fragmentation of a purely pluralist model; in other words, the text sets itself the challenge of a melting-pot synthesis. The melting-pot theorists discussed in the previous chapter privileged individual selves over culture groups as sites of synthesis; James's text goes further, laying the formal foundation for a noncoercive merging in a densely figured literary self.

To locate the self that will prove a formal basis for the synthesis of the text, James turns, paradoxically, to the site that puts traditional notions of selfhood in greatest jeopardy. *The American Scene* lingers upon (and returns to) irrepressible, unavoidable New York, a place characterized by "confusion carried to chaos for any intelligence, any perception; a welter of objects and sounds in which relief, detachment, dignity, meaning, perished utterly" (*AS,* 65). As setting, New York offers a material basis for discoveries of likeness between selves: early twentieth-century New York was already producing a popular consumer culture that was binding together the immigrant and laboring masses. In James's account, New York's continuous sensory assault challenges the boundaries between public and private, and thereby throws the very boundaries of the self into question. *The American Scene* registers this challenge to the self as a formal challenge to expression, as New York violates the boundaries of chapters, arguments, and timelines, "so little does any link in the huge looseness of New York... appear to come as a whole, or as final, out of the fusion" (*AS,* 89). This city operates according to a logic of excess. Such a New York is not unique to James's testimony: contemporaneous reports similarly dwell on the excesses of the New York scene. Ernest Poole's reformist novel *The Voice of the Street* (1906) represents the city in these terms:

> The street was racing and straining; it seemed to suck in all the crowds and sweep them on; with eyes fixed they hurried and raced as they had raced the mad day long. The street was fascinating. Lights gleamed from a thousand windows, from towers, from twentieth stories, from sparkling signs hung high in blue and red incandescents, from pawn-shops, lunch-rooms, cafes and saloons, from trolleys and street stands, from trains high up in the air and from holes that led into the subway. The roar was glorious! Nothing tired or sad or sentimental here; it was gay, throbbing, jerking, laughing, vibrating and thrilling with life. Life strung high! And soaring far above a thousand boy voices sang, "Extry! Extry! Extry!" All about graft, train smash-ups and strikes; about weddings, divorces and murders; football, prize-fights and horse races. "Extry! Extry! Extry!" And as fitting music to it all, a big street piano jerked out the quick nervous throbbing of rag-time. The street laughed and sparkled and swore, the street roared![11]

Poole's overwrought prose capably conveys the demands of the setting on the individual observer. The task of James's text is to find the expressive form that will neither hysterically reproduce the excessiveness of New York, as Poole's does, nor artificially impose a wholeness or finality that the "fusion" of the city resists.

The American Scene answers the challenge to literary form autobiographically: the text defers to James's process of devising a self that is equally responsive and resilient to the excesses of twentieth-century admixture. James's particular self meets with intimate complications in New York. Of the whole American scene, the city of New York is the place both most familiar to James (by dint of being his birthplace and childhood home) and most unfamiliar to James (by dint of bearing the most obvious traces of modern architecture, industry, and migration). In this zone of slippage and unreliability, the simplicity of familiar positions is compromised, and New York conveys this message to James in the most personal of terms. "One's supreme relation... was one's relation to one's country—a conception made up so largely of one's countrymen and one's countrywomen," he notes at the beginning of *The American Scene* (67); New York alerts him to a new way in which this relation is shared and transformed—by innumerable new countrymen and new countrywomen. By vividly displaying the new range of populations comprehended by the American identity, New York reveals the elasticity of American identity. While this elasticity fascinates James the cultural critic, the "huge looseness" of the city also poses a significant challenge to expression: "the impression... kept overflowing the cup and spreading in a wide waste of speculation" (*AS*, 64). As well as diffusing the critical attention, such looseness threatens to expand a shared relation, the basis of self-knowledge, into James's proverbial "loose baggy monster."[12] One fears, James writes, that "to touch it [the idea of the nation] overmuch, to pull it about, is to put it in peril of weakening" (*AS*, 67). An indefinite expansion of the idea of selfhood, through that expanded "supreme relationship," likewise threatens meaninglessness.

Against looseness and meaninglessness, *The American Scene* exhibits a kind of taut elasticity, a carefully choreographed and very literal performance of ambivalence. Both the text and the form of selfhood it models seem to pulse, their boundaries alternately expanding and contracting, their attention alternately comprehensive and minutely discriminating. In the phase of expansion, James's text enacts uncanny collapses of difference and sharings of identity. For instance, he writes that in wandering the "foreign" quarters of the city, "you recognize in them, freely, those elements that are not elements of swift convertibility, and you lose yourself in the wonder of what becomes, as it were, of the obstinate, the unconverted residuum" (*AS*, 95).[13] Appealing to the reader, James's "you" obscures the distinctness of the self in question, the self that in response to the differences of immigrants is already "lost" in wonder. "Which is *not* the alien," muses this interlocutor (*AS*, 95). Such merged identities are often precipitated by an "assault of suggestion," the scene's irresistible sensory and impressionistic claim on the wanderer (*AS*, 68). The violence of the assault and the intense strangeness of the momentary merging of selves then cause the viewer to recoil, contracting his attention. Shortly after the preceding reflections, the "observer gasp[s] with the sense of isolation," emerging from the solution in which he was dissolved and asserting his own difference from the faces around him—but also, ironically, confirming his turn as obstinate, unconverted, residuum (*AS*, 96). Through unpredictability and contradiction, the oscillating forms of self and text cultivate a tension that prevents loose meaninglessness.

Tensely shared identities do not produce elasticity easily, however. When James finds one of his most personal and yet most precarious identifications violently made collective, the assault proves a challenge to his ability to rebound into expansiveness. James "liked to think" of his "relation to New York as...almost inexpressibly intimate" (*AS*, 89); he hopes to rediscover an individual connection to the city of his childhood preserved, kept inviolate. Of course, New York denies him the nostalgic fulfillment of an unchanged intimate relation. Instead, he finds his private space opened up and shared in ways he never imagined. The relentless restlessness and disregard for the past that James noted in the American scene are directly focused at the self in New York; among the "checks and snubs" the city proffers, none is so affecting to him as "the rudely, the ruthlessly suppressed birth-house" in Washington Square (*AS*, 70). Indeed, James confesses, witnessing the blank new edifice that stands where his childhood home should be feels like "having been amputated of half my history" (*AS*, 71). He has been cut off from the physical trace of his past, and forced to conceive of the past as imaginatively manifested rather than physically grounded. Such alienation from his birthplace leaves him, ironically, in a marginal, tenuous position parallel to that of the newly arrived immigrant, the alien without a birthplace in the United States.[14] However apt the analogy may be, James's language of amputation suggests his skepticism about filling the void that has been left. Is this analogical relation (so central to melting-pot conceptions of being) an inadequate substitute for the intimate relations that once secured traditionally conceived selves?

"The Tremendous Force of Analogy"

Amputation, here, serves not only to evoke James's feelings at the erasure of his birthplace but also to trope the maimed and incomplete nature of the forms of connection reliant on the literary logics of the melting pot—here, analogy. This broader purpose of the amputation meta-trope becomes more clear in a short story that James published following his American trip. In "The Jolly Corner" (1908), Spencer Brydon returns to America after an absence of many years and finds his old house haunted by a ghost—an apparition of an alternate self, *his* self had he stayed in the United States, a ravaged and amputated man (he is missing several fingers). Oscillating between attraction and terror, Brydon finds himself "catching, as he felt, a moment back, the very breath" of his own double.[15] In "The Jolly Corner," evidence of the "suppressed" (the amputated fingers, like the birth-house of *The American Scene*) simultaneously acts both as evidence of the multiplicity of selves and as impetus for their disavowal. As the language of amputation suggests, the connective tissues that might yoke these multiple selves into a single person have been severed. New York's assault of suggestion has produced, as Brydon conjectures, "some different effect for my life and for my 'form'" (JC, 324). The self forced into the sharings of the melting pot emerges no longer whole—and with a new sense of the artificial coherence of "form" (thus Brydon's own scare quotes).[16] Brydon is averse to such high-cost sharings; he disavows his alternate, deeming him "the just so totally other person" as he stalks him using the metaphor of the hunt (JC, 326).

Navigating a "multiplication of doors" to a closed door at the end of a series of interconnected rooms (a series that brings to mind the tenement layouts that Jacob Riis described in *How the Other Half Lives,* save for its eerie emptiness), Brydon hangs back from confronting his alter ego. The closed door, the asserted boundary, the private space so unavailable to contemporary immigrants becomes, here, the means by which the anxious native-born dodges his relation to the other self. Brydon has imagined the other framed, contained, by a doorway, carefully distanced down a hallway. When he himself is *in* the chain of rooms, he retreats from the implied intimacy. He imagines the reopening of the door to this "chain of communication" as "the end of him," for his alternate will be "once more at large and in general possession" (JC, 336, 340). In one of his earliest dispatches from New York, James meditated vexedly on the "note of settled possession" among the "aliens" (*AS,* 67). Certainly, what for Brydon seems the "end" is, for James's accounts of New York, simply the end of the beginning (these musings conclude his February 1906 *Harper's* segment). Elsewhere, such a note is also narrated by Jane Addams as a beginning: their first night in the reputedly haunted Hull-House, Addams and her fellows inadvertently left a side door open. Having slept in a haunted house with the door open to the other, the residents awoke rested and unmolested, the feasibility of such sharing or "general possession" tested and proven. In "The Jolly Corner," however, Brydon takes the threat posed by openness to alternate selves in deadly earnest.

When his double reveals himself, Brydon's response is one of horror and refusal:

the bared identity was too hideous as *his*... The face, *that* face, Spencer Brydon's?—he searched it still, but looking away from it in dismay and denial. . . . It was unknown, inconceivable, awful, disconnected from any possibility—! He had been "sold," he inwardly moaned, stalking such game as this: the presence before him was a presence, the horror within him a horror, but the waste of his nights had been only grotesque and the success of his adventure an irony. Such an identity fitted his at *no* point, made its alternative monstrous. A thousand times yes, as it came upon him nearer now—the face was the face of a stranger. It came upon him nearer now, quite as one of those expanding fantastic images projected by the magic lantern of childhood; for the stranger, whoever he might be, evil, odious, blatant, vulgar, had advanced as for aggression, and he knew himself give ground. Then harder pressed still, sick with the force of his shock, and falling back as under the hot breath and roused passion of a life larger than his own, a rage of personality before which his own collapsed, he felt the whole vision turn to darkness and his very feet give way. (JC, 344)

Guarding that place denied to James (the house of his birth, the solid base of his identity), Spencer Brydon denounces the necessity of sharing it with another. The passage, of course, undercuts this intention at every turn; it is overfull with rhetorical connections between doubles, from repetition (presence, horror), to alliteration (dismay, denial), to rhyme (sick, shock), to irony. As Brydon backpedals, echoing prose mocks his desire to escape refraction. And yet the passage also sympathetically reflects Brydon's state of mind; its rapid shifts from questioning to exclamation and its torturous syntax dramatize his confusion. Brydon needs a coordinating conjunction, that linguistic feature that William James deemed constitutive of a world pluralistically conceived. Without the "and," Brydon is left with commas, piling words up paratactically without being able to explore a more full and nuanced relation between them. The rhetorical overload (unknown, inconceivable, awful; evil, odious, blatant, vulgar) mimics New York's effects of sensory "assault," in this case overcoming the vulnerable protagonist to the point of snuffing him out.

Brydon's vision of his alternate self reveals the inadequacy of response and reverberation in and of themselves. This passage demonstrates that without sympathy, response and reverberation can become defensive, even aggressive. While Brydon can accept mirroring ("the presence before him was a presence, the horror within him a horror"), he balks at the point at which perfect parallelism shifts to admit difference and complication (and, ironically, richer meaning): "but the waste of his nights had been only grotesque and the success of his adventure an irony." The question is, of course, whether analogy can serve to advance the connection from "identity," mere reflection or mirroring, to the sympathetic encompassing of difference that Brydon repudiates.[17] Certainly the story gives every indication that in repudiating sympathy, Brydon is struggling *against* the almost irrepressible analogical tendencies in language. Already contaminated by the language of commerce associated with his double (sold, waste, success), he finds himself with no viable exit strategy. While Brydon would have it that "Such an identity fitted his at *no* point, made its alternative monstrous," his phrase demonstrates his predicament. The rejection of "fit" precipitates a second clause in which the referent of "its" remains unclear: is the monstrous alternative an alternative to Brydon's identity, an alternative to "such" an identity, or an alternative to the rejected "fit"? (The rhyme between "fitted" and "its" further undermines his vehement rejection.) Brydon reverberates, here, but with outrage at the monstrous grotesqueries of his position. Indeed, the rage conveyed by this passage is amplified by the language's antagonistic, or undermining, relation to Brydon's disavowal. The intensity of Brydon's refusals mounts even as he seems to intuit that he has been "sold" even by language, that he is in fact bound by the "chain of communication." His aggressive denials, in other words, are fueled by the abstract and yet seemingly inescapable nature of the relation he is involved in. In a sense, Brydon both experiences and dramatizes how the melting-pot metaphor might become coercive in its own way.

While Brydon falls back before an imagined "assault" by his double, he yields in an effort to keep his sense of self intact and unsullied; unlike the restless analyst of *The American Scene,* he does not accede to either the incompleteness or the powerlessness of his self in face of the actions of metaphor. In fact, in the moments before his alter ego reveals his face, Brydon is overcomplete: he reflects complacently that the vision holds its hands to its face because "*he,* standing there for the achieved, the enjoyed, the triumphant life, couldn't be faced in his triumph" (JC, 343). Even when Brydon considers himself overcome, he does not loosen his grip on a solid, secure sense of self; as he faints, his exit is belied by the personal pronouns that foreground his continued sense of self: "His head went round; he was going; he had gone" (JC, 344). The limited and autocratic perceptions associated with disavowing the alter ego in "The Jolly Corner" stand as the story's cautionary lesson about anti-assimilationism. However, the story also adds necessary qualification to the scheme of oscillating assimilation and self-differentiation modeled by *The American Scene.* The new melting-pot process stirred up formidable passions, and Brydon demonstrates that these passions easily array themselves on the side of the old selfhood, that predictable individualist vehicle. No matter how "tremendous" is the impression conveyed by the "force of analogy," it still registers as an abstract or spectral alternative to fiercely held traditional conceptions of selfhood (JC, 329).

In *The American Scene*, James meditates on the spectral relations brought into being by melting-pot fusion by rendering the primal scene of immigration, Ellis Island, as a haunted house. Witnessing the arrival and processing of immigrants, James comes face to face with his own alternate selves. The American who "had thought he knew" what being American would entail is shaken by the vision of Ellis; he is "stamped" by the knowledge as is one "who has seen a ghost in his supposedly safe old house" (*AS*, 66).[18] That is, James asserts, despite the material regimes of power at work at Ellis Island, despite the ostensible regulation of immigrant bodies, something immaterial escapes regulation. Like Spencer Brydon, the native-born American starts in a position of supposed knowledge and security. However, in the Ellis Island haunting, the roles of "The Jolly Corner" are reversed. On Ellis Island the haunting performs the amputation, branding (stamping) its witness with the sign of a certain loss. To recognize the immigrant as the other self in the home is to lose one's sense of whole, singular selfhood. James forecasts a "chill" in the heart of the witness as the familiar breath is felt on the back of the neck; the chill signals the self's awakening from the warm, comfortable dream of the "close and sweet and *whole*...consciousness" (*AS*, 67). In other words, the ghosts of the Jamesian melting pot imply the necessary failure of those "hegemonic" ambitions that Eldon Eisenach has associated with Progressive reform.[19] Unlike Spencer Brydon, the Americans of *The American Scene* will not be allowed the "luxury" of denial (*AS*, 67). The relation implied by these ghosts and analogies, this scene asserts, does not lose but in fact *derives* its power from combined immateriality and intimacy.

After all, these Jamesian ghosts are familiars; they communicate intimate truths. As James wrote elsewhere, typical ghosts are "above all as little continuous and conscious and responsive, as is consistent with their taking the trouble...to appear at all" (*AN*, 174).[20] The ghosts that haunt the native-born American and Spencer Brydon, in other words, reflect back to them their own limitations: failures at continuity with the other, at consciousness, at responsiveness. The very discontinuity that James considers characteristic of ghosts evokes Spencer Brydon's refused "chain of communication" (JC, 336). When Brydon and his ilk resist connection with their "dark strangers," they undermine the alternative form of connection, even kinship, that the "assault of suggestion" represents. Where will and agency deform melting-pot ambitions for the self, ghosts emerge to disrupt the will and raise the prospect of the involuntary. Without the tensely elastic (and so often involuntary) experience of selfhood elaborated by *The American Scene*, James envisions a Brydon-esque existence at odds with the complicated nature of language, trapped within dead-end relations premised on the willful citation and reproduction of past plot conditions or character types.[21]

Melting-pot theorists, along with other Progressives, represented a continuum of opinions on whether the exercise of individual agency was necessary, advisable, or would lead to Brydonesque miscarriages. More often than not, this autobiography-rich period cast individual agency as the principal means by which the "necessary" relations of race and history could be rearranged. However, as W. E. B. Du Bois suggested in terms resonant with James's, individual freedom was a compelling objective only when it signified "not individual caprice or aberration but social self-realization in an endless chain of selves."[22] James's work elaborates this version of agency, charting the restless analyst's attempt to craft a position like the one that James described for his character Maisie, one in which "instead of simply submitting to the inherited tie and the imposed complication, of suffering from them, our little wonder-working agent would create, without design, quite fresh elements of this order—contribute, that is, to the formation of a fresh tie" (AN, 142). The critical terms in this explication of agency are "without design" and "contribute." Extreme expressions of individual agency, such as those of Spencer Brydon, are always suspect in James's work. The American Scene constitutes a formidable exploration of how analogy might assist melting-pot thinking in navigating the narrow way between the Scylla of self-surrendering disintegration and the Charybdis of naïve and coercive individual agency.

Under the "assault of suggestion," the restless analyst of The American Scene forms fresh ties through a logic of extension; in each moment the excess of sensory data expands, sprawling outward beyond the psychic and experiential confines of the moment. This sprawl extends the "chain of communication" in all directions and dimensions; the "too-defiant scale of numerosity and quantity—the effect of which is so to multiply the possibilities, so to open, by the million, contingent doors and windows," enables relations born out of unexpected contact (AS, 93). The American Scene elevates these relations born through accidental similarities and tricks of language by infusing them with multiply shaded and always-curious feelings. James's New York Edition preface to The Princess Casamassima insists on "the quality of bewilderment" in a text's central consciousness, imagining a text structured by a fine bewilderment as entailing "ever so many possible feelings, stretched across the scene like an attached thread on which the pearls of interest are strung" (AN, 66). Jamesian speculation here provides affective nuance to the melting-pot idealization of individual agency: "response" signifies both a form of individual action and an anti-individualist moment of being overcome through, and by, felt relations.

These moments of being modeled by the self of *The American Scene* are "externally related," syntactically dependent upon the action of a William Jamesian "and"; their relations are of "the strung-along type, the type of continuity, contiguity, and concatenation."[23] Used to characterize Jamesian pluralism, this statement is most often read as emphasizing contiguity. Henry James, on the other hand, takes up concatenation and, and as, continuity in his elaborations of melting-pot mergings. His "chain" of communication suggests not so much beads on a string as overlapping links, or a series of rooms with doors that can be either open or closed: external relation intersects with internal relation in these figures, as in the affective infusions to analogical relations that James's narrator performs. The oscillating self that *The American Scene* traces through scenes of excess does, however, align with William James's resistance to monism (what he termed "the all-form [that] allows of no taking up and dropping of connexions"). Indeed, in a moment of concatenated melting-pot and pluralistic conceptions, Henry James's text elaborates a form of being in which, in William's words, "a thing may be connected by intermediary things, with a thing in which it has no immediate or essential connexion. It is thus at all times in many possible connexions which are not necessarily actualized at the moment... the word 'or' names a genuine reality."[24] The reality of "or" names not only the improvisatory performances of selfhood represented in *The American Scene* but also the improvisatory literary form of the representation.

The threat of Brydon-esque assertion and foreclosure always trembles on the horizon of these moments of exquisite Jamesian receptivity. However, in the contraction of attention that predictably follows its dilation, the restless analyst shifts from superabundant response to "the inward, the philosophic" mode (*AS*, 93). In this mood, the emphasis falls upon the analyst, rather than his restlessness, and structural relations like analogy, metaphor, metonymy, and synecdoche become the text's primary modes of forging connections. James's restless analyst thus shows himself to have anything but Brydon's enraged and authoritarian relation to language (indeed, a reader might sometimes hope for a less loving relation!). Brydon refuses to allow analogies to dictate his intimate truths; *The American Scene*, on the other hand, labels this mood "inward," claiming for it a new and special status as a form of interiority. In this way, abstraction is domesticated, and even moments of contracted attention may be understood as performing a kind of relatedness.

The success of *The American Scene* at enacting an oscillating melting-pot model of selfhood can be tested on James's representation of his visit to the

Jewish quarter of Rutgers Street. Many scholars, dating back at least to Maxwell Geismar in 1963, see James's racism, nativism, and nostalgia manifested in these scenes.[25] Certainly James's dehumanizing references to animals and insects "swarming" suggests the intensity of his response to the perceived excesses of the scene (*AS*, 100).[26] In the ghetto, according to James, "multiplication, multiplication of everything, was the dominant note" (*AS*, 100). Multiplication assaults the self whose ideological premise is singularity; the analyst feels that self expanding and responds with figuration. What is critical to recognize in these scenes is that the threat of dehumanization menaces *both* the immigrant and the restless analyst; the danger is important precisely because it is shared. Both immigrant and Jamesian narrator must forge a "chain of communication" by which selves can come into contact without losing all semblance of personhood. For William Boelhower, these scenes emphasize the importunacy of "context"; however, I understand James's immigrant scene as foregrounding the literary means by which agents *share* context.[27]

James's famous description of the Rutgers Street scene bears the linguistic traces of multiplication, implicating him in its excessiveness; he does not stop with the repetition of the word "multiplication," but himself produces a barrage of troubling images, a figural excessiveness unusual even for him, through which to understand the scene before him:

> There are small strange animals, known to natural history, snakes or worms, I believe, who, when cut into pieces, wriggle away contentedly and live in the snippet as completely as in the whole. So the denizens of the New York Ghetto, heaped as thick as the splinters on the table of a glass-blower, had each, like the fine glass particle, his or her individual share of the whole hard glitter of Israel. This diffused intensity, as I have called it, causes any array of Jews to resemble (if I may be allowed another image) some long nocturnal street where every window in every house shows a maintained light. (*AS*, 100–101)

William James's "strung-along type" of being, which *The American Scene* uses to exceed the logic of reproduction and historical necessity, manifests itself here in the "long nocturnal street where every window in every house shows a maintained light." This street is the "chain of communication"; it is the corridor that Brydon shies from, for fear of sharing the series of rooms with his alternate self; it is a model for a fluid and yet particulate form of being. The lights in the windows flicker, maintained and yet mobile, constant and yet different from house to house. Indeed, what is inside the windows is not fixedly "other," for, only a page later, James reveals himself to be inside a window, "hung over the prospect from the windows of my friend" (*AS*, 102). Later, in one of the New York Edition's most famous articulations of artistic vision, James figures "windows" pierced in the "house of fiction...by the need of the individual vision and the pressure of the individual will" (*AN*, 46). The window from which James views the Jewish quarter, though, is that of a friend, and thus bespeaks a momentarily shared form of individual vision. His troping of Jewish continuity by the figure of window is further unsettled by his occupation of this same space. That which seems exclusive to an individual or group, in these sequences, turns out to be shared—albeit in awkward and often uncomfortable ways.

Analogically bound to immigrants through both his suppressed birth-place and his position at the window, James puts pressure on the process of figuration (and announces as much: "if I may be allowed another image"). His reflections teem with figures, mixing worms, glass, and dwellings, never pausing long enough to imply the sufficiency of any one figure. His utterance is made up of snippets and shards, just as the scene he watches is. Spencer Brydon may require the illusion of self-contained wholeness, but these snippets and shards—whether of Jewishness or of verbiage—firmly rebuke that fantasy. And yet the scene as James represents it is not one of committed fragmentation, either. In fact, the figures convey a various but interconnected impression; the images of glass, in particular, bring to mind the kaleidoscope, a creation of colored glass shards and mirrors. The "inward, philosophic" mood of contraction becomes, through this figure, a kind of reverie, and the associations of figures follow a kind of dream logic.

Like the restless analyst's attention, the kaleidoscope creates ever-changing patterns of glass and light. In each of its arrangements, the shards fall into relation with each other; in the next, they imperfectly assume versions of each other's positions, to entirely different effect. The kaleidoscopic nature of urban streetscapes was a common observation by the end of the nineteenth century: Charles Baudelaire, for one, described the urban observer as "a kaleidoscope gifted with consciousness, responding to each one of its movements and reproducing the multiplicity of life and the flickering grace of all the elements of life."[28] In *The American Scene* James's impressions gather and disperse in the same kaleidoscopic patterns as do the flows of humanity he watches; his writing follows the same fractured path, leaping from connection to connection, setting aside the narrative imperatives of coherence and wholeness.

Even the idea of dream logic, however, does not absolve James from responsibility for the foul figures he deploys with reference to Rutgers Street. Master perspective, kaleidoscope eye, glass blower, he fashions the figures that imply a single agent coordinating the reflective play of light on shards of glass. To shift from this Brydon-esque exercise of mastery to a mode in which Rutgers Street effectively, excessively, eludes representation by him, he confesses "there was too much in the vision," pronouncing the scene "phantasmagoric" (*AS,* 101).[29] Here phantasmagoria represents that which exceeds the individual perspective: that which can be grasped, imagined, approached only through a multiplicity of positionings. James relishes the term's excessiveness, down to its startling and "mouth-filling" substance (it signifies a continued play of language as well as a play of light).[30] He also plays on phantasmagoria's historical connotations as an arena of ontological uncertainty.[31] Appealing to a tradition of magic lanterns and other visual play dating back to the eighteenth century, the term "phantasmagoria" reframes the visual excess that James experiences as *pleasure,* particularly a pleasure of bewilderment, often shared in a social context.

But still, whose pleasure, what social context? James remains ambivalent, to say the least, about his feelings throughout his description of the Jewish Lower East Side, and what he describes as the "contented wriggling" of his subjects hardly constitutes pleasure. Indeed, while the Rutgers Street scene firmly anchors figuration and the flickering play of personae to the Jamesian melting pot, it fails to resolve the question of the nature and possibility of subjectivity in that melting pot. While these scenes may abstractly assist in comprehending a certain illogical logic of the melting pot, they are far less clear about the affective viability of such a model. Surrounded by visions of animals and insects, what form of human connection emerges? The James who seems trapped between self-loss and solipsism before this scene is neither indifferent to this question nor (ironically) alone in posing it. It is just because Spencer Brydon is alone in his old house that he reacts with such horror to the apparition whose face resembles "one of those expanding fantastic images projected by the magic lantern of childhood" (JC, 344). In the Rutgers Street scene, the question of what kind of fellowship can be brokered by plays of light and language remains the pressing one for James's melting-pot models of selfhood.

Of course, James is not alone in either posing these questions or failing to resolve them. The alienation from self and others that is so common to melting-pot texts often produces this simultaneous imperative for, and interrogation of, fellowship. As Jacob Riis worked on his famous account of the New York slum, *How the Other Half Lives* (1890), he found the project producing a peculiar dissociation in him. Riis's autobiography, *The Making of an American* (1901), recounts a magic-lantern episode of alienation similar to that experienced by James:

> I was haunted by a feeling that I would lose myself altogether, and got into the habit of leaving private directions in the office where I would probably be found, should question arise. It arose at last in a Brooklyn

church where I was making a speech with my magic-lantern pictures. While I spoke a feeling kept growing upon me that I ought to be down in the audience looking at the pictures. It all seemed a long way off and in no way related to me. Before I knew it, or anyone had time to notice, I had gone down and taken a front seat. I sat there as much as five minutes perhaps.[32]

For Riis, prolonged engagement with the immigrant ghetto prompts a fundamental confusion of self and other, a confusion mediated through the flickering refracted light of the pictures he projects during his lectures. The alienation coincides with an intense need to join in the social pleasure of shared visual display, and to abandon the commanding perspective of the stage master. This anxious loss of the steering self passes quickly in Riis's autobiography; in this anecdote, his abdication of leadership produces monotony, literally, as the pictures in the slide show no longer change, and he awakes to the fact that he is needed on stage. Riis was far less willing than James to experiment with relinquishing social leadership and recognizing the limits of individual agency. Nonetheless, this anecdote suggests that even Riis was subject to the dream logic of the melting pot, in which social pleasure balanced subjective experiences of alienation and fragmentation.

Away from the crowds of New York, home in the relative solitude of Lamb House following his trip, James used his correspondence to continue feeling out a means of sharing social pleasure in unmoored certainties about subjectivity. Like Spencer Brydon, he is alone in his old house experiencing visions, but unlike Brydon, he does not cast them as horrors:

I have more impressions than I know what to do with or can account for—and this in spite of finding that, also, they tend exceedingly to melt and fade and pass away, flicker off like the shadows from firelight on the wall. But I shall draw a long breath when I have worked them off... it may be very fantastic and irrelevant stuff I am producing—for I don't see, I repeat, where it all comes from. And the queerest part of the matter is that, though I *shall* rejoice when it is over, I meanwhile quite enjoy doing it.[33]

Familiar notes infuse this chatty epistle—the melting, the flickering, the fantastic, the obscured origins. Above all, however, James emphasizes pleasure— he anticipates rejoicing when he completes his account of his American travels, but also enjoys his composition. The echoing "joys" bridge the different stages of the self, implying that the social pleasures (of watching a magic lantern show, say) can be cultivated in a playful exploration of one's own bewilderment and internal dissonance; one can be social even when solitary. The personal intimacy of epistolary address influences the form of analysis: rather than chasing down the least implication of a figure, James's intelligence ranges like the magic lantern's play of iridescence on a wall, there for both his own and his correspondent's enjoyment. This strategy involves a kind of sleight-of-hand, in which the logical and philosophical problems of a theory of selfhood are not so much solved as they are transformed into entertaining puzzles. James's use of "phantasmagoria" in *The American Scene* aims for this kind of effect; it casts his American experience as an early twentieth-century version of the visual trick or trompe l'oeuil, whose bewildering effects affectively unite its audience. The phantasmagoria signifies a kind of visual play that disdains individual control and mastery in favor of the pleasure of the visually unusual, the excessive, the unreal. Fact and fiction interpenetrate, and the spectator is robbed of his or her certainty, amputated of explanations. Rather than structuring perception, phantasmagoria releases it to range freely, associating the violation of boundaries with communal delight rather than anxiety.

James's turn to the nonsense word "phantasmagoria" also signals both the elasticity and the limits of language before the pleasures of melting-pot complexity. The melting-pot projects that James undertakes in *The American Scene* rely in large part on the unbiddable powers of language, especially analogy. However, as the scene at Rutgers Street suggests, words like "confusion" and "swarm" cannot be fully alienated from their origins; as with James and his immigrant interlocutors, ghostly traces of early allegiances linger. At times *The American Scene* seems to reach for a new form of analogy, one that advances the logic of metaphor to the point that, through innumerable and intense new connections, it blasts away the calcified accretions of words. James attempts to be sympathetic to the possibility (one, according to James, "not directly adverse to joy,") that in the land of the melting pot, words, like persons, might come utterly unmoored:

> it is as if the syllables were too numerous to make a legible word. The *il*legible word, accordingly, the great inscrutable answer to questions, hangs in the vast American sky, to his imagination, as something fantastic and *abracadabrant,* belonging to no known language, and it is under this convenient ensign that he travels and considers and contemplates, and, to the best of his ability, enjoys. (*AS,* 93)

The abracadabrant represents the linguistic version of the phantasmagorical. It imagines a loosening of limits, the possibility of new and unknown forms. Abracadabrant, phantasmagoric, the numerous syllables jostle socially in James's chosen terms. Even the words model social pleasures, multi-syllabic enjoy-ments, unfamiliar and inscrutable though the companies they model may be. As James's comment implies, this form of connection is more or less robust according to the interlocutor's "ability" to enjoy. Paradoxically, the limits of words are not inherent, but traceable to the individual affective investments through which James imagines them producing new forms of connection.

To sidestep his own limited ability to "enjoy" under the abstract sign "belonging to no known language"—to project a form of representation that is disrespectful of the ways affective investments limit words—James's narrator performs something like what William James's *Varieties of Religious Experience* termed *"self-surrender."*[34] Henry James also performed this self-surrendering in his correspondence, as his comment that while in the United States he "failed to arrive at a single conclusion, or to find myself entertaining a single *opinion"* suggests.[35] These attempts to uncouple subjective enjoyment from individual ability both explain and evince the peculiar impulse-to-abstraction that permeates *The American Scene*. Ultimately, such gestures offer pleasures more theoretical than actual. "Play," in these schemes, connotes mobility more convincingly than it does pleasure; James's many reassurances that pleasure is in fact possible, is surprisingly available, is indulged in now and then, prove remarkably tepid evidence of joy. The theoretical problems of the melting pot have simply been advanced a step: if the question of how flexible melting-pot selves might forge social connections is solved by appealing to affect, particularly pleasure, then the question of pleasure poses the next theoretical hurdle. Given that the melting-pot self that James imag-ines is perpetually overcome and surrendered, then must that self's feelings and pleasures also be overcome and surrendered? If so, then are they the kinds of feelings and pleasures through which social bonds can be experienced? A system in which "one story is good only till another is told" implies ruth-less turn-over, as James ruefully observed, faced with America's mania for newness (*AS,* 61). Should the melting-pot self be prevented from becoming an assembly-line of personas, or even a conspicuous consumer of transient interpersonal pleasures?—and if so, how?

In contemporaneous sociology, George Herbert Mead was theorizing a "social self," a place of analogy and role-playing, in which experiences of selfness and otherness are never fully separate. He anticipated that when "an essential problem appears, there is some disintegration" of the habitual orga-nization of the self:

> in a sense the old self has disintegrated, and out of the moral process
> a new self arises.... To leave the field to the values represented by the

old self is exactly what we term selfishness.... Where, however, the problem is objectively considered, although the conflict is a social one, it should not resolve itself into a struggle between selves, but into such a reconstruction of the situation that different and enlarged and more adequate personalities may emerge.... [T]he old self should enter upon the same terms with the selves whose roles are assumed.[36]

Mead's theory of the social self articulates a melting-pot protocol in which *within the context of the self* early settlers claim no priority over new arrivals, but persist and interact with them on a basis of equality. In Mead's view, the social self no longer privileges a historical narrative of originality (the "old self"), but neither does it privilege a narrative of progress (the "new self"). As if in response to James's problem of sundered feelings due to self-surrender, Mead recommends a more tempered self-surrender, a kind of social accommodation that avoids Brydon-esque triumph without entirely dissolving affective links. This solution works, to the extent that it does, because it re-embeds the abstract logical problems of the melting-pot self in the imperatives of its social and cultural context, making them problems that can be addressed through a Progressive "reconstruction of the situation."

To speak of situation or context in this age, Jane Addams emphasized, was to speak socially. The moral imperatives of the melting-pot era were paradoxically grounded in specific social engagement even as theorists aspired to their "social" expansion beyond the conditions of that specific engagement. "The latter day moral ideal is in reality that of a social morality," she imagines her contemporaries arguing: "Cast our experiences in a larger mould if our lives are to be animated by the larger social aims."[37] Henry James conceives of proto-Meadian "*different and enlarged and more adequate*" selves in Addams's "larger mould," as it were. Mead and Addams embed logical problems in social contexts in order to imagine ethical responses. James embeds his own logical problem (that of exceeding affective limits without constructing feeling as disposable) in a literary context in order to imagine a formal response.

"Stirred Sensibility"

When planning his return to the United States, James cast his imaginative response in terms of feeling: his "sensibility vibrates" at the idea of an American visit.[38] Later, describing the formal organization of his novel *The Princess Casamassima,* James reveals the extent to which he relied upon feeling as a mode of connection: a fine consciousness might be trusted to put out "ever so many possible feelings, stretched across the scene like an attached thread on which the pearls of interest are strung" (*AN*, 66). Forms, literary and social, are not only woven together by the threads of feeling; in James's melting-pot imagination, form embeds and exercises the fine feeling required to generate, comprehend, and represent the further connections he projects.

Forms need not play this role, of course: for James the hotel culture of New York offers the most awful vision of the unfeeling forces of social and intellectual consolidation at work at the turn of the century. As in the writing of Theodore Roosevelt, in the hotel-world of New York, James gets the "sense of a promiscuity which manages to be at the same time an inordinate untempered monotony. . . . A 'mixed' social manifestation . . . blissfully exempt from any principle or possibility of disaccord with itself" (*AS*, 80). In the hotel-world the discord and dynamism of American culture are managed into normalcy, accommodated and made banal. This is a system of total synchrony—it eliminates the danger, ambivalence, and play of feeling that James valued in other quarters of the city. "Disaccord with itself," the oscillating tension that characterizes the form of *The American Scene,* is the primary loss in this system, and when disaccord is lost, so is interest (to monotony) and fellow feeling (to simultaneity).

James explicitly connects this hotel-world with the Americanizing schemes of immigrant assimilation favored by Henry Ford and Theodore Roosevelt. He extends his defense of disaccord and critique of monotony to the sphere of immigrant assimilation, whose very atmosphere, he accuses, washes "colour" out of the European immigrant:

> like . . . the tub of hot water that reduces a piece of bright-hued stuff, on immersion, to the proved state of not 'washing': the only fault of my image indeed being that if the stuff loses its brightness the water of the tub at least is more or less agreeably dyed with it. That is doubtless not the case . . . since we surely fail to observe that the property washed out of the new subject begins to tint with its pink or its azure his fellow-soakers in the terrible tank. (*AS*, 98)

As against this observation of the "terrible tank," suddenly the "aquarium" of the New York Ghetto, where "innumerable fish, of overdeveloped proboscis . . . bump together," takes on new meaning (*AS*, 100). James's Lower East Side remains a "social caldron" where, in the words of Abraham Cahan, "a human hodgepodge with its component parts changed but not yet fused into one homogeneous whole" still persists.[39] Criticizing an assimilative climate that undervalues disaccord, James embeds disaccord in the "fine feeling" that structures his melting-pot literary form. Such a form is fluid, but it also continually visits the "bumps" of the immigrant scene on the reader.

Throughout *The American Scene,* James resists the role of "high-stationed orchestral leader" with "colossal extended arms" (*AS,* 82), through which the various manifestations of early twentieth-century American culture are harmonized into a "gorgeous golden blur" (*AS,* 81). His text is organized much like the jagged up-ended comb that James accused the New York skyline of being; when his impressions of New York exceed the confines of a single chapter, or hopscotch between various visits, James underlines the tension produced by this site's excessiveness. "Disaccord with itself" is constitutive of this form and the selfhood it performs. James will not weaken it by pulling it about too much; instead, the Jamesian form turns to overflow to prevent the monistic Bergsonian "gorgeous golden blur." *The American Scene* unites Jamesian theory and praxis, staging the "living and breathing and feeling and moving great monster" in ways responsive to its own "interesting and quite unexpectedly and almost uncannily delightful and sympathetic" tenor.[40] That is, the text formally enacts the mutually constitutive tension between sympathy and disaccord.

New York itself suggests this formal possibility to James. In Central Park, just steps away from the homogenizing glow of the Plaza, James locates a melting-pot tableau in which disaccord is not only possible but also pleasurable. He describes walking in the park as like making, "in the most agreeable manner possible, the tour of the little globe. And that, frankly, I think, was the best of all impressions—was seeing New York at its best; for if ever one could feel at one's ease about the 'social question,' it would be surely, somehow, on such an occasion" (*AS,* 133). Suddenly the James who has been "assaulted" by the "bristling" aspects of the city imagines himself at his ease. He credits this shift to the park's emphasis on form, its creation of a sense of "occasion," of "manner," of the "tour," by which James's minglings with "the inconceivable alien" are shaped by shared leisure (*AS,* 66).[41] Put at his "ease" as by a good host, James finds the discomfort produced by the inconceivability of the other lessened. The result is less a gorgeous golden blur than it is a brief moment of social enjoyment, like Jacob Riis's sharing of his audience's enjoyment of the graceful play of light.

The park plays a role in James's narrative that museums, libraries, and schools play in so many immigrant narratives: such public spaces are, as Walter Lippmann pointed out, the sites at which Progressive-era America imagined "collective property." In other words, civic spaces constitute an assault upon "absolute possession," aiming to literalize the evacuation of the traditional possessive individual that melting-pot ideas conduct more figuratively.[42] Collective-property spaces perform their work on the self in an expressly public context, and while they reach far into the private self in their implications, they do not violate the privacy of the self in the ways that James found so unsettling. Like the park, these spaces orchestrated leisure as a form of pleasurable, figurative acquisition: visitors collected sights, sounds, skills, languages, but never retained exclusive control over them. As John Dewey's and Jane Addams's work suggests, Progressive-era theorists of public life were particularly interested in infusing such places of "collective property" with an ethos of reciprocity.

James understands Central Park as accommodating the foreign masses without managing them in Americanizing ways; the play of color that he celebrates in the park suggests that the tub of hot water has not succeeded in stripping all color from these fabrics (*AS*, 98). Indeed, Frederick Law Olmsted described his designs for the park as attempts to defuse the managerial tone of urban life and to cultivate sympathetic response: in the park, he wrote in 1870, "we want the greatest possible contrast with the restraining and confining conditions of the town, which compel us to walk circumspectly, watchfully, jealously, which compel us to look upon others without sympathy."[43] Though Olmsted did not intend quite the jostling contrasts that James saw at play in the park, his design for civic feeling resists the ritualized hospitality of the "hotel-spirit" and its "gorgeous golden blur." The slowly evolving forms that Olmsted privileged in his landscape designs emphasize process and change; they model an aesthetic compatible with a mutualist, melting-pot form of assimilation.

The Central Park that James, uncharacteristically decidedly, proclaims the "best of all impressions" and "New York at its best," was a much-changed space from the Central Park of bourgeois display from his childhood.[44] As conceived by Olmsted and Calvert Vaux's design of 1858, Central Park was to serve a wealthy and leisured class as a refuge from the chaos of the nineteenth-century city. By the 1870s park attendance was growing rapidly, but in a way that threatened, according to many including Olmsted himself, to bring the chaos into the park. In 1878 the Sixth Avenue elevated line shortened the trip from lower Manhattan to the park by twenty minutes; a contemporary observer suggested that 80 percent of the visitors to the park on a Sunday were workingmen and their families.[45] In the 1880s restrictions on public concerts in the park on Sundays were lifted for the sake of the working poor, and by the 1890s keep-off-the-grass regulations were lifted. By 1891 *Munsey's Magazine* described the crowded late-century park as quintessentially vaudevillian, based on "the marvelous variety of its scenery and embellishments"; the Mall's "monuments of foreigners" and "imported music discoursed by a band principally composed of imported musicians" marked it as a hub of "cosmopolitanism."[46] Immigrant and working-class visitors from the tenements of the Lower East Side would enter the park from the same Fifth Avenue entrance as did the monied, keeping the vastly separate classes of the city within each other's ken, as a *Sun* reporter noted in 1893. In 1904, the same year as James's visit, the leader of the Nineteenth Assembly district organized a picnic at the park for thirteen thousand West Side children: the group processed to the park together, led by Irish, German, Italian, and African-American May Kings and Queens.[47] Many contemporary commentators considered the park a unique ground for transcending the ethnic and racial insularity that characterized city neighborhoods of the period.

Reached from so many different angles and used in so many different ways, the park was evolving in unexpected ways by the end of the century. In his correspondence Olmsted raged about the demands placed on public parks:

> Suppose that you had been commissioned to build a really grand opera house; that after the construction work had been nearly completed and your scheme of decoration fully designed you should be instructed that the building was to be used on Sundays as a Baptist Tabernacle, and that suitable place must be found for a huge organ, a pulpit and a dipping pool. Then at intervals afterwards, you should be advised that it must be so refitted and furnished so that parts of it could be used for a court room, a jail, a concert hall, hotel, skating rink, for surgical cliniques, for a circus, dog show, drill room, ball room, railway station and shot tower?[48]

The park, like the imagination of the restless analyst in turn-of-the-century New York, was beset from all sides. James was fascinated by the *means* by which Central Park accommodated its crowds. He, too, used the vaudevillian trope to explain the form of accommodation modeled by the park; according to him it resembled:

> an actress in a company destitute...of all other feminine talent; so that she assumes on successive nights the most dissimilar parts and ranges in the course of a week from the tragedy queen to the singing chambermaid. That valour by itself wins the public and brings down the house—it being really a marvel that she should in no part fail of a hit....You are perfectly aware, as you hang about her in May and June, that you *have,* as a travelled person, beheld more extraordinary scenery and communed with nature in ampler or fairer forms; but it is equally definite to you that none of those adventures have counted more to you for experience, for stirred sensibility—inasmuch as you can be, at the best, and in the showiest countries, only thrilled by the pastoral or the

awful, and as to pass, in New York, from the discipline of the streets to this so different many-smiling presence is to be thrilled at every turn. (*AS*, 132)

James's comparison sets us down in a "chain of communication" of the figurative sort; he describes the park's likeness to a performer whose business is likeness. In this corridor of metaphor, potential sites of response are multiplied; "to be thrilled at every turn" by "this so different many-smiling presence" is quite different from the traditional binary of spectator responses excited by "the pastoral or the awful." The observing position here entails not distancing spectatorship but participation, a shared turning (out, around, and into). This is a scene of Jamesian "stirred sensibility."

In *The Tragic Muse* (1890), James had imagined another actress, Miriam Rooth, who, it seemed, "was always acting... her existence was a series of parts assumed for the moment, each changed for the next, before the perpetual mirror of some curiosity or admiration or wonder—some spectatorship that she perceived or imagined in the people around her."[49] This actress exists in a symbiotic relation with the audience, whom she imagines and who imagines her—even in the passage above, in which observation is refracted through an adjacent consciousness. The mutuality of this dynamic keeps the actress mobile, changing from part to part and spectator to spectator. A devoted admirer later feels that acting is too dull a word to convey what it is that Rooth does:

> her changing face affected this particular admirer at least not as a series of masks, but as a response to perceived differences, an intensity of that perception, or still more as something richly constructional, like the shifting of a scene in a play or like a room with many windows. The image she was to project was always incalculable, but if her present denied her past and declined responsibility for her future it made a good thing of the hour and kept the actual peculiarly fresh. (*TM*, 359)

Unlike masks, which are imposed from without, Rooth's transformations are "responses" generated from a complex interaction of interior and exterior worlds. Her being is "constructional," that is, both constructed and constructive. Bound by neither past nor future, the self proposed by Rooth's figure avoids the traps of determinism to represent the very form of non-chronological relational selfhood explored by melting-pot thinkers. As "a thing alive, with a power to change, to grow, to develop, to beget new forms of the same life," her performance yokes form and agency (*TM*, 315). These *formal* implications, in turn, are cast in intellectual terms: Rooth speaks of "stir[ring] [people] up so they'll have ideas" (*TM*, 219). It is not incidental that such a form of selfhood is marked Jewish in James's 1890 novel, or that it is *not* explicitly marked Jewish in *The American Scene*. James's later work hinges on his recognition that he is implicated in such a model of selfhood, and that his prose forms are implicated in Miriam Rooth's "scenic" theatricality. When James turns to New York's Central Park, he creates a figure that reveals the formal sympathies between the Roothian performance and his own work.

From nothing save its own scarce resources and its sympathetic response, the actress-park of *The American Scene* manages to accommodate all those who have turned to it. "It has had to have something for everybody, since everybody arrives famished," James observes admiringly; "it has had to multiply itself to extravagance, to pathetic little efforts of exaggeration and deception, to be, breathlessly, everywhere and everything at once" (*AS*, 132). (To read James's correspondence concerning his own compositional efforts is to be reminded of this language of exertion and insufficiency in the face of endless demands.) The park is driven to its extremes of self-transformation by what is, at base, an ethos of responsive feeling. The valor of this performance, which runs the gamut from tragedy queen to singing chambermaid, inspires a response in its own right. These conditions develop a Jamesian "chain of communication."

While the figure of the actress may well be in keeping with the excesses James elsewhere associated with the American scene, James's description of the park insists upon the destitution of the scene. The lack of resources available to the performer evokes James's famous litany of artistic resources missing from the mid-nineteenth-century United States. However, *The American Scene* makes conditions of possibility from what were once considered conditions of impossibility. Indeed, amenities (although, admittedly, not the kind of traditional high-cultural amenities that James yearned for in his 1879 essay *Hawthorne*) seem part of what makes the scene at the Waldorf-Astoria so insupportable to James. The "golden glow" facilitated by the hotel-world's ability to supply its guests contrasts sharply with the shabby inadequacies of a park whose green spaces were compared by one 1895 critic to vacant lots in the tenement district.[50] In the sumptuous hotel-world, there is no question that any parallel to a theatrical company would entail an ample supply of leading ladies, each with her own rigid specialization. Only the inadequacies of a park facing extreme demands enable the comparison to the actress required to assume all roles. The scene's simultaneous superabundance of suggestion and delinquency of amenities enables both the "valour" of the performer and the feeling of the respondent. Unlike rural New Hampshire, whose utter absence of "forms" James traced to individual senses of entitlement, the park proliferates with forms by dint of its enthusiasm but utter confusion about how to meet its responsibilities to others.

By going to extremes, the park meets, matches, and assimilates its "polyglot" crowd, which James concedes "has none but the mildest action on the nerves.... They become for you practically as your fellow-spectators of the theatre, whose proximity you take for granted while... the variety of accents with which the air swarmed... make it a question whether the Park itself or its visitors were more polyglot" (*AS*, 132–33). In this mise-en-scène, James himself assimilates the fact of his fellowship with recent immigrants more ably than in many other parts of *The American Scene*. In fine melting-pot fashion, as James and crowd momentarily merge as "fellow-spectators," the accented English (and other languages) of the crowd merges with the "accents" of the park's performance. The air swarms with "accents" become mobile; language, no longer the victim of the "torture-rooms of the living idiom" that James located in East Side coffee-houses, gestures toward the "accent of the very ultimate future" that James imagined speaking "ethnic synthesis" in no "existing literary measure" (*AS*, 106). The sudden agency of language in the park unites James, his fellow-spectators, and the actress-park in their heroic responses to the "syllables... too numerous" of the American scene (*AS*, 93). The theatrical idiom of the park casts the formal challenge of melting-pot expression as a shared one: unlike the immigrant autobiographer Constantine Panunzio, who understands it necessary to learn all parts, James and his companions here scramble to learn any parts of an ever-changing script, each of them catching syllables here and there.[51]

James's autobiography *A Small Boy and Others* describes him as a young theater-buff who was "more interested in the pulse of our party [of spectators]... than in the beat of the drama and the shock of its opposed forces" (*SB*, 163). The Central Park sequence of *The American Scene* similarly positions James's lifelong commitment to the theater as an appreciation of its capacity to transgress boundaries between individuals through feeling, to stage performances that enter the audience and register in its "pulse." The drama, here, principally consists of neither beat nor shock, but of a capacity to craft an arena in which that tense oscillation (here, pulsing) of response and disavowal includes a "stirred sensibility" that bonds selves and parts of selves together in fleeting pleasure.[52] In a similarly synthetic gesture, George Herbert Mead proposed considering the drama as a figure for figuration: to his mind both drama and analogy involve similarly social forms of expression and interpretation.[53] When James addresses the problems of a selfhood conceived through analogy with the formal strategies of the theater, he suggests just such a melting-pot compatibility.

Through the figure of the park, James salvages feeling and representation from the threat of the gorgeous golden blur. With Central Park's mediation, *The American Scene* imagines and performs a melting-pot selfhood that shuttles between various positions and personae, without utterly sacrificing the emotional and representational values of older forms of selfhood. This selfhood, and the formal program that James embarked upon after returning home, constitute his responses to the aesthetic destitution that he saw in the Progressive-era United States. Both Central Park and the later Jamesian texts drawing on its formal devices exemplify not only the melting-pot turn in James's imagination and literary expression but also the basis for ideas of identity that retain a hold on American culture even a century later.

"The Open Cup of *Application*"

Central Park, and the Progressive-era melting pot more generally, prodded James to experiment with merging spectatorial and participatory sensibilities. Following *The American Scene,* he elaborates this fusion with more explicit reference to literary form; it is as if he returned home intending to address what it would mean to write like the park. James's preface to *The Golden Bowl* describes the New York Edition in terms that go straight to such a question. After years of "cultivation of unacquaintedness" with his works, he writes, they seemed strange and threatening to him (much as New York did earlier).[54] He discovers that revising entails surrendering oneself to an alien text, as he once surrendered to the melting-pot scene, and with similar effects: "the act of seeing it again, caused whatever I looked at on any page to flower before me" (*AN,* 339). This process has little in common with the grand orchestrations that James earlier ("broodingly") associated with rewriting. Rather, the revision that he undertakes after his American trip transforms the novel into a participatory form, in which James is as much a part of the crowd as he is the anxious lead actress of a destitute company. Revising a novel requires him "to get nearer all its elements," which implies a close approach to both text and question of revision, but also an intimate drawing-together of component parts (*AN,* 338). This process reveals writer, reader, and text as each other's too-often disavowed alternate selves. Revision no more rewards an individual's self-assertion over his pages (or a coercive conception of what is owed to an individual) than did the American scene. Instead, it is an organic process, one by which the scene asserts agency, flowering, multiplying, swarming, and readers become "participators by a fond attention" (*AN,* 62).[55] Like melting-pot assimilation, that is, James's modernist revisions introduce unsettling strategies of sharing, discovering new, unfamiliar forms in old scenes.

The process of revision was not all cast as park-like accommodations, however: in a letter to Scribner's outlining his vision of a New York Edition, James emphasized the selections and omissions required to produce the edition. Of course, as David McWhirter and Michael Anesko have argued, the market played a critical role in determining the size and shape of the edition.[56] However, James sold Scribner's on an edition whose final constitution remained vague; the undisclosed nature of the exclusions to be performed casts the relation of the part to the whole as a fundamental formal question for the edition. The excluded texts, along with Spencer Brydon's repudiated "black stranger" in "The Jolly Corner," suggest that James's melting-pot modernism participates in the constitutive racial exclusions Kenneth Warren has traced through James's realism, and Matthew Jacobson has traced in turn-of-the-century immigrant assimilation. Like *The American Scene,* the New York Edition represents a Jamesian melting-pot modernism that is formally both expansive and amputated.[57] These exclusions are historically contingent—their necessity is of the moment rather than logical or philosophical—but they are also the exclusions through which melting-pot modernism achieves its fullest Jamesian articulation.

Simultaneously sprawling and abbreviated, the form of this edition telegraphs the changeability of literary form and the shaping effects of imaginative participation, all while struggling with the nature and meaning of the exclusionary selections that constitute the edition. James's preface to *The Golden Bowl* famously frames the edition through analogy, casting it as a process of tracing an old path through a snow-covered scene:

> my exploring tread, for application to it, had quite unlearned the old pace and found itself naturally falling into another, which might sometimes indeed more or less agree with the original tracks, but might most often, or very nearly, break the surface in other places. What was thus predominantly interesting to note, at all events, was the high spontaneity of these deviations and differences, which became thus things not of choice, but of immediate and perfect necessity: necessity to the end of dealing with the quantities in question at all. (*AN,* 336)

At many points James is no longer in step with his other self. These deviations from the origin are necessary means to the "end" of "dealing" with the text; the "dealing," an act of reading, response, and interpretation, of course simply registers as a new beginning. Divergence may be both spontaneous and necessary, but it is not cast as a matter of "choice"; James imagines forms

of individual agency that differ in important ways from traditional individualistic self-direction. Such a process of encountering old and new positions
combines exteriority and interiority, with the "exploring tread...break[ing]
the surface" to suggest how play on surfaces so often reveals depths that are
fundamental to "dealing." For writers considered later in this study, what
James implicitly puts down to "necessity" here will become central matters
of interrogation: racial exclusion, for James Weldon Johnson; the deviation
of present from past, for Willa Cather; the obscuring of market forces by the
individual narrative, for Gertrude Stein. The James of the prefaces anticipates, to some extent, the emergence of these concerns, but also leaves them
aside in the process of articulating the literary-formal parameters of melting-
pot modernism.

For the James of the critical prefaces, "dealing" with a literary work
entails reconceiving of what it means to be faithful to one's origins, much as
an assimilating immigrant might do. Like immigrant autobiographers, James
insistently begins his narratives (here, prefaces) with origins, pointing, when-
ever possible, to the kernels to which his texts may be traced. The textual selves
being profiled in James's accounts remain faithful to their origins in a figurative sense, but also deviate from previous versions. Through the New York
Edition, James elaborates a formal version of a self that endures despite—or,
in fact, thanks to—different iterations. In this model, the "essence" of the
self entails "follow[ing] up the formidable process" that James associated
with his American trip.[58] One stays "true" to such a selfhood through regular formal renovation, especially in the sense of continually adopting and
discarding different versions. For James the New York Edition constitutes
a sustained response to the question that forms "the whole of [the artist's]
life intellectual," for it enables both persistence and newness, a selfhood that
is both familiar and other: "The 'old' matter is there, re-accepted, re-tasted,
exquisitely re-assimilated and re-enjoyed...perforating as by some strange
and fine, some latent and gathered force, a myriad more adequate channels"
(AN, 339–40). The repeatedly emphasized prefix "re" establishes revision
as a Jamesian form of citation, in which the past (assimilated, past tense) is
recuperated, as well as made something to which one can contribute (say, by
the application of a prefix). In tension with this lovingly recuperative "re" is
the "re" that marks the unavailability of its object, the impossibility of stepping perfectly in old tracks or words. This tension consists of a large part of
the "force" by which the "myriad" new "channels" slice through divisions,
creating "chains of communication" between old versions (of selfhood, of
form) and new ones.

This revision-infused concept of literary work intersects with melting-pot discourse in ways that extend far beyond analogical resonance. Certainly, the impossible "re," the perfect stepping in old tracks, was no more possible for the self-alienated immigrant autobiographer, or the changed immigrant gazing in confusion upon the "homeland" to which he no longer felt the same connection, than it was for the reader and literary critic. But when James explains that no fiction can be understood through a reductive inquiry into its origins (that is, no "real person" is ever "transplanted" into the world of fiction), he does so in extended and explicit melting-pot terms:

> No such process is *effectively* possible, we must hold, as the imputed act of transplanting; an act essentially not mechanical, but thinkable rather—so far as thinkable at all—in chemical, almost in mystical terms. We can surely account for nothing in the novelist's work that hasn't passed through the crucible of his imagination, hasn't, in that perpetually simmering cauldron his intellectual *pot-au-feu,* been reduced to savoury fusion. We here figure the morsel, of course, not as boiled to nothing, but as exposed, in return for the taste it gives out, to a new and richer saturation. In this state it is in due course picked out and served, and . . . a poor importance [will] attend it, if it doesn't speak most of its late genial medium, the good, the wonderful company it has, as I hint, aesthetically kept. It has entered, in fine, into new relations, it emerges for new ones. Its final savour has been constituted, but its prime identity destroyed—which is what was to be demonstrated. Thus it has become a different, and, thanks to a rare alchemy, better thing. Therefore let us have as little as possible about its 'being' Mr. This or Mrs. That. If it adjusts itself with the least truth to its new life it can't possibly be either. (*AN,* 230)

This sequence most clearly registers the infusion of the melting pot into James's conceptualization of literary form. Here the figures of alchemy and cooking interpenetrate, as they did in *The American Scene;* here the "prime identity" is destroyed but a newer and richer saturation is achieved; here the new life is adjusted to, in just the way that any number of James's contemporaries would have spoken of immigration. By virtue of James's late position in the "polyglot crowd," his own figure maps onto those of his literary "morsels." The use of melting-pot language of transmutation has the effect of casting the literary imagination as a crucible in which abstract chemical (quasi-mystical) forces are at work, and to which James is equally subject. A melting-pot aesthetic theory presumes, if not the death of the author, then at least his radical reconception as, paradoxically, one who *also* speaks, however codedly, of his "late genial medium."

By figuring the literary imagination in chemical terms, James participates in the scientific enthusiasms of the Progressive era, the very enthusiasms that (ironically) led to the framing of immigrant assimilation in the language of alchemy. Like the sociologist Sarah Simons, James privileges "chemical" over "mechanical" combination. In James's argument, the relation between "real" person and literary person is "essentially not mechanical, but thinkable rather—so far as thinkable at all—in chemical, almost in mystical terms" (*AN*, 230). Mechanics involve an attention to the application of forces (an author upon his materials, a nation upon its immigrants); chemistry, instead, attends to changes in form, combination, separation, diffusing interest in causality into a broader interest in process. Force and causality both represent significant blind spots in the melting-pot model, and James's melting-pot literary theory represents a good site for their interrogation. James's literary theory shows that the failure to fully engage the political and moral problems of Jim Crow America that Kenneth Warren associates with James's realism is, instead, symptomatic of the failure to come to terms with force that theoretically underpins Jamesian literary modernism.[59] In what follows I will consider the extent to which James's theoretical intertwining of form and selfhood might require, or even justify, such a problematic lack of curiosity about the exertion of force.[60]

By intertwining a rebuke to mechanics with an elevation of chemical science, James strikes a distinctly Progressive-era note. Walter Lippmann's *Drift and Mastery* (1914) contains a most un-Jamesian celebration of science as a means of "mastery," but, more significantly for us, does so through a suggestive repudiation of "mechanical" science. Lippmann rejects the over-faithful "following of...analogy" on the mechanical side of science: to him a "real scientist" knows how to navigate the fluidity of analogy, recognizing both its promise and its limits.[61] Analogy *properly* conceived stars in Lippmann's celebration of scientific thinking (as it does in Jamesian form and melting-pot thinking), for its mobile evocations of likeness very easily shift into non-dogmatic suggestions of like*i*ness: "around each observation there gathers an aura of conjectures. The scientific discoverer can penetrate the crevices of fact with moving guesses; each experiment is suspended in pregnant hypotheses."[62] Lippmann's phrase combines the preternatural mobility of the guesses with the stillness of the suspended experiment, the fecund promise of pregnancy with the threatened barrenness of the unproven hypotheses: each state shifts into its other. As in James's insistence that literary transformation be understood "in chemical, almost in mystical terms," Lippmann's version of science merges into mysticism (the "aura"). In the passive construction "there gathers an aura of conjectures," Lippmann performs the sacrifice of causal precision that is required to diffuse responsibility for imagining transformation and thinking transformatively.

Analogy enables James and Lippmann to share in the turn-of-the-century promise of science and to extend that promise to their readers. However, that promise is bought at some cost. This chain of scientific communication may purport to intervene in, and reconceive of, traditional forms of authority, but it leaves the concepts of authority and coercion relatively unscathed. Lippmann's celebration of "mastery" cannot pre-empt, and may even prepare the ground for, the idealizations and abuses of power central to so much modernism. In the New York Edition, science offers James a tantalizing opportunity to figure transformations without linking them causally to any single agent. The question raised by this strategy, of course, is: to what degree is James's use of these figures compromised by an evasion of questions of authority in the way that Lippmann's is?

In James's preface to *The Ambassadors,* scientific figuration offers the means to imagine changing form as a natural reaction rather than a traumatic imposition:

> [Strether] had come [to Paris] with a view that might have been fig-
> ured by a clear green liquid, say, in a neat glass phial; and the liquid,
> once poured into the open cup of *application,* once exposed to the
> action of another air, had begun to turn from green to red, or whatever,
> and might, for all he knew, be on its way to purple, to black, to yellow.
> (*AN,* 314)

Obscuring the agency of experimenters, chemical and textual, James's preface both describes a self released from containment and mobilizes the *means* of that self's transformation and release.[63] The figure is introduced in a hypothetical tone ("might have been figured") but quickly shifts into actual deployment (or *application*), changing its own nature and that of the matter it works upon. Both novel and preface here serve as kinds of laboratories, in which chemical transformation trumps mechanical containment. It is not simply the view that changes upon exposure to "another" air; through the action of figuration, the *forms* of being themselves shift. For the reader, a liquid becomes a view, air becomes experience, an open cup becomes application. Figuration is itself a version of the "the open cup of *application,*" the process by which liquids become "exposed to the action of another air." Figuration *acts,* counts as a primary agent, one that produces an uncharted and unpredictable process like the one it represents.

Fixing agency upon the process of figuration (rather than upon any individual artist or actor, or even upon a material social context) produced significant opportunities in the theorization of melting-pot selfhood. James's prefaces make it more clear than *The American Scene* did: to his mind coercive social power cannot be expected operate directly, or even predictably, through the vehicle of figuration. When figuration is understood as a primary causal force, transformations are driven by the haphazard logic that infuses New York's "assault of sensibility": surprise encounters produce unexpected relations. While a sense of the past assists in the understanding and appreciation of changes that have taken place, it offers no predictive advantage.[64] Who knows whether the liquid is "on its way to purple, to black, to yellow"? The individual self remains estranged from such insight or influence: "for all he knew," any new connection, new form, might be produced by the illegible, abracadabrant play of language upon his being. Freedom is bought, here, at the cost of individual responsibility, which James instead diffuses across the abstract forces of representation.

The testimony of a contemporaneous immigrant scientist suggests why this chemical confusion of mechanical causality appealed to thinkers as different as James and Lippmann, despite its troubling implications for the analysis of power and responsibility. In his Pulitzer Prize–winning autobiography *From Immigrant to Inventor* (1924), Michael Pupin, the famous Progressive-era engineer, explains that scientific investigation (like literary matters of form and figuration) ignores what seem to be fundamental questions; it self-consciously neglects the big questions for small advances on more utilitarian questions:

> When we told them that the electrical science was one of the most exact of all physical sciences, some shook their heads and exhibited considerable scepticism. One of them asked me: 'Doctor, do you know what electricity is?' 'No,' said I, and he added another question: 'Then how can you have an exact science of electricity when you do not even know what electricity is?'... It is a difficult thing to make unscientific people understand that science studies first and foremost the *activities of things and not their ultimate nature.*[65]

For Pupin as for a generation of thinkers elaborating on the melting-pot metaphor, the "ultimate nature" of the immigrant was as unknowable (and uninteresting) as the "activities" in which he was involved were all-consuming. Appraisals of causality trace activities back to their originators: in this sense they are of a kind with, and inexorably extend into, inquiries into "ultimate nature," and cannot be the province of either scientist or melting-pot modernist.

Certainly in his fundamental theory of prose—that "the grave distinction between substance and form in a really wrought work signally break[s]
down" (*AN,* 115)—James concurs with Pupin and other melting-pot theorists that "substance" (or ultimate nature) is interesting only insofar as it is
accessible through "form" (the activities or outward life of things and texts).
James's aesthetic practice is in line with Pupin's belief that one must strive for
precise knowledge without pretending a knowledge of "ultimate natures,"
and indeed, that both experiment and expression come closer to truth when
they attend to activities rather than pursuing ultimate natures. James's literary theory translates the pragmatic (sociological, ethnographic) insight that
attending to the immigrant's activities is the only way to begin understanding
her nature into a fundamental modernist aesthetic principle: understanding
what the text *does* is the only way of understanding what it *is.*

In these discussions text and immigrant come to occupy strangely symmetrical positions. Indeed, James's prefaces of the New York Edition register
the influence of the melting pot through a peculiar formal twist: they cast the
literary text as agent in its own right, figuratively merging the forms of text
and person. As Dorothy Hale puts it, the Jamesian "appreciation of alter-
ity" passes through a "sequence of transmutation" in the prefaces, producing
what she terms "a self-expressive art work."[66] James's texts talk back to him
in the prefaces (more often than not challenging his ordering vision, just as
the immigrant inhabitants of New York did). While his texts might design
to entertain, James ironically notes, they are signally *not* the "living doll" that
"would speak and act and perform" without requiring "anything like reciprocity" (*AN,* 189). Instead, James casts his texts as his "progeny" (*AN,* 337)
and speaks of the edition, its act of revision, as a "living affair" (*AN,* 342). In
his final preface (to *The Golden Bowl*), he gives his clearest acknowledgment
of the text as a "doing" agent: "to 'put' things is very exactly and responsibly
and interminably to do them," he concludes (*AN,* 347). He is careful not to
imply that the text is a neutral conduit for its author's "doing": in keeping
with the diffused agency and inscrutable power dynamics of his model, he
asserts that texts continue to act without their authors' interference, leaving
those authors "all license of disconnexion and disavowal" (*AN,* 348). Texts
are, in other words, "first-order" agents: their activity and intentionality can
no more be traced back to a single authorizing source than can the activity and intentionality of immigrant agents be traced back to a single racial
or cultural origin. Like the immigrant on the fire-escape of Rutgers Street,
like the "black stranger" encountered in a corridor of one's own abandoned
house, James's textual agents demand a social connection: we are asked simply
"to feel" for these "performances." By the "lightest touch" of the central

consciousness, here writer and elsewhere melting-pot subject, "the whole chain of relation and responsibility is reconstituted" (*AN*, 348).

"Certain Precious Discriminations"

If James seemed to accept, even welcome, the diffusion and postponement of agency resultant from melting-pot theories of selfhood in his New York Edition prefaces, his series of late-life autobiographies suggest that agency continued to prove an unnerving question for him. These autobiographies extend James's engagement with the melting-pot predicament. (Indeed, as we shall see, they diffused that predicament, dragging sometimes unwilling James family members into James's complicated versions of selfhood and responsibility.) James's preface to *The Ambassadors* defines autobiography as a means of choosing "*not* to make certain precious discriminations" (*AN*, 321); his autobiographies, appropriately, are so radically unfinished that they fail to make critical discriminations between selves, both the selves represented in the text and those involved in its construction and consumption. Roles blur and merge, marking the autobiographies as James's latest and most extreme interrogation of the implications of melting-pot models of selfhood and formal experimentation. Both *A Small Boy and Others* (1913) and *Notes of a Son and Brother* (1914) were written in part to memorialize James's recently deceased brother William. They are, in James's word, "experimental" texts, ones that embed his social objective in a context of literary-formal innovation.[67] This late autobiographical exercise vividly evokes a problem in James's delicately crafted aesthetic performance. On the one hand, "not to make certain precious discriminations" between selves means succeeding at the form of melting-pot mixture that James had refined; on the other hand, because these discriminations have value to some, James's disregard for them has troubling implications.

James explained the form of *Notes of a Son and Brother*, the second volume of the autobiography, as an attempt to see "if I might live, by the imagination, in William's so adaptive skin."[68] The experimental form of *Notes of a Son and Brother* involves Henry James assuming his brother's voice, acceding to what he tropes as the "ghostly appeal" of old letters, and including these letters in the text, interweaving his brother's changing voices with his own (*NS*, 42). Because agency is even more obscure in *Notes of a Son and Brother* than in many of James's other figurations, the text testifies to the "illegible amputations" securing James's artistic project. That is, the text is silent on how Henry James's "concession" to the "ghostly appeal" merges with his *response* to that appeal—or, how he rewrites his brother's letters. In this case his silent participation in the correspondence clearly constitutes a significant exertion of force.[69] To accept operations of force being obscured here as they were elsewhere in the Jamesian melting-pot project means accepting Henry's right to exercise such power over William's voice.

William's son Harry, for one, was disturbed by the liberal revisions his uncle made to William's letters. Henry James justified his rewritings to his nephew by appealing to the feeling behind them: "it was as if I kept spiritually replying to this [request for protection by WJ] that he might indeed trust me to handle him with the last tact and devotion—that is to do with him everything I seemed to feel him *like*."[70] This response to Harry intertwines the idea of "stirred sensibility" with a melting-pot insistence on *likeness*, rather than identity. In effect, James argues that by rewriting his brother's letters, he retains for William in death the mobile identifications that he practiced in life; Henry thus repudiates the still, fixed self of the letter for a self that is constantly, multiply, "like." Indeed, when Henry James describes his identification with William, he uses terms familiar from his melting-pot texts: William has an effect akin to "the action of colouring-matter dropped into water or that of the turning-on of a light within a window," two figures Henry James earlier used to trope the immigrant presence (*NS*, 15).

This late skirmish with Harry James is superabundant in its suggestion. On the one hand, it confirms James's consistency in his commitment to melting-pot merging. He uses feeling to extend abstract metaphorical theories into very intimate territory, and thereby gives affective as well as intellectual heft to melting-pot ideas. The run of texts from *The American Scene* through the autobiographies confirms him as a major articulator of melting-pot thinking. His late autobiographical acts, however, also confirm that the action of the melting pot, even via an intimate and sensitive conduit, can come off as intellectual and aesthetic imperialism. Despite his sympathetic intent and his apparent innocence of force, Henry's chemical fusions read as mechanical impositions of force to his nephew. This is not to say that the insights or the aspirations of melting-pot thinking must be dismissed altogether—simply that even in the hands of James, one of their most sensitive propounders, melting-pot ideas still exhibit ethical and logical vulnerabilities. James elaborated a sophisticated framework of melting-pot ideas and both theorized and modeled the usefulness of these ideas for literary modernism—where their strengths and their flaws can still be discerned. Indeed, these strengths and flaws extend even to contemporary theorizations of merging and fusion; for that reason, we cannot afford to unqualifiedly embrace or reject them. Instead, we must subject them to the kind of close reading that Jamesian texts demand of us.

For James, this late stage of his melting-pot project infuses his renovated ideas of selfhood with new feeling, but is finally most significant in literary-formal terms: "I think I am nonetheless right as to the passages hanging better together so with my own text, and 'melting' so with my own atmosphere. . . . I have had to the last point the instinct and the sense for fusions and interrelations, for framing and encircling. . . every part of my stuff in every other."[71] The "melting," "fusions," and "interrelations" of these final works complete the promise of the "renovation of one's grab-bag" that James imagined waiting for him in the turn-of-the-century United States. His investigation ended here, but many of his questions and strategies were picked up and adapted by members of a cohort profoundly influenced by both melting-pot thinking and Jamesian literary modernism. As I will show in the following chapters, ghostly traces of the Jamesian "grab-bag" mark the work of James Weldon Johnson, Willa Cather, and Gertrude Stein.

✪ CHAPTER 3

James Weldon Johnson's Integrationist Chameleonism

James Weldon Johnson was committed to racial integration. His fidelity to this objective, which he saw as entailing the construction of a racially egalitarian American state and culture, was unmatched among African American intellectuals of his generation. This integrationism represents the melting-pot impetus in Progressive-era race relations; it has, most famously, been decried by Harold Cruse as preventing the emergence of an autonomous ethnic culture, but it has also been associated with "New Negro" self-deception by critics such as David Levering Lewis and Henry Louis Gates, Jr.[1] More recently, however, George Hutchinson (who provides a helpful guide to critical debates over Harlem Renaissance interracialism) has argued that the historical complexity of race is best understood through intellectual nexuses such as Johnsonian integrationism, "those moments when and places where the intertwined discourses of race, culture, and nation were exposed to questioning, to skepticism, to transformation, however small and localized, and when possibilities for coalitions of cultural reformers were envisioned and exploited."[2] This chapter focuses on just such a moment and place, showing how deeply Johnson was engaged with melting-pot ideas and how this engagement embedded concerns about racial equity into modernist literature, culture, and politics.

James Weldon Johnson's prominence in the National Association for the Advancement of Colored People—he served as the executive secretary of the organization for almost ten years, 1920–1930—speaks to his embrace of the Progressive-era integrationist ideals that organization represented. Unlike many of his peers, despite significant disillusionment he remained true to Progressive-era assimilationist ideals well past the First World War and through the interwar period. Unlike Henry James (but like Willa Cather and Gertrude Stein), Johnson lived and worked both in and beyond the formative years of the melting pot, and the intellectual influence of that early moment can and should be traced through his later work. Johnson insisted that African Americans had "woven [themselves] into the woof and warp of the nation."[3] In other words, his concern was *not* whether African Americans *could* be admitted into the melting pot, for he believed they were excellent examples of the vitality of cultural mixture. Rather, Johnson was concerned with whether or not African Americans would receive credit for their ongoing contributions to cultural mixture, and whether they ought to intervene in, and change the nature of, the *process* of cultural mixture. As both a writer and a political activist Johnson worked to change political, social, economic, and aesthetic conditions so as to better reflect ongoing cultural interweaving, and so as to ensure that the interweaving observed certain ethical principles. His work in imagining and promoting a shared civic culture resonates with melting-pot efforts like those of Jane Addams and John Dewey. He approached integration as melting-pot thinkers approached assimilation: that is, he understood cultural merging to take place at a formal level. Johnson's melting-pot modernism is most distinctly registered in his decision to advance his political and cultural agendas through sustained experimentation at the level of expressive form. His writings both theorize and wage a formal campaign for equity on behalf of black America.

Johnson was a polymath—educator, lawyer, songwriter, journalist, novelist, anthropologist, historian—but the roles for which he is best known, executive secretary of the NAACP and senior statesman of the Harlem Renaissance, bespeak the close ties that he perceived between political activism and artistic innovation. This chapter explores the generic and expressive variety through which Johnson advanced his ideas of cultural fusion, a merging conceived not in terms of the physical mingling that Charles Chesnutt prescribed in his essay series "The Future American" (1900), but in expressive terms. (Johnson characteristically declared that one could "*write so as to fuse* white and black America."[4]) In a 1922 editorial for the *New York Age,* Johnson laid out the shared forms by which cultural fusion was enacted: "Peoples are not related and united by physical aspects or even by blood. They are united by common cultures, common ideas, common ideals, common languages, common educations."[5] Johnson's career consists of an extraordinary array of efforts to "relate" and "unite" through the sharing of these "common" forms. Here I will be focusing in particular on his project to embed something a little *less* common in the melting-pot language of fusion. As the bleak racial politics of the post-Reconstruction United States taught him, "common" cultures could serve to unite peoples only if more explicit attention was given to the power imbalances that prevented equitable cultural sharing. This chapter will both elaborate and interrogate efforts by Johnson to attend to these power imbalances, to address them, and to craft a racially inclusive melting pot.

Johnson's *New York Age* editorial emphasizes the word "common," evoking not only the spirit of shared or public goods that infused theories of the melting pot, but also the disrespect that such projects so often faced (Henry James, for example, had no great love for the "common"). Johnson understood that there had long been cultural traffic across the color line in the United States; while that traffic destabilized the color line, racial boundaries were still policed by violence and prejudice. For that reason, Johnson could not afford to be as neutral as a Jamesian melting-pot subject about the operations of power; as long as inequitable racial relations persisted, cultural plunder would pre-empt interracial cultural weaving. In the pages that follow I will show how Johnson took a formal program not dissimilar from James's melting-pot experimentalism and attempted, through it, to fashion new awareness of the ways in which force impacts melting-pot ideology. Johnson's explicit and sustained attention to asymmetrical power relations is unusual among melting-pot modernists. He neither simply wishes to include "black and yellow" in his melting pot through simple declaration, as Zangwill does, nor wishes to deny the possibility of cultural intermixture across racial boundaries, as Robert Park does. Johnson's writings address asymmetries of power by attempting to devise equitable means for interracial sharing, considering both the feasibility and the consequences of embedding equity concerns in melting-pot models.

While James, then, ends his career by responding to the intellectual challenge of the melting pot with a celebration of its fluid conceptions of self and expression, Johnson ends with a pointedly different response to this challenge. Johnson's latest works celebrate the fluid forms of *African American* selfhood and of *African American* artistic expression, developed in the face of persistent racial inequality that extended into the conception of the melting pot. Johnson's cultural pride becomes only more pronounced and more forcefully articulated as his career progresses, but this should not be taken as constituting a repudiation of melting-pot integrationism. Rather, it represents a necessary means of transforming inequitable cultural plunder into reciprocal melting-pot "gifts." In other words, Johnson works on the same paradox that Eric Sundquist points to at the foundation of W. E. B. Du Bois's career: "that cultures could be learned, shared, and made universal, but that the hierarchy of racism left the dominant culture ignorant of the singular spiritual heritage that the institution of slavery had embedded within its own nation."[6] In Johnson's case, cultural pride and programs of cultural education do not reflect an insistence on static or even coherent cultural blocks; rather, they are the means by which power and inequality can be taken into consideration in order to advance cultural integration.

Recognizing, along with Jane Addams and W. E. B. Du Bois, that a viable program of cultural sharing must genuinely appreciate a wide variety of cultural "gifts" as such, Johnson advocated a version of assimilation that celebrates difference.[7] Despite their very different stances on the question of the melting pot, Johnson's integrationism here is not so different from Randolph Bourne's famous theorization of a national community of equal rights without cultural uniformity in the essay "Trans-National America" (1916).[8] For Bourne and his generation, wartime hysteria proved that Progressive-era assimilation theorists were willing to dispense with rights and protections for disempowered groups. Yet Johnson's work shows that on some fronts, at least, considerations of rights, equity, and power were being brought to bear upon melting-pot thinking even before the war. Such a program was by no means either easy or successful, as Johnson's career shows; he spent many years and ranged over many expressive forms in his attempts to insert explicit considerations of justice into a paradigm whose abstract espousals of free-floating egalitarianism often fell short on such considerations.

This chapter traces the pursuit of formally flexible literary egalitarianism through Johnson's career. I begin by sketching the resonance of his earliest Tin Pan Alley song-writing with melting-pot thinking, in order to fully convey his indebtedness to the model. I then turn to his faux-autobiography *The Autobiography of an Ex-Coloured Man,* showing how it questions two different tendencies in melting-pot thought: first, it skeptically exposes melting-pot ideas of selfhood as both subjectively unpersuasive and logically incoherent; second, it seriously interrogates the capacity of melting-pot modes of subjectivity to mount any kind of ethical critique or resistance to the violence of racism. From this devastating assessment of melting-pot thinking, I go on to trace Johnson's proposed alternatives: the delicately theorized performances of egalitarian literary experimentalism represented by his editorial and anthologizing work. Throughout the many phases of his career, Johnson remains committed to enacting a melting-pot literary and cultural synthesis, but he insists on doing so in terms that remain alert to, and guarded against, the force exerted by both hate and inequality. Johnson provides a particularly important example of melting-pot modernism because he pursues the political objectives claimed by so many Progressive-era reformers to their literary implications. Engaging explicitly, and not always forgivingly, with the applicability of immigration-based models of cultural sharing to the rapidly hardening racial divisions of the post-Reconstruction United States, he represents an indispensable melting-pot voice.

Race into the Melting Pot

Johnson never again raised the melting-pot vision of "common cultures" so playfully, in such a Jamesian fashion, as he does in "Under the Bamboo Tree" (1902), a song that he composed with his brother, J. Rosamond Johnson, and Bob Cole. In his later criticism Johnson insisted that popular "lighter music" of African American origin, like this song, deserves greater recognition as "a form of art"; in his autobiography he self-consciously reflects on the cross-cultural collaboration that brought about such art: "fused and then developed, chiefly by Jewish musicians... it has become our national medium for expressing ourselves musically in popular form."[9] Johnson's days as a writer in New York's early twentieth-century popular music industry exposed him to a paradigmatic site of American cultural intermixture, and his representation of the industry both nods to its ethnic and financial particulars and extracts from these dynamics the national "ourselves." Cole and Johnson's "Under the Bamboo Tree" became a great hit (so popular that Yale based cheers for the annual Yale-Harvard football game on it). It remained such a sophisticated and enduring testament to Johnson's variety of talents that it was sung at a New York dinner in his honor in 1931.

Through its refrain, "Under the Bamboo Tree" transforms the love story of a "Zulu from Matabooloo" into a melting-pot meditation on multiplicity, self-division, and social connection:

> If you lak-a-me, lak I lak-a you;
> And we lak-a-both the same,
> I lak-a say, this very day,
> I lak-a change your name;
> 'Cause I love-a-you and love-a-you true
> And if you-a love-a-me,
> One live as two, two live as one
> Under the bamboo tree.[10]

"Lak," or like, is the dominant note of this refrain. In a love song it denotes affection, but its connotation of likeness, or comparability, is also strongly in evidence here (from "*lak* I lak-a you"). The word recurs over clauses and lines, becoming the basis for both shared meanings and shared sounds; by echoing through the song, it enacts similarity as well as connoting it. However, repetition also draws attention to the different meanings taken on by the word in different contexts; likeness, here, is quite distinct from identity. "Lak" is, in fact, non-identical to "like" as we know it, and also non-identical to the vernacular pronunciation that, in Johnson's estimation, dialect spellings were never capable of adequately invoking. "Lak," then, also signifies a lack—the missing familiar, the botched identity. Both the repetition and the unfamiliar pronunciation transform the word, reminding listeners that, literally, "likeness" can be foreign.

To "lak-a-both the same," as in this song's refrain, is a complex process that resists perfect transcription. All three terms, like, both, and same, can indicate commonality, but their combination suggests that they do not express the very *same* sameness. Bringing them together, Johnson's song points to the difference in their similarities. Being combined thus transforms the words ("change[s their] name," in the words of the song); indeed, the transcribed elision ("lak-*a*") that recurs through the refrain suggests the physical changes to the word caused by proximity to other words. The chiasmus of "One live as two, two live as one" enacts this transformation, a "crossing" characteristic of melting-pot experience. In the chiasmus, words figuratively and literally assume the positions of their fellows. The two clauses have independent grammatical viability and meaning, and yet their power is amplified by their combination. This chiasmus creates new meanings: foremost among these is the confusion of "one" and "two," mediated by the "as." In this context individuality becomes doubleness, while connection produces merging. However, as the "as" reminds us, this process of merging remains one oriented to likeness, rather than identity; no wholesale collapses of difference have taken place.

Indeed, the "Zulu from Matabooloo" remains a thoroughly alien figure, despite the familiar mergings and doublings that he mediates for the popular singer. In his later writings Johnson proved as skeptical about the assumptions of racial connection implicit in African colonization schemes as he was adamant about the "Americanness" of African Americans. In this light, the words "Zulu from Matabooloo" go beyond playful rhyming to evoke the "*abracadabrant*" illegibility that confronted Henry James at the scene of immigration. Despite "sharing" the words of the Zulu, the singer and writer remain profoundly estranged from his position. The play of language has produced a fleeting experience of pleasure, but it has not suggested this figure as a truly viable "alternate self." Artful, sophisticated, even evocative of feeling, the song may be a "common" leisure product, but its formal effects have been bought at the price of political or ethical vigilance. That is, the problem that haunts much of Henry James's late work is front and center in Johnson's early work, and might even be said to constitute the central aesthetic and political question of his career.

Johnson's *Autobiography of an Ex-Coloured Man* (1912) probes this dilemma, considering the threefold challenge of integrating a recognition of asymmetries of power, a commitment to ethical action, and a privileging of changeability into aesthetic and political representation. The *Autobiography* considers a prewar period in which cultures might circulate with increasing freedom, as the success of Tin Pan Alley and ragtime suggested, but persons could not, given ongoing racial violence and the segregation legally formalized by the landmark decision *Plessy v. Ferguson* (1896). African Americans, that is, found themselves largely in the position of the "Zulu from Matabooloo," rigidly held apart by an omniscient policing perspective even as their words and songs were "shared." Johnson, however, perceived an opportunity to use the self-conscious formal experimentalism of contemporary melting-pot theories against the racial boundaries that limited equitable cultural fusion. To make good on Israel Zangwill's inclusion of "black and yellow" in his melting pot, in other words, what was signified by black and yellow must be transformed, made abracadabrant. Johnson's song, with its emphasis on "lak," offers a new entrée into W. E. B. Du Bois's hope, articulated in *The Souls of Black Folk* (1903), "that some day on American soil two world-races may give each to each those characteristics both so sadly lack."[11] Both thinkers tap into the language of the common fund, transforming a national conversation fixated on deficits in post-Reconstruction black culture into an occasion for mutually transformative barter. If "world-races" might be conceived of as connected through complementary incompleteness, then perhaps the isolated cipher of the "Zulu from Matabooloo" might be introduced into a more cosmopolitan system of exchange. Johnson's 1912 novel considers whether such mutual giving could take place without reinscribing existing racial inequities.

As its title suggests, *The Autobiography of an Ex-Coloured Man* takes up the autobiographical form that was central to both immigrant literature of the melting pot and Henry James's late experiments. First published anonymously, Johnson's text was taken by many as an authentic autobiography. Indeed, Johnson instructed his first publishers to avoid "giving any impression that it is fiction."[12] Playing on the demand for melting-pot autobiographies and the market's historical resistance to non-autobiographical texts by African Americans, Johnson's novel merges the conventions of slave narratives with those of immigrant autobiographies. First-person literary forms had long been used to combat prejudice, on the premise that special access to the interiority of individuals whose inner lives were in question would constitute a basis for new sympathy, cultural inclusion, and reciprocity. Johnson's text, however, exposes this premise to the anxiety initiated by the cipher in "Under the Bamboo Tree." *The Autobiography of an Ex-Coloured Man* installs the "lak" where the authentic interiority ought to be found, offering special access to a narrative that marshals the rhetoric of authenticity in singularly unconvincing ways. Of course, the *Autobiography* is no more slave narrative or melting-pot autobiography than it is autobiography at all; by the time it was republished under Johnson's name in 1927, its false performance of autobiographical interiority was immediately recognizable as such.[13] In 1912, however, *The Autobiography of an Ex-Coloured Man* used the uncertainties generated by its unclear degree of imposture to drive a wedge between theories of melting-pot being and ideas of authentic selfhood.[14] *The Autobiography of an Ex-Coloured Man* shows that autobiography is unsuited for the integrative work it is so often called upon to perform: to begin with, it cannot convincingly represent the more contingent forms of selfhood proposed in the melting-pot model; and were it ever able to do so, it would be fatally compromised in its ability to argue for the more equitable politics needed to achieve melting-pot objectives.

The *Autobiography* ultimately fails to present an articulation of selfhood free from either the ethical traps of Henry James's diffuse creations (the "Zulu from Matabooloo" problem) or the ontological traps of more "straight" ethnic autobiography. Through its failure, however, it mounts a compelling critique of the centrality of autobiography in the melting-pot age. This is not to say that Johnson utterly abandons the individual-form so central to Progressive-era theories of cultural merging. None other than W. E. B. Du Bois had met white Progressive racism with an insistence that "the ideal ought to be that a man should be treated as an individual," suggesting that the individual-form might be both the means and the end of struggles for Progressive-era racial equity.[15] *The Autobiography of an Ex-Coloured Man* represents Johnson's experiment with what being "treated as an individual" signifies in integrative terms—specifically, with how and why an autobiographical account might be taken as a "composite and proportionate presentation of the entire race."[16]

"The Inner Life of the Negro"

The Autobiography of an Ex-Coloured Man opens with a preface (signed by the publishers, but dictated to them by Johnson himself in a letter of

February 17, 1912) that announces in the tone of the circus barker that "in these pages it is as though a veil had been drawn aside: the reader is given a view of the inner life of the Negro in America" (*Ex,* xl). This bombastic claim of authoritative insight serves as an introductory caution, for it demonstrates the easy match of false clarity with disingenuous integrationism. These "publishers" are not utterly dishonest, however; both W. E. B. Du Bois and Johnson's narrator represented that which lies behind the veil as equally a particular individual consciousness and an entire arena of cultural experience. According to this consensus *the* "inner life of the Negro" is at once singular in the sense of being individually unique, and singular in the sense of being archetypal (Robert Park's abstract mask). Johnson's novel takes this idea seriously: it collapses the two realms into each other, making the inner life of the individual and the inner life of the group indistinguishable. The many merge into the one in an archetypally indistinct melting-pot subjectivity, one recognizable from multitudes of immigrant autobiographies. That this merging is heralded and enabled by the venal publishers, however, suggests that it is considerably less innocent than melting-pot theorists imagined. This warning constitutes only the beginning of Johnson's interrogation of melting-pot versions of subjectivity.

Johnson's fictional publishers represent the unusual subjectivity of the *Autobiography* as acting in contradictory ways. On the one hand, the publishers claim, the autobiographical narrative "initiate[s]" the reader "into the freemasonry...of the race," so immerses him in its subjective particularity that he can claim a part of it (*Ex,* xl).[17] On the other hand, they add, the autobiographical narrative gives the reader "a glimpse behind the scenes of this race drama...[he is] taken upon an elevation where he can catch a bird's-eye-view," or given a kind of authoritative, commanding non-participant position (*Ex,* xl). The publishers seem untroubled by the merging of these different perspectives. And they are not entirely wrong here, either: the unpredictable merging of subjective and objective perspectives does represent the distinctive literary device of the *Autobiography.* The text explores the autobiographical equivalent of free indirect discourse, as it were. By doing this it reverses the movement of texts like James's *American Scene;* rather than finding subjectivity where documentation was expected, the *Autobiography* produces documentary objectivity out of a domain of pure self. This sleight-of-hand constitutes the *Autobiography*'s first major interruption of the logic driving the autobiographical regime of the melting pot.

Johnson's faux-autobiography takes to an extreme the autobiographical tendency to use the outside world to talk about inner states. The *Autobiography* flagrantly performs a melting-pot generic blending, showing up the cacophonous possibilities of such blending; it merges autobiography with the documentary ethos so popular in turn-of-the-century American writing, proposing to treat subjectivity as simply another dangerous space to be mastered and represented through the techniques of a diligent realism.[18] The narrative opens with the narrator's titillating revelation that he is "divulging the great secret of my life, the secret which for some years I have guarded far more carefully than any of my earthly possessions" (*Ex,* 3).[19] The narrator's announcement builds on the promises of revelation in the publishers' preface. However, the exact nature of this innermost knowledge is never specified. The *Autobiography* reveals many secrets, but it ultimately never identifies which is the "great secret": that the narrator, according to law and social convention, is black? Or that he now lives as a white man, his mother's race suppressed? What is the "common," public knowledge (the subject of documentary), and what is the innermost knowledge (autobiography)? (The answer here surely differs according to implied audience, reinforcing the segmented nature of the "public" in the early twentieth-century United States.) Ultimately, however, the passing narrative implied in this breathless confession is less important than the narrator's promise that his text will reveal all. The ethos of confession that structures the autobiography itself creates "common" knowledge, for the great revelation dissolves the boundaries constituted by disparate knowledges: the divide between origins and contemporary activities collapses. In that sense the great secret is that there is no longer any great secret, no longer any division to protect. Publication is the engine of integration here; the subjectivity that welcomes merging finds its being in and through autobiography.

This logic is put into practice in one of the *Autobiography*'s critical scenes of subjectification and self-consciousness: after a teacher implies that he is not, as he assumed, white, the young narrator rushes to a mirror and gazes at his reflected self. Here revealed secrets do helpfully rupture the boundaries of the sovereign self, introducing new perspectives, voices, and self-identifications into the individual's repertoire. The narrator looks "long and earnestly" into the mirror, and as he does so, recalls that he has "often heard people say to my mother: 'what a pretty boy you have!'" (*Ex,* 17). While the earnest gaze recalls that of the well-meaning Progressive, this sequence is palpably Du Boisian: to begin to think of himself as black is to approach himself through the eyes, and voices, of others. In the moment of discovery, the self is surrounded, hearing voices despite his position alone in front of the mirror, approaching himself through a variety of senses. Perception mediated by others—other perspectives, other senses—appears to be the means by which the narrator can integrate new knowledge and old beliefs. (In that sense it may even constitute a version of the "intimate contact" that Du Bois saw as necessary to "realizing" the truths of existence behind the Veil.) In Johnson's mirror scene, auditory and visual impressions mingle; subjective and external data interpenetrate just as melting-pot thinkers imagined self and other might interpenetrate.

Yet the narrator who emerges from this scene is a narcissistic creature, one who in repeatedly demanding of his mother "am I a nigger?" shows no awareness that her tears are not for him alone, or that he has any emotional or ethical responsibility to another (*Ex,* 18). Indeed, in its introduction of questions of race and prejudice into the scene of internal division, Johnson's mirror scene constitutes an important intervention into a common melting-pot trope.[20] In Abraham Cahan's *Yekl* (1896), when Gitl tries on a hat before her mirror she signals her transition from racially marked greenhorn to melting-pot assimilator. The sociologist Charles Horton Cooley's 1902 theory of a "looking-glass self" made no reference to race:[21]

> as we see our face, figure, and dress in the glass, and are interested in them because they are ours, and pleased or otherwise with them according as they do or do not answer to what we should like them to be; so in imagination we perceive in another's mind some thought of our appearance, manners, aims, deeds, character, friends, and so on, and are variously affected by it.[22]

Johnson's novel considerably complicates these versions of assimilation. When Johnson's narrator tries to understand blackness by means of his youthful reflection, the mirror makes manifest an externalized version of Cooley's looking-glass self. What W. E. B. Du Bois rendered in more subjective terms, as double-consciousness, Johnson's novel transposes into a more literal register. Through the revelation of his teacher, Johnson's narrator simultaneously joins a community with shared, common knowledge (of his racial "identity"), and experiences his separation from that community by virtue of the knowledge they share. For the first time, he becomes "conscious" of the ways in which he is seen, and measures himself according to those expectations (*Ex,* 17). Yet despite this growing consciousness, this scene capably evokes how melting-pot modes of being can be totally hospitable to prejudice. The word "nigger" rings tauntingly in his ears, but he soon re-uses the word himself in his mother's company. Without additional racial self-consciousness, this expanded form of inner life offers few protections against racist abuses.

The communal constitution of self that the narrator experiences at the mirror extends throughout the text of the *Autobiography;* the narrator never untangles his own inner life from the versions of inner life that he observes

in his travels. His continual construction and reconstruction of his subjectivity produces the episodic form of the *Autobiography*. This autobiography is a
catalog of visible or audible phenomena, a chronicle of the matter of culture
in a racialized United States. Johnson parodies a melting-pot mixture of
muckraking journalism and assimilative autobiography through a discontinuous series of exposés of "inner life." In this generic blend, the narrator
derives his authority to speak not from a self-justifying subjectivity, but from
his external experience. He offers inside information about the "race struggle" as inside information about his self, but he never convincingly asserts the
self-consciousness that might prove resilient to prejudice or racial hate.

Instead, following the publishers' promise that the reader will be "initiated
into the freemasonry of the race," Johnson's narrator obligingly leads the
reader through a variety of cultural sketches (*Ex*, xl). Each begins with an
initiation into an esoteric realm, and each proceeds through a full assimilation by the narrator, in which he convincingly assumes manners that he has
only recently encountered.[23] Only full assimilation following the initiation
can be trusted to produce the collapse of "insider" and "inside," thereby sus-
taining the *Autobiography*'s idea of subjective interiority as constituted by
full access to the "inner life of the Negro in America." In one exemplary
instance, the narrator is initially put off by the loud talking, "rolling '*caram-
bas*,' menacing gesticulations with knives, forks, and spoons" of a dinner-time
ritual at a Jacksonville boarding house for Cuban-American cigar-makers
(*Ex*, 68). However, after spending a short time among these men, the narrator learns the intricacies of cigar-making, Floridian labor practices, and
the social and political priorities of the Cuban-American community; he
soon becomes an integral part of the dinner-time ritual that so daunted him
earlier. In official recognition of his mastery of the language and manners of
this society, he is selected as "reader," an insider position in the cigar factory.
He is fully assimilated, and carefully documents both this culture and the self
it produces for him.

Yet despite this and the many other cultural immersions the narrator
undergoes, he never fully assumes an identity, if what is meant by that is
developing an enduring attachment to a certain position. In the same period
as his cigar-making apprenticeship, the narrator also gains access to the "best
class" of African Americans in Jacksonville (by teaching music). He lays out
an elaborate description of this society as well, noting that his assimilation
into it progressed so far that he was engaged to be married to a young school-
teacher. Then, having lost his job at the cigar factory, he suddenly decides to
go North. There he plunges into new circles and makes no further mention
of those he has left behind. These "inner lives" pass from the scene without

leaving any lasting impression on the narrator. The subjectivity along which all of these identity changes are strung is a slim thread indeed, with little other than the narrator's expressed "I" carried from episode to episode. This speedy turnover represents the fullest satirical exaggeration of the melting-pot logic of cultural role-playing (though it does not play out exactly as most melting-pot theorists imagined: such dispatch with cultural materials might come closer to the Americanization movement's sense of the dispensability of certain pasts). By virtue of these rapid shifts between states, Johnson's novel calls into question the quality and depth of the inner life allowed by melting-pot theories.

In a 1922 letter to Carl Van Doren, Johnson wrote that he had considered "The Chameleon" as a title for the novel; the narrator's behavior certainly justifies such a title.[24] In Johnson's exaggerated version of the adoption and abandonment of cultural roles, neither individuals nor cultures command lasting allegiance, even when they are experienced intimately. Whether he is faced with the ins and outs of the gambling underworld or those of the disaffected leisure class, the narrator learns to assume and remove identities as if they were garments, of sorts. He is introduced to, and shocked by the strangeness of, a society; he begins cataloging its manners, and soon finds himself fitting in so well that he beats the locals at their own game. While the narrative remains attentive to race, it does so in a way that makes evident that the narrator is no more "naturally" at home in the world of black New York musicians than he is in the whites-only smoking compartment of a Pullman traveling from Nashville to Atlanta.[25] In both cases, he pauses, studies, and makes himself at home. The *Autobiography* exhibits the same formal dynamism as its protagonist, shifting from sentimental to documentary to confessional registers, assuming and then setting aside the codes of each mode. (The habits of attention and study that make for successful passing do also make for excellent documentary: that Johnson reprinted the description of New York's Tenderloin nightlife in his cultural history *Black Manhattan* testifies to the accuracy of the narrator's accounts.) In this sense, Johnson's novel is not so much a "novel of passing" as a novel of passing, and passing, and passing.

This extreme melting-pot changeability proves troubling in ethical terms, however. In *The Souls of Black Folk,* W. E. B. Du Bois describes the "loving emphasis and deeper detail" needed to counter the ethical limitations of the documentary impulse (*SBF,* 15). Johnson's novel only approaches such love and depth ironically. Du Bois's text both uses documentary forms and anti-sociologically insists on the transformative powers of feeling (in this respect revealing a melting-pot kinship with Henry James's work). Johnson's radically different approach centers on an unsympathetic narrator, the kind of autobiographical "composite" that Edwin E. Slosson, writing for the *Independent* at the turn of the century, suggested "one is not apt to fall in love with."[26] At his worst, the narrator of the *Autobiography* comes off as a self-satisfied bigot; at his best he is a peculiarly cool customer, one whose blankness seems calculated to leave the reader cold. The flatness of Johnson's narrator eerily re-creates the effect of Johnson's earlier "Zulu from Mata- booloo," but it in fact telegraphs an important shift in Johnson's thought: the Zulu remained estranged from the reader *despite* having made his per- spective available to be shared; the narrator of the *Autobiography* is estranged from the reader *because* he is so promiscuous in perspective. Through the failure of sympathy—both on the part of the narrator and with respect to him— Johnson critiques melting-pot models of assimilation. By relying on ideas of sympathetic response, melting-pot theories avoided theorizing a more structured, and therefore restrictive, interpersonal ethics. Johnson uses the failure of sympathy as a fulcrum by which to shift from an investigation of the *logics* of melting-pot assimilationism to an indictment of the *ethics* of melting-pot assimilationism.

The Autobiography of an Ex-Coloured Man takes up the idea of sympa- thy ironically: in this novel sympathy is physiological, in the sense of being responsive to the environment. The narrator's sympathies can be elicited by context (as a child pianist, he performs the requisite melodramatic feelings) or by company (he mirrors his mother's sensitivity and love, his fellow cigar- makers' bonhomie, his benefactor's delicacy and refinement). This version of sympathy represents an extreme instance of the melting-pot focus on "activities" rather than "ultimate natures"; the symmetries and convergences explored by the *Autobiography* are behavioral, produced in and by specific environments.[27] In Du Boisian terms, the narrator emphasizes, but with no particular love; he renders detail, but not particularly deeply. His alliances are fleeting and instrumental, and his responses to his surroundings flicker over him like the play of light on a wall. This narrator registers Johnson's critique of theories that insist on fluidity as the foremost property of the new self. Here, a selfhood constituted, like Henry James's autobiographical figures, through the play of responses, identifications, and identity sharings, seems fundamentally stunted by its indifference to principles that constitute full humanity. The sympathy of which it is capable is, like the subjectivity that it manifests, theoretical, viable in name only.

Johnson's narrator, lacking independent interiority, is confused about his status as an ethical agent: he puzzles, when he resolves to go to the American South to gather African American folk expression, whether it was "more a desire to help those I considered my people, or more a desire to distinguish myself, which was leading me back to the United States?" (*Ex*, 147). These narrower ethical questions of individual motivation are soon shunted aside, however, along with the unresolved although troubling ethics of an "inner life" constituted in melting-pot terms. Johnson's novel instead focalizes the more pressing ethical crisis of melting-pot subjectivity through a vivid and horrifying scene of racial violence. In the face of such violence, Johnson's novel suggests, the whole question of the "inner life" recedes in importance, and the ethical demands of an outer life move to the fore.

"Playing with Fire"

The narrator of *The Autobiography of an Ex-Coloured Man* witnesses a lynching during his journey through the South, and he is shocked and shaken by it. The lynching constitutes both the formal and the ethical crisis of Johnson's novel: it is the site at which Johnson develops his fullest indictment of melting-pot models of integration, particularly their blindness to asymmetrical relations of power and to the role of violence in producing and policing Progressive-era understandings of difference. Johnson's narrator already knows that such things happen: by the early twentieth century, public exposure of lynching was such that even the narrator's "slow-witted" friend from Luxembourg can plausibly ask him if, indeed, "they" burned a man alive in the United States (*Ex*, 136). Lynching had come under public scrutiny through a variety of efforts: in the 1890s, for example, Ida B. Wells had made her name publishing graphic descriptions and denunciations of Southern lynching in both her ill-fated Memphis newspaper, the *Free Speech*, and in Northern magazines and pamphlet form. In the *Autobiography* Johnson begins a project that extends through his NAACP articles on lynching (published in the *Crisis* and *Current History*), one that analyzes how lynching stages the conflict between a Jamesian-style "assault of suggestion" and the imperative of moral and political response. In the plot of the *Autobiography* the lynching leads away from interiority-intensive questions of motivation, because it demands that ethical concerns be recognized as not exclusively matters of interiority. It is through lynching, in other words, that Johnson's critique of existing models of integration shifts from questions of the subjective life to questions of public life.

The lynching perfectly encapsulates the horror through which regimes of racial discipline flourished in the Progressive-era United States; it halts the formal changefulness of *The Autobiography of an Ex-Coloured Man* just as it would halt the boundary-crossing of any assimilating agent. The narrator refuses to continue his risky task of uncovering and representing the "inner life" of blackness, and instead announces his decision to assume a white identity. As a result, the novel of modernist chameleonism stalls, for its assumption and abandonment of modes is tethered to the mobility of the narrator. The kind of boundary-policing that shores up a static and secure white identity requires that, following the narrator's choice to live as white, his narrative "be brief and touch only on important facts" (*Ex*, 192). (The sentimentalism to which this post-chameleonic narrative of courtship regresses is a nicely nineteenth-century touch.) By stalling at this stage and in this way, *The Autobiography of an Ex-Coloured Man* suggests that lynching functions less as a mode of shoring up whiteness (though it does reduce mobility back and forth across the color line) than as an ethical and aesthetic limit that must be anticipated and met by any serious integrationist philosophy.

For the narrator, the lynching transforms the matter of being from a question of surface play to one of deep seriousness, from a question of integrationist selfhood (with social connection experienced through the ever-shifting similarities of the melting pot) to one of "identity." The narrator cannot imagine the extension of self-conscious playfulness into the disciplined space of the lynching. Thus the lynching sequence brings the forms of autobiographical constructionism central to melting-pot thinking to a boundary that the melting pot must not blur, a difference that the melting pot must not assimilate. The narrator discovers that his model of integrative selfhood is ineffective when it comes to proposing limits or resistance to violence and injustice. The *Autobiography* hints that, in face of the continued existence of violence and injustice, the contingent forms of selfhood that the narrator pursued previously in fact constitute forms of escapism (enabling maneuvers like passing); melting-pot being is thus not simply ethically naïve, but ethically bankrupt.

These intertwined ethical critiques emerge most forcefully from the texture of the *Autobiography*'s lynching sequence. This sequence begins as many representations of unfamiliar persons and spaces do in the *Autobiography*: with the narrator's attentive, quasi-documentary sketching of contextual detail. The tone suddenly shifts, however, as the narrator identifies the lynching victim, who is "too stunned and stupefied even to tremble," and the narration then takes on that stunned stupefaction:[28]

Fuel was brought from everywhere, oil, the torch; the flames crouched for an instant as though to gather strength, then leaped up as high as their victim's head. He squirmed, he writhed, strained at his chains, then gave out cries and groans I shall always hear. The cries and groans were choked off by the fire and smoke; but his eyes, bulging from their sockets, rolled from side to side, appealing in vain for help. Some of the crowd yelled and cheered, others seemed appalled at what they had done, and there were those who turned away sickened at the sight. I was fixed to the spot where I stood, powerless to take my eyes from what I did not want to see.

It was over before I realized that time had elapsed. Before I could make myself believe that what I saw was really happening, I was looking at a scorched post, a smouldering fire, blackened bones, charred fragments sifting down through coils of chain; and the smell of burnt flesh—human flesh—was in my nostrils.

I walked a short distance away and sat down in order to clear my dazed mind. A great wave of humiliation and shame swept over me. (*Ex,* 187)

Compared to the attention that he has lavished on settings like the cigar factory, ragtime club, and religious revival, the narrator's *restraint* here is shocking. This scene, which will be epochal in his life, passes with extraordinary rapidity. Two sentences are given to the attitudes of the victim, and one to the attitudes of the crowd. The flames leap; the cries are choked off; and it is "over before I realized that time had elapsed."[29] In its effects on the narration and on the form of the novel, this scene proves to be Johnson's own kind of "scene of excess," but it is distinct from the Jamesian version of excessiveness in several ways. To begin with, the excessiveness of the lynching scene must be inferred from its representational opposite, the uncharacteristic restraint of the narrator. Johnson's lynching scene is further unlike Henry James's scenes of excess in that it ultimately limits the witness's psychic and physical mobility. James's figurative amputation (of his birth-place) freed him to haunt the American scene in new ways; this other amputation, not figurative enough, stops its witness in his tracks. Johnson's narrator is condemned to monotony and entrapment: he "shall always hear" those cries, unable to slip their grasp as he has done with so many other affiliations. He, like the victim of the lynching, is "fixed."

The narrator asserts his "I" throughout this passage, attempting to separate himself from the crowd, but as we have seen, he has little facility for doing so. Instead, his chameleonism re-emerges, with troubling results. Ever environmentally and socially responsive, as he stands by and observes the lynching he is effectively made over in the image of the lynchers. Johnson's text capably conveys how the logic of spectatorship produces complicity in such events, but it also demonstrates how spectatorship extends beyond the visual realm: by the end of the lynching, the outward traces of the scene—the scent of charred flesh—are "in" the narrator, assimilated by him, part of his "inner self." An integrative self, however committed to equality and social justice it might be, seems powerless to resist this violence. Theories of integrative self-hood, equally, seem muted and complicit when faced with the lynching.

Johnson was by no means the first person to note that Progressivism, even melting-pot Progressivism, had a blind spot where racial violence was concerned. The lynching scene of *The Autobiography of an Ex-Coloured Man* entered an already active debate on the question. None other than Jane Addams, who had published a denunciation of lynching in the *Independent* in January 1901, had been called to task by the anti-lynching writer Ida B. Wells in those same pages. (The *Independent* was one of the publications that Johnson reported subscribing to while posted in Venezuela between 1906 and 1909.[30]) As Wells pointed out, Addams's spirited opposition to lynching silently acceded to a central, false, racist narrative: that the victims of lynchings had committed crimes (most often assault on a white woman) for which the lynching served as illegal punishment. Addams, in other words, had herself been swept into a kind of complicity with lynching, in that she accepted its narrative frame even as she challenged its ethics and its efficacy.[31]

Wells's article in the *Independent* extended her argument from *A Red Record: Tabulated Statistics and Alleged Causes of Lynchings in the United States, 1892–1893–1894* (1895), in which she confronted the silent complicities of lynching culture, North and South. For Wells, anonymity (central to integrative mobility in *The Autobiography of an Ex-Coloured Man*) represented a literary form of complicity with racial violence.[32] Wells's lynching coverage assiduously avoided such silent complicity, forgoing the uncredited source, repudiating the unidentified assumption that mars Jane Addams's contribution to the lynching debates. *A Red Record* aims to expose the "open secret" of the too-often anonymous lynching mob. Yet even when documenting the manic mood of a mob at a notoriously horrifying lynching in Paris, Texas, Wells could not "identify" the crowd in the same way as the lynching victim (whose name, Smith, she notes). Instead, a violent frenzy makes the crowd preternaturally mobile, while its victim is immobilized: "Every man, woman and child in that awful crowd was worked up to a greater frenzy than that which actuated Smith's horrible crime. The people were capable of any new atrocity now, and as Smith's yells became more and more frequent, it was difficult to hold the crowd back."[33] When the crowd cannot be held back, it breaks all bounds, assimilates all positions (save that of the victim, whose racial difference is thereby marked).[34] The voracious assimilativeness of the mob incorporates all participants into a faceless mass. This aspect of the scene at Paris explains Wells's resistance to anonymity in lynching reportage. To be a witness in that context is to be conscripted as a participant, a lyncher.[35] While Wells fiercely resists that position, Johnson's anonymous narrator experiences it in terror and disgust.

Wells's lynching writings insisted that the crowd *is* the lynching, in some fundamental sense. The crowd speaks of the identity and purpose of the event more eloquently than either victim or mode of torture does.[36] It is the *origin* of the event, and in this context, *contra* Jamesian melting-pot logic, origins do matter. When such brutal force is exerted, it can only be met, or even stopped, once traced back to its exact origin. Wells's writings clarify the predicament faced by Johnson's narrator at the lynching: a melting-pot indifference to origins, force, or even identification means complicity in this horror. The most basic logic of lynching aims to fix, isolate, and reveal: *that* is blackness, it asserts; *that* is "not us." Wells, however, sensed the more insidious threat of the scene: the capacious "us," crowd-assimilativeness, creeping complicity, silent accessions to the logic of lynching (such as Jane Addams's, but also implicit in anonymous spectatorship).

Though Wells's insights did not translate into radical generic transformation in her writings, Johnson did experiment with ways of representing racial violence so as to subvert creeping complicity. "The Lynching at Memphis," which he published in the *Crisis* in 1917, shows Wells's influence in its considered approach to documenting the spectacle. Published at the outset of Johnson's involvement in the NAACP's anti-lynching campaign, only five years after the publication of the *Autobiography,* this article takes up the unanswered ethical challenge of the *Autobiography*'s lynching scene. "The Lynching at Memphis" adopts a singularly unusual strategy for an article with such a title: it does not depict the actual lynching. Johnson's article aims to draw attention to the event, but to avoid a re-performance of the violence. The closing paragraph reads as follows:

> Out on the Macon Road is the spot where Ell Person was burned. It is in the bottom lands of the Wolfe River, about fifteen miles from the heart of Memphis. A long wooden bridge with iron railings stretches across the stream and the lowlands. The spot is down in a hollow twenty feet, perhaps, below the level of the road, and on the left side and at the near end of the bridge as approached from the city. For a wide space around, the trees had been felled to give the view to a larger crowd. All the paraphernalia of the unspeakable orgy were still there; the log of a great tree placed on the ground; an iron rail taken from the bridge and driven down with its base supported by the log, its top supported by a long piece of timber bracing it from the back and by

wires which had been strung around it and fastened to the log. At the base of this iron rail to which Ell Person had been chained the earth was still black and charred; at its top, placed there to mark the spot, there floated an American flag.[37]

At the site where the lynchers meant to stabilize the "truth" of blackness, there is nothing: the flag, though mobile, is blank, inscrutable, contested (maybe even menacing, ironic). The figurative sites of blackness are like this literal site, Johnson's paragraph implies: they are neither the immobilized victim aimed at by the lynchers nor the authentic "inner life" fetishized by autobiography, but rather places that can be reached only by orienting one-self by a series of landmarks. This site is both otherworldly and banal, but it is above all accessible. The passage gives a fine attention to the instruments of stabilization (that is, of torture)—but firmly frames them as instruments, as process, rather than an end. It resists reproducing either the victim or the act. I will not burn the man again for you, Johnson's article wordlessly avers, repeating his narrator's earlier refusal. If you want objectification, I will give you objects, not black bodies. This article will not "give the view to a larger crowd."

The last paragraph of Johnson's "Lynching at Memphis" insists that the lynching scene must be understood in ethical terms, as the chronicle of "force" that Henry James's version of melting-pot mobility could not accommodate. Here a documentary emphasis on the outer life helps to amass the material evidence of the crime. The evidence, however, signifies in figurative ways that exceed its materiality. In the physics of the arrangement, one beam "supported" by another, Johnson conveys the complex assortment of forces, brought to bear from all corners, that goes into the production of racial violence. These objects are drawn from everyday life, from the surrounding landscape. Through them, the "unspeakable orgy" asserts itself in its very unspeakableness. The iron rail links the charred ground and the national flag figuratively as well as literally: the horror of the occasion appropriately exceeds direct representation here. Knowing the way in which spectacu-larization amplifies the assault, Johnson's article staunchly resists the public display of violence and victim; this restrained documentary stops short of more broadly disseminating both victimization and guilt.

And so we return to our own earlier site of refusal: when the narrator of *The Autobiography of an Ex-Coloured Man* stumbles away from the scene of the lynching, he knows that he has crossed a limit. His overwhelming feel-ings of shame suggest that it is an ethical limit. The narrator suffers from the residual effects of melting-pot mobility: roles at the lynching merged terrifyingly, mingling witnessing with participation, vulnerability with victimizing. The horrifying possibility that he could himself be the victim of a lynching is matched only by the horrifying implication that he might equally be—indeed, has been—part of a lynch mob. Even the scant description that he offers marks him as one who was not entirely overcome and senseless during the event, one who in fact observed and did not intervene. As a result, what little description the narrator engages in tends to minimize the role of the crowd of which he was part. The fuel "is brought," passively obscuring the bringers; the flames do the horrifying work. The narrator represents even the victim as a more active participant than he; the victim squirms, writhes, and rolls his eyes, while the narrator, self-reportedly "powerless," remains "fixed to the spot." This remarkable choice of language reflects the narrator's fear of occupying the position of victim, fixed to the spot as if to the post. It also, however, signals a troubling willingness to occupy the position of victim *figuratively* in order to obscure his complicity with the lynchers. Melting-pot mobility offers the narrator an out here, a slight remission of his bystander's guilt, and he grabs it. This evasion of responsibility secures Johnson's ethical critique of melting-pot subjectivity.

The Autobiography of an Ex-Coloured Man uses lynching to assess the uses to which the language and strategies of the melting pot can be put, and it produces a damning report. As he stands before the lynching, the responses of the narrator are expressed in the language of sympathy—of transference—of fleeting and figurative occupation of others' positions. Even the shame he expresses is mobile: he is ashamed for his race, ashamed for his country, ashamed at his participation, ashamed at his powerlessness. The narrator uses this language, and assumes these positions, to facilitate an open and fluid movement between perspectives, which in turn allows him to avoid taking responsibility for the moments he safely spent as a white spectator.[38] Melting-pot fluidity serves him quite well in this evasion. The optimistic visions of integrationist boundary-crossing are all very well, Johnson's novel suggests, but they do not of themselves dismantle a racist society, and are too often simply turned to its ends.

The narrator's judgment-neutral, culturally fluid version of selfhood proves totally unable to resist or even properly interrogate a cultural form like lynching. Faced with the charred post of the lynching, having witnessed a scene of extraordinary brutality and savagery, he senses that these Southern whites hold repugnant views. However, he also, quizzically, concedes that "from a certain point of view... they are picturesque" (*Ex,* 189). That is, in a system in which an open and quasi-ethnographic approach to difference prevails, there is unnervingly little basis for distinguishing the behaviors of these lynchers from the (equally picturesque) Jacksonville cakewalks that he detailed—and joined—earlier in his narrative.[39] While, as he alleges, a crime such as lynching should never be tolerated in a "civilized" nation, his earlier travels across value systems have resisted just the kind of judgment that produces comparative estimates of civilization. In other words, Boasian anthropology, here, is with the lynchers.

The lynching becomes a means for Johnson's novel to contrast direct and indirect modes of critique. Certainly, the narrator argues against lynching, much as Wells, Addams, and other muckraking Progressives had. However, the novel proposes a more trenchant and innovative critique when it elaborates the response to lynching that most naturally follows from the logics of melting-pot integration. The inadequacy of that response clearly indicates the inadequacy of melting-pot versions of integration when it comes to racial violence and inequality. Before the narrator conceives of his plan to flee and take on the identity of a white man, he attempts to reflect on the scene, to analyze it as if it were like any of the other scenes he has documented and explicated for his audience. This project falls flat. "The Southern whites are in many respects a great people," he opines. "Looked at from a certain point of view, they are picturesque" (*Ex*, 189). The narrator's lackluster commentary reveals the flaws in the melting-pot objective of opening "certain points of view" to wider audiences. He cannot bear to make this "certain point of view" available to his readers, and he winces with shame at the possibility that he has already done so. As the narrator attempts to understand the terror of the lynching scene through the lens of the picturesque, there is a perceptible grinding of literary gears.[40] He suggests that one might appreciate the white Southerner as one would appreciate a fine performance at the theater, or as the "ordinary peace-loving citizen" might "sit by a comfortable fire and read with enjoyment of the bloody deeds of pirates and the fierce brutality of vikings" (*Ex*, 189). In the familiar and lurid light of the fire he evokes, suddenly the reader of Progressive anti-lynching journalism feels the sting of complicity. "We should shudder with horror at the mere idea of such practices being realities in this day," the narrator finally admits (*Ex*, 189). This shudder communicates the collapse of the picturesque that aestheticizes difference, and the failure of the narrator's attempt to assimilate what he has witnessed to familiar literary conventions.

A great deal of melting-pot writing purposefully suppressed the shudder of horror evoked by difference through a variety of literary devices—or at the very least imagined controlling and directing such a shudder into the appropriate political channels. Progressive-era intellectuals saw overcoming the horror of the other—the transformation of Henry James's Spencer

Brydon into "the restless analyst"—as a first step toward tolerance in both the self and the polity. Ironically, however, by relaxing prejudice through suppressing the horror response, a great deal of melting-pot writing made itself unfit for other political purposes. Muckraking journalism resembles anti-lynching writing in that it aimed to excite public opinion against certain insupportable practices (legal and financial exploitation of the poor, political corruption); it differs from anti-lynching writing by aiming to excite righteous indignation rather than outright horror. Anti-lynching literature could not so temper itself as to be satisfied with indignation. Its subject was horrifying, and so at odds with value-neutral or even difference-curious representation. Johnson's lynching scene in *The Autobiography of an Ex-Coloured Man* uncovers the paradoxical complicity of the celebration of difference in a system of racial terror. The lyncher could no more be accepted as a form of "alternate self" for melting-pot fusion than the "cultural gifts" of lynching could be accepted as appropriate contributions to a communal cultural fund. Melting-pot thinking seemed to provide no alternatives to this, however.

Because assimilated behavior (assumed manners) effectively constitutes the narrator's subjectivity throughout the *Autobiography,* in the wake of the lynching he finds himself without a place from which to denounce those manners. Johnson's novel suggests that the melting-pot subjectivity constructed through taking the outer life as the inner life offers no way to get further out—to refuse, resist, critique, or construct alternatives. In order to denounce the barbarism of Southern whites, the narrator must call upon a secure, independent component of his subjectivity, one that does not shift based on each new set of cultural mores that it assimilates. The lynching, paradoxically, does appear to offer one secure identity—a white one—and once the narrator assumes this secure position he is stuck there, an undistinguished if agonized white spectator. Following the lynching the narrator proves strangely unchameleonic, uncharacteristically out of sync with local manners. He returns to New York, and yet remains "completely lost" (*Ex,* 192). Inadequate to resisting racial horror, melting-pot adaptability collapses in its wake.

This sudden halt to Johnson's novel tropes a refusal shared by many lynching texts. Ida B. Wells's *Red Record* notes a similar reaction on the part of the witness whose testimony she used to indict the crowd at the lynching in Paris, Texas: "When asked if he should ever return to Paris, Mr. King said: 'I shall never go south again. The impressions of that awful day will stay with me forever.'"[41] Lynching circumscribes King's mobility, fixing him as it "fixed" Johnson's narrator, setting in place a script that refuses emendation. Johnson himself was a victim of racial violence in his youth in Jacksonville, and when he finally related the experience in his autobiography, *Along This Way*, he did so in tones that echo his narrator's:

> For weeks and months the episode with all of its implications preyed on my mind and disturbed me in my sleep. I would wake often in the night-time, after living through again those few frightful seconds, exhausted by the nightmare of a struggle with a band of murderous, bloodthirsty men in khaki, with loaded rifles and fixed bayonets. It was not until twenty years after, through work I was then engaged in, that I was able to liberate myself completely from this horror complex. (*ATW*, 170)

In his dreams Johnson seems condemned to repeat this horrifying script without intervening. He ultimately regains his mobility through "work," activities that date to either the anti-lynching activism that he spearheaded for the NAACP throughout the 1920s, or his parallel project of anthologizing African American artistic expression. The question of "either," however, is a false one; Johnson's liberation from the horror is constituted through the unexpected coherence of anti-lynching activism and anthologization. The indictment of melting-pot subjectivity that characterizes *The Autobiography of an Ex-Coloured Man* gives way, in Johnson's work of the 1920s, to the elaboration of a more resistant, self-aware, and ethically responsive form of integrationist thinking. This later version of integrationism follows the Jamesian model in self-consciously turning to questions of literary form.

"Symbols from Within"

Throughout Johnson's tenure as leader of the NAACP, the organization continued to publish information, particularly on the topic of lynching, to advance its political cause. In response to a 1921 complaint that "restating known facts" about lynching was not bringing about the desired political effect, Johnson wrote that his campaign aimed "to root out the thing which makes possible these horrible details. I am of the opinion that this can only be done through the fullest publicity."[42] Johnson's use of the word "publicity" recalls the narrator of the *Autobiography*'s sense that selfhood is constituted through publication of the "great secret." In Johnson's post-*Autobiography* lynching work, however, this publicity does not focus on the "horrible details," but applies itself to something antecedent to those details, "root[ing] out the thing which makes [them] possible." As an objective, "rooting out" is both analytical (in its attention to identifying origins, tracing causal forces) and active. Unlike simply "bringing to light," rooting out presumes that representation can strive for more than faithful reproduction. If lynchings are the toxic foliage of this plant, they flourish in the light, under traditional documentary scrutiny. To root out the plant through publicity means baring the roots to the air, *un*covering the enabling conditions rather than merely (in Jean Lutes's words) "covering" the lynchings. Johnson's expression recognizes that events like lynchings have deep and often complex systems of roots, are grounded in a particular soil and intertwined with other parts of the cultural environment: that lynchers, ultimately, are interesting not as individuals, but as manifestations of a corrupt culture. Such an analysis puts the "public" back in "publicity," understanding structures that extend beyond, and exert force upon, the individual-form as vitally relevant to public life. Bringing its analysis to bear upon the processes rather than the products of racial violence, such a strategy uses the process-mindedness of the melting-pot moment to exceed the ethical limits of melting-pot subjectivity.

The specifics of this strategy emerge in Johnson's major project of the 1920s, a series of anthologies that constitute a groundbreaking publicity campaign for African American artistic expression: *The Book of American Negro Poetry* (1922), *The Book of American Negro Spirituals* (1925), *The Second Book of American Negro Spirituals* (1926), and the revised and expanded *Book of American Negro Poetry* (1931). These anthologies testify to Johnson's belief that African American artistic achievements represented the most eloquent arguments against lynching and racial prejudice. They are also Johnson's extended, and eloquent, version of W. E. B. Du Bois's query in *The Souls of Black Folk:* "Our song, our toil, our cheer, and warning have been given to this nation in blood-brotherhood. Are not these gifts worth the giving? Is not this work and striving? Would America have been America without her Negro people?" (*SBF,* 207). As Russ Castronovo argues, the editorial program Du Bois adopted at the *Crisis* through the teens and twenties represented an aesthetic response to the crisis of lynching.[43] Along similar lines, the Johnsonian integrationist program proposes that the more successfully one answers Du Bois's question in the affirmative, the more forceful and effective one can be in eliminating violence and prejudice.

Johnson wishes to install egalitarianism in the cultural mixing of the melting-pot era, but his egalitarianism does not entail either reflexive repudiation of force or the regulation of cultural mixtures. These forms of policing would have resonated far too closely with the rigid and exclusionary prejudice that African Americans struggled against in the Progressive era. Instead, in keeping with the melting-pot ethos of reciprocity, Johnson emphasizes actions, commensurate with but opposed to, the actions undertaken in the name of racial subordination. These later texts address the question of *how*

one can effectively intervene in the process of cultural mixture; more specifically, how one can take action that, on the one hand, is not repressive, but, on
the other hand, eliminates the passive complicity with repugnant positions
that afflicted the narrator of the *Autobiography*.

In response to these questions, Johnson's anthologies integrate folk and
vernacular materials with high art, emphasizing the ways in which these
varied literary forms exert force. As an editor, Johnson revised, expanded,
and serialized his anthologies, using their changing forms to model forces of
changeable combination rather than of rigid (purity-minded) canonization.
The anthologies thus emphasize the dynamic, active nature of literary expression. For Johnson as for Henry James, texts are characterized by a capacity to *do*. Like any other force, their force must be approached and exerted
with caution and ethical consciousness. However, in the Johnsonian integrationist program texts also represent the possibility of more expansive public
actions than those available to individual persons. Less firmly tethered to the
individual subjectivities that make agency so problematic, texts in Johnson's
anthologies seem to extend the promise of a third position, one that meets
(and exerts) force neither as the fluid yet ethically impotent narrator of the
Autobiography does, nor as the unrealistically self-determining David Quixano
of *The Melting-Pot* does.

Johnson elaborates this integrationist third position in familiar melting-
pot language, however. Just as Henry James used chemical language to consider the nature of force in literary form, and Zangwill and Robert Park used
the alchemical figures of melting pot and crucible to reform selfhood and
experience, so Johnson used the language of alchemy to explain the nature
of force and form in African American art. In his preface to *The Book of
American Negro Poetry* (1922), Johnson, like James, casts art as the product of melting-pot transformation: according to Johnson the artist runs
his material "through the alembic of his genius."[44] The artistic production of African Americans, in particular, demonstrates a capacity that "is
more than adaptability, it is a *transfusive* quality" (PNP, 697: my emphasis).
The word "transfusive" plays upon the transformations troped in alchemical
metaphors, but it also linguistically transposes art into the place of blood.
Like Franz Boas, who charted the sharing of myths and languages, Johnson pledges himself to a vision in which art may be transferred like blood,
from the interiority of one being to another. The anthologies offer literary transfusion as a significant form of integrative action. In a landscape
marked by lynching, in fact, the anthologies constitute indispensable traces
of force—not only of the current configurations of power but also of the
ways in which power has been successively transfused, until it came into its

most recent configurations. Johnson's prefaces use the anthologies as occasions to recognize power not as timeless and transcendent, but as working to contingent, changeable ends.

Johnson's writings on literature consistently emphasize the power and influence of art in the struggle for integration. His preface to *The Book of American Negro Poetry* is only one of the places in which he asserts that "the status of the Negro in the United States is more a question of national mental attitude toward the race than of actual conditions," and that the single best opportunity for African Americans to make over the national imagination is "the production of literature and art" (PNP, 688). In the series of anthologies beginning with *The Book of American Negro Poetry,* Johnson casts his campaign of artistic education and cultural pride in formal terms:

> What the colored poet in the United States needs to do is...find a form that will express the racial spirit by symbols from within rather than by symbols from without, such as [dialect]....He needs a form that is freer and larger than dialect, but which will still hold the racial flavor; a form expressing the imagery, the idioms, the peculiar turns of thought, and the distinctive humor and pathos, too, of the Negro, but which will also be capable of voicing the deepest and highest emotions and aspirations, and allow of the widest range of subjects and the widest scope of treatment....In stating the need for Aframerican poets in the United States to work out a new and distinctive form of expression I do not wish to be understood to hold any theory that they should limit themselves to Negro poetry, to racial themes; the sooner they are able to write *American* poetry spontaneously, the better. Nevertheless, I believe that the richest contribution the Negro poet can make to the American literature of the future will be the *fusion into it* of his own individual artistic gifts. (PNP, 713–14, my emphasis)

The closing remarks of this passage balance cultural nationalism with a distinctly melting-pot appeal to fusion. Melting-pot thinking also informs Johnson's language of "racial flavor," for, as the example of Henry James shows, in melting-pot discourse the alchemical figure often shades into a conception of the nation as cultural stew. Johnson no more wants the racial flavor dissipated than James wanted the cultural "dye" from immigrant fabric to be lost in the massive bath of his contemporary United States. For Johnson, symbols must come "from within" if they are to act as the basis for cultural transfusion; like the idea of transfusion, "within" puts language usually associated with biological being to use in evoking a figurative and changeable inner life. Located in symbols, imagery, idioms, and turns of thought—*gifts*—Johnson's "within" represents a cultural imaginary or imagined self that he constitutes in peculiarly formal terms.[45]

The demands on such a form are great, and Johnson's statement above frames those demands as actions that the form must undertake: it must express, hold the flavor, voice, allow the widest range. In these actions it must evince the taut elasticity that Henry James theorized, being both free and large enough to convey the full range of experience, and yet structured and continuous so as to make manifest its African American origins.

The preface to *The Book of American Negro Poetry* shows Johnson antici-pating the African American vernacular forms that he brought to national attention in the two-part *Book of American Negro Spirituals* of the mid-1920s. Certainly his prefaces to *those* anthologies suggest his excitement about an expressive form that seemed to meet the demands for both integrative fluidity and anti-racist eloquence. Faced with problems of transcription, he still praises the spirituals' "subtle and elusive" nature. (Given that the narrator of the *Auto-biography* describes being "fixed" by the lynching, it is not surprising that John-son celebrates the resistance of these forms to "fixation.") In fact, the famous anthologies of spirituals showcase forms whose distinctive characteristic is that of eluding the straight documentation that the *Autobiography* proposes.[46] That they are "freer," capable of the "widest scope," constitutes their power.

Johnson's prefaces to his anthologies of spirituals associate the force and agency of his material with its vernacular, improvisatory status. For this rea-son I want to consider Johnson's framing of the spirituals as continuous with his framing of another vernacular religious form, the sermon. While I do not want to imply that these forms are equivalent in Johnson's practice—indeed, his nuanced and detailed treatments of the two forms make it impossible to do so—it is fair to say that when taken together, his framings of these two forms amount to a theory of black vernacular religious expression. For Johnson, these forms represent means of avoiding the ethical lapses of earlier integrative theories, while still guarding valuable ideas of individual flex-ibility and communal combination. In other words, for Johnson a variety of vernacular religious forms occasion "the first-run event of an African *critical* subject-position" in the United States that Hortense Spillers associates with the sermon.[47]

Before the narrator of *The Autobiography of an Ex-Coloured Man* is brought up short by the lynching, he glimpses the kind of critical subject position afforded by black vernacular religious expression. Collecting African Ameri-can folk materials at a "big meeting" in the South, the narrator diligently yet skeptically documents the rhetorical forms used by a preacher—but finally finds himself just "swept along" by "the torrent of the preacher's words, moving with the rhythm and glowing with the eloquence" (*Ex,* 177). The "torrent" complicates the matter of tabulating styles or even registering the content of the utterance; it sweeps bystanders into participation in ways uncannily similar to the lynching. Johnson elsewhere describes preaching as an "electric current [run] through the crowd": it is a force that *passes*.[48] Unlike the lynching, however, there is no individual endpoint to the circuit of energy created by preacher and worshippers, no terminus at which the electrical current is grounded, as in the lynching's charred victim. Rather than horror, vernacular religious expression summons up "one of the most thrilling emotions which the human heart may experience": its ethical intervention is humanization through ecstatic feeling (*Ex,* 181).

According to the *Autobiography,* sermons exert force through form rather than content: their "eloquence consists more in the manner of saying than in what is said" (*Ex,* 176). From the late teens through the twenties, Johnson took up this anti-racist form and experimented with its modernist aesthetic implications, composing a series of "sermons in verse." According to Johnson's autobiography *Along This Way,* he started "The Creation," the first of these poems to be composed, in 1918, in response to an electrifying sermonizing performance. Johnson's preface to *God's Trombones* (1927), his collection of sermons in verse, describes this experience as being moved by a force both *inside* him and outside of his conception of individual agency. He is, "perhaps against my will, deeply moved; the emotional effect upon me was irresistible" (*GT,* 7). In this formulation, the self is made mobile, stirred, but neither by identifiable external force nor by deliberate act of will. The form of the religious expression creates an emotional force that is felt individually, but exercised collaboratively.

The poems of *God's Trombones* both testify to the affectively based force of African American vernacular religious expression, and investigate what it might mean for a melting-pot modernist to wield such a volatile force. Through these poems, Johnson addressed his lingering questions about the ethics, aesthetics, and logistics of melting-pot integrationism. His poetic experiments take up these questions in three interrelated ways. First, *God's Trombones* explores how vernacular religious forms enable cultural fusion; second, it demonstrates the assimilative range of vernacular religious forms, especially their ability to accommodate expressive innovations; third, it represents religious expressive forms as historical archives of force (particularly the forces of fusion and innovation). In these three ways, *God's Trombones* registers as a melting-pot literary experiment, one by which Johnson enacts the provisional integrationist modernism that his critical writings refined throughout the 1920s.

The fusionist impulse of *God's Trombones* is evident from its opening: "Listen, Lord—A Prayer" evokes (and describes) the anticipatory emotional state of the religious assembly through the voice of an anonymous individual participant. As if broadcasting the subjective blankness of the narrator of *The Autobiography of an Ex-Coloured Man,* the congregant of "Listen, Lord" describes the congregation as coming together "Like empty pitchers to a full fountain."[49] Here the "empty pitchers" figure complicates Johnson's imperative that writers attend to "symbols from within" (from the preface to *The Book of American Negro Poetry;* Johnson quotes it again in the preface to *God's Trombones*). If congregants are "empty pitchers," then these symbols must come from a "within" understood primarily in cultural-fusionist, not biological or essentialist terms (*GT,* 8). The "within" elaborated by the poems of *God's Trombones* is not a place furnished with a set of known symbols, but a place through which encounter and fusion continually "fill the fountain" (or, in melting-pot terms, the "fund"), thereby fashioning new symbols. Johnson represents the persons of the congregation and the vernacular religious expression as mutually constituting, filling and giving form to each other through their encounter. By installing reciprocity as the basis of the vernacular religious form, *God's Trombones* attempts to secure the ethical parameters of the form, tethering flexibility to solidarity in a way that the *Autobiography* could not.

In the subsequent poems, the voice of the "old-time Negro preacher" assists in returning writer and reader to a historical scene of cultural fusion. (In the preface to the collection Johnson insists on the figure's significance as a cultural mediator: "through him... the people of diverse languages and customs who were brought here from diverse parts of Africa and thrown into slavery were given their first sense of unity and solidarity": *GT,* 2.) The preacher evoked in Johnson's poems achieves his "transfusive quality" (from the preface to *The Book of American Negro Poetry*) through his range of emotional reference, by which he cites and combines the varied emotional states of his listeners: he "intoned, he moaned, he pleaded—he blared, he crashed, he thundered" (*GT,* 7).[50] (According to the preface, the title *God's Trombones* evokes the "amplitude" of preachers' voices, for the trombone is "the instrument possessing above all others the power to express the wide and varied range of emotions encompassed by the human voice": *GT,* 7.) The flexibility, virtuosity, and range of reference of Johnson's preacher-figure call to mind the narrator of *The Autobiography of an Ex-Coloured Man;* however, the preacher more clearly guides that range of reference with ethical purpose. The preacher conveys a "sense of unity" to his congregants, employing the force of *feeling* to combine his listeners into a resilient community.

This language of range and flexibility, especially as it pertains to emotional response, characterizes Johnson's discussions of a variety of vernacular religious forms: his preface to *The Second Book of Negro Spirituals* (1926) points to the "sensitiveness and quick response to the whole gamut of human emotions" evident in the spirituals.[51] His integrationism manifests itself in an amplitude understood as "human" range rather than culturally particular content. Johnson's writing on the spirituals finds the interiority necessary for "symbols from within" in the depth of feeling so lacking in *The Autobiography of an Ex-Coloured Man*. The *gamut* of "human emotions" spanned by these forms includes emotions responsive to, resistant to, and even covetous of the power that went unregulated in other melting-pot theories. This deep emotional archive of "common" humanity does not entirely subsume difference in humanist universalism, however. Johnson regularly balances his universalism with pride in the role that African Americans play as special guardians of this humanist archive.

God's Trombones cites the full range of traces of enslavement borne by sermon-forms, but it prioritizes the improvisational force with which slaves met enslavement and forged new cultural bonds. This means that Johnson's poems cast African American vernacular religious forms as actively combining historical citation with change and innovation—indeed, as actively demonstrating how innovation may function as a form of historical citation. The preface to *God's Trombones* frames the poems as attempts to evoke the exploratory capacities of vernacular forms, rather than as strict acts of preservation. After all, old-time preachers do not allow themselves to be dictated to by a text: for them "a text served mainly as a starting point" for movement to places unforeseen by textual origins (*GT*, 4). Meter and line length do not determine rhythmic patterns; the syncopation characteristic of preaching tempos involves "the crowding in of many syllables or the lengthening out of a few to fill one metrical foot" (*GT*, 11). These textual and metrical elasticities signal the assimilative capacities of the form. By underlining the improvisatory eloquence of the sermon-form, Johnson articulates a means by which "symbols from within" might indicate a historical tradition, an originary text, but not a bounded cultural group. By foregrounding the ways in which the mundane is converted into the timeless, vernacular religious expressions abstract away from a particular community of believers, even as they enable particular expressive innovations. The action of vernacular religious forms is oscillating, in the Jamesian sense, for it moves between historical attentiveness and modernist inventiveness, cultural particularity and universalist human range.

A particular instance of this oscillation suggests the very fine line trodden by Johnson's integrationist vision. In the preface of *God's Trombones*,

Johnson describes trying "sincerely to fix something" of the old-time preacher, underlining the fact that he "is rapidly passing" (*GT,* 11). That one may be "sincere" about such fixing suggests that, despite its troubling associations with the lynching in *The Autobiography of an Ex-Coloured Man,* the process of trying to "fix" has not been abandoned. In speaking of fixing "something," Johnson implies an imprecise process that differs from the totalizing fixing of the lynching—it is, instead, a version of the "freer and larger" expressive form that Johnson seeks (PNP, 713). The sincerity of the attempt to fix is balanced by the irony (doubleness) always in play with the word "passing" (here passing as a temporal rather than a racial action). Fixing stands here for the kind of archival work that Johnson envisions for his expressive form; through emotional investment (sincerity), it loosens ideas (including that of fixity) from their earlier connotations, even while citing those connotations in a kind of ethical due diligence.

The language and the concerns of "Under the Bamboo Tree," of *The Autobiography of an Ex-Coloured Man,* and of the NAACP lynching writings continue to resonate through Johnson's later work. These echoes raise topics that have neither been fixed in their meaning nor become fluid enough to pass entirely from scrutiny. Indeed, as language and concerns are extended across different texts they become peculiarly vulnerable as far as interpretation is concerned. Ironically, it is this very vulnerability of the figure that is neither entirely fixed nor fully passing that constitutes the force of Johnson's work. Like the "subtle and elusive" swing of the spirituals, the power of these texts emerges from that which cannot be transcribed, the balance of continuity and change constituted by echoes and improvisation.[52] Thus the integrative force that Johnson devises attends to ethics by insisting on simultaneous faithfulness and improvisation in one's relation to an ever-elusive, ever-"passing" text. Participants in vernacular religious forms are responsible to and for each other and the text—in religious, ethical, and historical senses. Johnson imagines readers like congregants, forever responding to and citing his texts, but also inevitably losing and twisting parts of them.

With *God's Trombones,* Johnson imaginatively exerts a force to parry racial violence; in his prefaces, however, he is even more explicit, focusing on raising consciousness in response to such threats. His critical writings model the kind of intelligence, vigilance, and insistence by which he imagined an integrative program would keep force within ethical bounds. The preface to *The Second Book of Negro Spirituals* clarifies where progress has been made, but cultural criticism is still needed: the spirituals "have exerted a gentle and little-considered influence for a good many years. For more than half a century they have touched and stirred the hearts of people and effected a softening

down of some of the hard edges of prejudice against the Negro."[53] Over time
the effects of vernacular forms (including, but not exclusively, the spirituals) have registered within, at a kind of unconscious, emotional level.[54] The
next task for both art and criticism is to promote self-consciousness, a more
"considered" engagement with these forms. Johnson's late integrative work
combines the anti-racist gentleness of vernacular forms with the alertness of
cultural criticism.

In this way, Johnson's later works suggest that melting-pot thinking must
better emphasize *awareness* in order to live up to its egalitarian rhetoric. The
half-conscious action of sympathetic response is available to even the rudder-
less narrator of *The Autobiography of an Ex-Coloured Man;* it is by no means
so powerful as awareness, according to Johnson. He celebrates the new hearing that the spirituals received in the 1920s as a "reaction far different from
the sort produced by their first popularity; the effect now produced upon
white hearers is not sympathy for the 'poor Negro' but admiration for the creative genius of the race."[55] The force exerted by African American vernacular
forms evolves gradually and cumulatively out of historical collaborations; the
spirituals themselves help "produce" the intelligence and awareness needed
to interpret them. In Johnson's narrative, sympathy is but a way-station along
the route to the expressive forms that best advance an integrationist agenda.
Johnson's Harlem Renaissance role of public intellectual, of literary and cultural critic for black America, thus represents a reasoned response to both the
ethical and the aesthetic challenges of Progressive-era melting-pot thinking.

Like Henry James in the New York edition, teaching his peers how to
reconceive of the novel form, the Johnson of the prefaces instructs his readers in the recognition and interpretation of African American contributions to a common cultural fund. In fact, Johnson's autobiography, *Along
This Way* (1933), wryly positions him as writer of endless prefaces, for a
series of works that "needed" the background and reading protocols he
could give; he recalls wondering "if I was condemned to do a preface for
every book that I should write."[56] The prefaces attend closely to the intertwining of historical circumstance and formal expression, the play of forces
that is archived in literary form. Acting as guides to the reader faced with
unfamiliar forms, as teachers to the melting-pot participant overwhelmed
by integrationist fusions, the prefaces draw on a history of cultural fusion to
illuminate the new modes of thought and experience that such fusions make
possible. The prefaces shape and reshape the anthologies, the contents of the
anthologies, and the audiences of the anthologies with every new edition.
Most important, they are conjectural, supportive, supplemental, *introductory:*
they self-consciously model an important distinction between documentary

and criticism, aligning the formal reflexiveness of criticism with an ethically vigilant integrationism.

Johnson's most eloquent and self-conscious argument for this version of integrationism appears among the final paragraphs of his magisterial history *Black Manhattan* (1930). It is worth quoting at length:

> Forces are going out that are reshaping public sentiment and opinion.... Through his artistic efforts the Negro is smashing...immemorial stereotype faster than he has ever done through any method he has been able to use. He is making it realized that he is the possessor of a wealth of natural endowments and that he has long been a generous giver to America. He is impressing upon the national mind that he is an active and important force in American life; that he is a creator as well as a creature; that he has given as well as received; that his gifts have been not only obvious and material, but also spiritual and aesthetic; that he is a contributor to the nation's common cultural store; in fine, he is helping to form American civilization. (*BM,* 283–84)

The paragraph insists on form in familiar Johnsonian terms: as conduit of force and as arena of reciprocity. Johnson's integrative aesthetic program emphasizes the politics of formal self-consciousness: he speaks in terms that resonate with those employed by Jane Addams and Robert Park in their melting-pot literary theories, but that emerge from a career of attentiveness to the operations of power. This paragraph balances historical awareness with an insistence on future change and innovation. The pattern of doublings (creator as well as a creature; given as well as received; not only material, but also spiritual), as well as the syntax that builds pause for reflection and emphasis, evokes both maintained difference and balanced, equitable combination.

The terms of this paragraph also resonate because they are so familiar to Johnson's longtime reader. He has used these phrases before. In his preface to *The Second Book of Negro Spirituals,* he writes:

> [the spirituals] have been, perhaps, the main force in breaking down the immemorial stereotype that...the Negro, intellectually and morally empty, is here to be filled, filled with education, filled with religion, filled with morality, filled with culture, in a word, to be made into what is considered a civilized human being. All of this is, in a measure, true; but in a larger measure it is true that the Negro is possessed of a wealth of natural endowments; that he has long been a generous giver to America; that he has helped to shape and mold it; that he has put an

indelible imprint upon it; that America is the exact America it is today because of his influence. . . . This awakening to the truth that the Negro is an active and important force in American life; that he is a creator as well as a creature; that he has given as well as received; that he is the potential giver of larger and richer contributions, is, I think, due more to the present realization of the beauty and value of the Spirituals than to any other one cause.[57]

The passage also appears, in much this form, at the beginning of chapter 30 of Johnson's autobiography, *Along This Way*. The parts of this passage that are not shared across its different incarnations resonate elsewhere in Johnson's work. The preface to *The Second Book of Negro Spirituals* maintains that the openness of the self to being "filled" remains "in a measure, true"; Johnson himself remains (in a measure) true to the version of improvisational melting-pot selfhood, the self forever filling and refilling, that he first sketched out in "Under the Bamboo Tree" and *The Autobiography of an Ex-Coloured Man*. He does not repudiate the idea of the "empty vessel," in other words. His later writings, however, foreground the active intelligence and equal collabora-tion that must characterize an integrative "filling." Similarly, Johnson uses melting-pot language of plasticity to describe culture, and the self's place in culture, even in the later writings: the African American is shaper, molder, creator, giver. To these terms he adds "human" and "American," with the full discourse of rights and equity that he insists they must live up to.

The phrase that most palpably binds these different versions of Johnson's integrative argument, revealing their shared character, is "a creator as well as a creature." (These words also echo in the preface to the revised edition of *The Book of American Negro Poetry*.[58]) This phrase maps the transformation of a word (through subtly new letters) just as it conveys the transformative nature of African Americans. The two roles played by the African American are no more incompatible than are the two modes of signification, connota-tive and denotative, figural and literal, deployed by the sentence. The roles are played in tandem, expressing the realization of the self before the mir-ror, enacting the double consciousness that is fundamental to melting-pot experience. The close juxtaposition of the words reveals their shared lexical origin and their invariable interconnection. The phrase "creator as well as a creature" is shared across Johnsonian texts just as a cultural practice might be shared by participants in the melting pot. Like the many silent citations of African American cultural materials, however, the repeated phrase exerts a most elusive force; it constitutes its own subtle argument for close and criti-cal attention.

Johnson's practice of literary recycling makes a mockery of ideas that forms or concepts are proprietary—can an idea such as this one be copyrighted, when it exists in so many incarnations? Which statement is the authoritative one? Through such repetition across his writings, Johnson creates a kind of meta-textual synchrony and multivocality. It produces effects that are not always harmonious; what, for example, are we to make of the seemingly incompatible claims that it is theater—or that it is the spirituals—or that it is poetic expression—that has, *above all,* brought about the recognition of African Americans as equal contributors to the cultural melting pot? Such a question cannot be resolved, though together the claims do produce a strange effect of equality-among-firsts. The tone of conviction in Johnson's pronouncements must be reconciled with the peculiarity of multiple forms occupying the position of "single" most important form. Of necessity, this strategy explodes any possibility of sovereign singularity; no singular utterance, nor single identity, can be understood to exclude other utterances or identities. No preacher commands a vernacular form, no autobiography encapsulates the melting-pot experience. In this way Johnson attempts to guard against implying the dominance of any single version of rights or ethics. In each of these claims, his tone unwaveringly conveys his belief that he is right; brought together, these incompatible claims subtly emend this message, making it into a matter of plural "rights." This is Johnson's distinctive innovation when it comes to imagining a non-coercive ethical structure for integration.

Johnson did not reserve his practice of re-use for this passage alone. Citation is, in fact, the distinctive formal attribute of his nonfictional writings. In some cases, as in these, he cites silently, incorporating and re-using the words that represent his most eloquent statement on an issue. In other cases he cites forthrightly, including (in quotation marks) a description from *The Autobiography of an Ex-Coloured Man* in *Black Manhattan,* or a statement from his preface to *The Book of American Negro Poetry* in his preface to *God's Trombones.* Most provocatively, he meditates upon the question of form itself in terms shared by both *The Autobiography of an Ex-Coloured Man* and his poem "O Black and Unknown Bards": "How did it catch that subtle undertone,/ That note in music heard not with the ears?"[59] In such a case, it becomes clear that chameleonism on the part of the cited words is a formal strategy itself. That "subtle undertone," which does not register on the ears, is created at least in part by the echolalic cross-reference that infuses Johnson's work. As citations are successively redeployed, the identity of the quoted material both remains constant and is transformed by its redeployment. The citational form is, in Johnson's words from the preface to *The Book of Negro*

Poetry, both free and large and still holds the flavor. The practice of citation makes multiple meanings something to be anticipated and explored across Johnson's writings. Pursuing a favorite statement of his leads not to a single "inner truth" so much as to a hall of mirrors. The free and large range of reference required for this reading (instead of a single text, Johnson sends us to his entire body of work, and beyond that, to the vernacular and poetic forms he collected) holds the flavor by insisting on the ethical framework that he knew melting-pot thinking required.

As my discussion of Cather in the next chapter suggests, the mode of integrative citation by which Johnson sustained himself ethically and aesthetically was hardly unassailable. Imagining cultural "gifts" circulating as freely as Johnson's words in his work made many Americans, both native-born and immigrant, black and white, fear for the loss of the ethical rudder that coherent traditions provided. In "Trans-National America," his most direct argument against the melting pot, Randolph Bourne warned, "Just so surely as we disintegrate these nuclei of nationalistic culture do we tend to create hordes of men and women without a spiritual country, cultural outlaws, without taste, without standards but those of the mob."[60] For Johnson integrative ethics were best served by imagining inherited traditions as diffuse and amenable to critical acts of deconstruction, combination, and reinterpretation. However, the logical, ethical, and aesthetic questions raised by conceiving of individual or cultural pasts as transferable constitute the basis for the melting-pot experiments of Willa Cather's career.

❦ Chapter 4

Recollection, Reform, and "Broken Time" in Willa Cather

James Weldon Johnson's integrationism relied on a logic shared by a great deal of melting-pot writing: he turned to cultural activities of the *past* to construct parameters for present cultural syntheses. Like so many immigrant autobiographers of the Progressive era, Johnson saw cultural synthesis as entailing not the repression of personal and group histories, but their broader dissemination. The better that white audiences understood, and self-consciously adopted, the formal devices of the spirituals, his logic went, the better (and more equitably) assimilation would work. However, such a view was hardly uniformly agreed upon: in the context of immigration, for example, Anglo-conformity Americanizers did imagine a near-total suppression of different cultural practices and languages; cultural pluralists, on the other hand, argued that cultural "inheritances" required more active preservation. Horace Kallen framed his famous objections to the melting pot most forcefully in terms of the past: he accused melting-pot assimilation of aiming for "the complete cutting-off of the ancestral memories of the American populations" (*CD*, 112). This chapter uses Willa Cather's novels, as well as writings by a cluster of other melting-pot thinkers, to consider this topic of significant disagreement.

Rather than focusing on Kallen's dramatic accusation of "complete cutting-off," however, I will explore the means by which Progressive-era thinkers attempted to imagine combining histories in an ideally inclusive melting pot. When settlement workers, immigrant writers, and even W. E. B. Du Bois spoke of the cultural "gifts" contributed by minority populations, they emphasized the importance of (in Jane Addams's words) "respect for the achievements of one's fathers, the bringing together of the past with the present."[1] In the last chapter I argued that James Weldon Johnson's practice of citation represents one means by which past customs and beliefs might be taken up and integrated into new contexts. When Kallen objected to culture conceived of as "a sort of independent variable which might be put on and laid off like a garment," rather than as an unchanging inheritance such as represented by a grandfather, he spoke to the disrespect, even violence, that he saw in this instrumental relation to the past (*CD*, 215).[2] As even this schematically sketched disagreement suggests, considering whether, and how, personal and cultural pasts might be integrated requires engaging with a variety of conceptions of the very nature of the past. Willa Cather's novels did just that.

In a series of speaking engagements in her home state of Nebraska in fall 1921, Cather made her stance on immigrant heritages clear: "The Americanization committee worker who persuades an old Bohemian housewife that it is better for her to feed her family out of tin cans instead of cooking them a steaming goose for dinner is committing a crime against art."[3] The *Omaha World-Herald* reported Cather's remarks as condemning "the indiscriminate Americanization work of overzealous patriots who implant into the foreign minds a distaste for all they have brought of value from their own country," which "retarded art in America."[4] Cather's words yoke immigrant heritages and American artistic expression: Anglo-conformist assimilation, by conceiving of the United States as (in Henry James's memorable formulation) "the tub of hot water" that strips the dye from "a piece of bright-hued stuff," consigns Americans to a cultural and intellectual life as if, in Cather's words, "out of tin cans."[5] Here the tin cans evoke Jane Addams's fear of too-rigid forms. According to Cather, sophisticated and formally flexible art will come only when Americans embrace "all [that foreign minds] have brought of value from their own country." The argument here is not simply aesthetic: it is distinctly temporal, having to do with how to import heritage to a new country (and a country of the new). Again, the tin cans point to questions of preservation and transportation. Cather's fictions constitute an extended aesthetic response to the questions of temporality involved in melting-pot models of assimilation.

In the melting-pot model, the immigrant past—that is, what Cather terms "all [that foreign minds] have brought of value from their own country"— diffuses throughout American culture. As Robert Park's *Introduction to the Science of Sociology* (1921) defines assimilation, it is "a process of interpenetration and fusion in which persons and groups acquire the memories, sentiments, and attitudes of other persons or groups, and, by sharing their experience and history, are incorporated with them in a common cultural life."[6] Through this "sharing," distinct cultural heritages become accessible to a variety of different agents. In the melting pot elaborated by Israel Zangwill, the assumption of new cultural material often entails discarding or disregarding certain elements—his protagonist David Quixano, most famously, must assimilate to American culture by putting aside the Old World enmities of pogrom-ridden Kishineff. Theories of melting-pot assimilation understand the past as alienable, something that can be both picked up and put aside. This vision produces considerable contradiction on the question of the nature of the past. On the one hand, the past is cast as immutable heritage, a garment transferable because already fully formed; on the other hand, it is cast as a story (Park's memory, sentiment, attitude) told in the present, and hence always changing. In either case, the model opens itself to accusations like Kallen's (that it falsely recasts relationships of necessity as consensual relationships).

Alive to the contradictory, contested nature of the past in the melting-pot model, Cather's writing mounts more than a simple argument for, or even demonstration of, the "inclusion" of immigrant heritages. As a whole Cather's work recognizes inclusion as merely an introductory term, one whose parameters must be defined, and which may well involve a Jamesian oscillation between merging and separation, a Johnsonian balance of historical citation and contemporary innovation.[7] Cather made her reputation with her modernist novels *O Pioneers!* (1913) and *My Ántonia* (1918), which give serious and appreciative attention to immigrant contributions to American culture. However, her later novels show the melting-pot inheritance embedded in pluralistic *anti*-melting-pot ideas. *The Professor's House* (1925) and *Death Comes for the Archbishop* (1927) resonate with contemporaneous popularizations of Horace Kallen's pluralism: they focalize important questions about the losses entailed in melting-pot assimilation, and about the nature, quality, and viability of Progressive-era conceptions of the past. Even as they testify to the ongoing claims of melting-pot discourse, then, Cather's writings also point forthrightly to the limits—philosophical and historical—of the paradigm.

My aim here is both to elaborate melting-pot models of historical preservation and redistribution and to explore the ways in which Cather's writings uncover logical and affective problems in those models. James Weldon Johnson's writings put specific histories—of racial violence and exploitation, of innovative vernacular expression—to use, building protections for difference into integrationist thinking. Cather's work spends more time questioning the nature and limits of these histories. Can the steaming goose not only be saved for the Bohemian family but also be metaphorically offered up for general consumption? What does it mean to redistribute cultural "gifts," if they are successfully introduced into a cultural "fund"? Can histories be shared—and if so, with what effects? As well as showing a new course through Cather's work, these questions make up an indispensable element of any inquiry into melting-pot thinking.

Cather's literary explorations of the melting-pot past were initiated in Samuel S. McClure's *My Autobiography* (1914), which she ghostwrote. In the same year that Cather began McClure's autobiography, the ardent assimilationist Mary Antin declared that her autobiography helpfully alienated her from her own past, claiming that "a long past vividly remembered is like a heavy garment that clings to your limbs when you would run."[8] As Cather tried on McClure's voice, the Antin-like idea that a past might be assumed and removed likely proved a compelling notion. For Cather, McClure's autobiography offered a medium in which assuming a past proves to be the very way of keeping it fresh and vital. However, McClure's autobiography also suggests a utilitarian, rough-and-tumble approach to the past, one that implicitly accedes to the Americanizer's push for "tin cans" by emphasizing the use-value of the past. Indeed, by the end of McClure's autobiography his anti-nostalgic stance marks him as a likely proponent of canning the past, if that would only make it more useful to contemporary endeavors.

Cather's later novels turn away from McClure's instrumentalism, instead using the formal experimentalism of the melting pot to join James and Johnson in transforming life writing. Her novels *The Professor's House* and *Death Comes for the Archbishop* do not directly address the immigrant scene or self, but they do very clearly extend investigations that Cather initiated in her life writing–inspired works *My Autobiography* and *My Ántonia*. Where many Progressive-era writers approached debates over the nature of the past through the form of the self, then, Cather embedded her responses in the structures of her novels. In Cather's hands, aesthetic form begins doing the work that the self-form did for so many immigrant autobiographers; in novels where no discernable, or at least traditional, immigrant figure appears, the historiographical crisis of the melting pot nonetheless registers, at an aesthetic level. But Cather reaches this late formal strategy through a familiar route, beginning where so many Progressive-era intellectuals initiated their investigations of the melting-pot model: the autobiography.

The Melting-Pot Autobiography

In the fall of 1912, following six years working as an editor at *McClure's*, Cather quit magazine work to pursue her own writing. However, she agreed to work with S. S. McClure on one last project: as she completed *O Pioneers!*, her first major modernist novel, she also drafted McClure's *My Autobiography.*[9] This classic early twentieth-century immigrant autobiography recounts McClure's emigration from Ireland and his rise to success in the Progressive-era United States; nothing in the text suggests Cather's role in its composition. The project obviously required Cather to give voice to an alien past, and it represents a fascinating early experiment in which to ground her subsequent novelistic innovations. The intertwining of ghostwriting and immigrant autobiography cannot help but be ironic and citational in its approach to history. McClure's autobiography goes further, however, and overtly proposes an irreverent and open-ended relation to the past—not only privately, to his ghostwriter, but publicly, to his readers. Taking for granted what Henry James thrashed out so painfully in *The American Scene,* McClure narrates his autobiography as if he were a spectator (or ghostwriter) of his own life.[10] This style of narration focuses less on plot points than on exploring the means by which personhood is constituted. The creative and communal relation to the past that this text models is unusual in the context of Cather's writing, but it is textbook melting pot.

Though it is not one of the melting-pot autobiographies that Horace Kallen took to task in "Democracy *Versus* the Melting-Pot," McClure's *My Autobiography* perfectly anticipates, and participates in, the dynamic Kallen diagnosed: it casts the past as a matter of consent and contemporary construction, rather than of necessity. *My Autobiography* even attempts to loosen the fetters of necessity as far as chronology is concerned, narrating events in a seemingly haphazard order that requires creative reconstruction from readers. The plot of the autobiography is episodic, Jamesian in its refusal of progress and causality if not in its density. Even in moments of crisis, McClure gives readers little direction: he leaves the United States for Ireland, his immigrant dreams in tatters—he fortuitously finds his way back again—all without any mention of the "final" resolution toward which these events tend. (As both McClure and his readers know—from the title of the periodical in which the autobiography first ran!—about his success with his great muckraking periodical, such a strategy may seem a little disingenuous.) Instead, collapsing his experience, his narration, and the reading of his story into a rough contemporaneity, McClure expresses happy surprise at every new turn of events. He resists the temptations of the retrospective glance and historical synthesis, often describing his encounters with characters without revealing the ways in which their relationships with him will later evolve. (For example, he chronicles his early interactions with a Professor Hurd of Knox College without noting that the man would later become his father-in-law; only when McClure describes his relationship with Harriet Hurd does this relation come out.) As a result the reader experiences a past that seems as open as present experience. All of these strategies end by dramatically understating the forces of necessity, historical or otherwise. But McClure adamantly resists the idea of an already-formed past that needs only simple transcription, or an authoritative autobiographical voice that "owns" that past.

My Autobiography reflects on its innovative relation to the past by both describing and sampling a form of biography that Ida Tarbell developed under McClure's management. According to McClure, Tarbell used contemporary collaboration to reanimate the past in her biography of Abraham Lincoln. She approached her topic as an investigative reporter, collecting and publishing "portraits of Lincoln... from all sorts of obscure sources; people sent them in from all over the country" (221). "The story" here is a synthesis, coordinated by a nodal individual who collects cultural material from "obscure sources" and then disseminates this material through publication. In this model Tarbell resembles the James Weldon Johnson of the anthologies and prefaces. She collects impressions to make the past experiences of one group or individual available to others. In melting-pot terms, this approach expands the appeal and range of the cultural inheritance, amplifying the value of the "gift" by creating new understandings of old material.

McClure's autobiography engages in a similar rewriting of the past. In the final installment of the serialized autobiography, McClure published a selection from the copious correspondence that he received while serializing the text. The book edition weaves McClure's correspondence together with his autobiographical narration.[11] McClure narrates the past by engaging directly with his correspondents. For example, in response to a letter in which Dr. F. J. Scott "hope[s] you will mention" a horse-trading trip to his father's farm, McClure expands on the scene (*SSM,* 114). This narration recognizes no exclusive claims on the past. The autobiography's melting-pot version of history emphasizes how porous the boundary is between personal histories and public ones.

The coordination of correspondence is only one way in which McClure's autobiography approaches questions of history through a quasi-editorial method. The book represents an impressively layered editorial project (through McClure, Cather, editors at *McClure's* magazine, where it was serialized, and editors at Frederick A. Stokes, where it was published in book form). Like

Henry James's novels of the New York Edition and James Weldon Johnson's anthologies of poetry and spirituals, McClure's past represents a text shaped by contemporary critical encounter.

The figure of the editor, it turns out, constituted an irresistible trope for melting-pot histories. The editorial role seemed to offer just the arm's-length approach to the past that was required to enable the mixture of histories. In *The Americanization of Edward Bok* (1920), the autobiography of the Dutch immigrant who edited the popular *Ladies' Home Journal,* Bok discussed why the figure of the editor so often came into play when diverse histories were being assimilated. He claimed that an editor ideally acts as a "pivot," on whom "everything turns."[12] A capable editor focuses on temporal shifts, anticipating the literary and cultural desires of a public that "knows what it wants when it sees it, [but]...never wants the thing that it does ask for, although it thinks it does at the time" (Bok, 163–64). The public is trapped in the present, according to Bok; however, the editor, the pivot, both sees historically and, ironically, recognizes the discontinuous nature of history. Editing, in other words, requires an extraordinarily nuanced awareness of time and one's place in (and out of) it. If the editor as theorized by Bok sounds uncannily like Mary Antin's immigrant, or James Weldon Johnson's black vernacular artist, it is because they share his interest in proposing innovative ways of navigating the melting pot's fraught relation to time.

McClure's unusual approach to history does not date from his time as an editor, however; he is first primed for his later historical project when, as a boy, he works as a peddler. He describes peddling as work "exactly suited to my nature and my needs, that could be taken up and dropped again at will: a means of making money that was easy, pleasant, nomadic, and especially adapted to broken time" (*SSM,* 118). Like the "swing" and syncopation that James Weldon Johnson locates in the spirituals, the "broken time" of peddling provides McClure with a metaphor and a rhythm, forms of agency through which he navigates an entry into the daunting nineteenth-century marketplace. This "broken time" represents an assimilation-temporality opposed to the "clock time" that so many industrialists attempted to inculcate in newly immigrated laborers.[13] Yet young McClure must eventually graduate from peddling to professional writing, where he finds structure and repetition in keeping with an industrial workplace. He casts the anxiety of his early professional days in historical terms: the weight of the past feels overwhelming in New York, where it seems that "everything had been done, as if there were no further possibilities of expansion," or as if the long-standing prose traditions of the city, as well as its journalistic and publishing establishment, leave no space for a newcomer (*SSM,* 171). As a young professional McClure suffers from the predicament of the immigrant: he is offered few opportunities for significant "doing," and sees only things that are "done." He must free himself from the force of the "done," overcoming what he terms "the delusion of the completeness of the world"; he does this by imagining the "broken time" of peddling transposed to this urban, professional milieu (171).[14]

To "do," and thereby overcome his historical anxieties, McClure devises a handful of techniques that reproduce the effects of "broken time" in his professional efforts. These techniques come together in his first great business success, the newspaper syndicate. He runs his business from his domestic space, his schedule is forever mixed up, and he and his wife do "every kind of office drudgery, all the things that in an ordinary business there are half a dozen people to do...the office-boy's work and the clerk's work and the stenographer's work...from eight in the morning to ten o'clock at night" (*SSM,* 175). McClure here represents the grueling home-work conditions that afflicted so many immigrant families as an opportunity for innovation: these unconventional hours represent the closest urban-industrial alternative to the "broken time" of the peddler. And just as he switched from peddling coffee pots to handkerchiefs (or from studying to peddling) as a youngster, he now juggles multiple different identities within the field of his new venture. He plays the roles assumed by half a dozen people in a conventional business. His syndicated texts, in turn, assume positions for which they were not necessarily originally conceived (for syndication respects no boundaries of heritage or expertise, authorial intention or audience). This celebration of some of the immigrant scene's most troubling labor practices suggests the extent to which melting-pot thinking was bound up with the market, a question that I will take up in greater detail in the next chapter. McClure's willingness to make an advantage of these adverse labor conditions (he emphasizes the accessibility and transferability they enable) speaks both to his genuine desire to transform workers' relations to the conditions of their labor, and to the ways in which such genuine desires could quickly shade into justifications of unjustifiable conditions.

As editor of *McClure's,* McClure refined these techniques into formal strategies that translated "broken time" into both literary product and labor conditions. He promotes a genre he calls the "*McClure* article," which recreates the "broken time" of the peddler by, ironically, insulating his writers from the importunacy of the market. He puts them on salary, reasoning that the deadlines of piece-work produce linear temporal attitudes and correspondingly linear research processes, while salaries encourage writers to cast about in unusual directions to find their material. The *McClure* article, he argues, amasses a rich fund of knowledge for communal consideration: its preparation entails "the accumulation of knowledge and material enough to make a book" (*SSM,* 245). McClure understands a salary as buying a more broadly envisioned past for his articles; salary-work produces writing founded in an archive of original research, writing that reconceives the past rather than simply reproducing established wisdom.

However, despite McClure's enthusiasm about his editorial work, his auto-biography fails to infuse this part of his narrative with the kind of personal passion that his peddling days evoked (even in his correspondents and read-ers). The descriptions of editorial work may be theoretically persuasive, but they lack emotional immediacy, as did many melting-pot employments of the editor figure (including Jacob Riis's autobiography *The Making of an American,* which declares Riis the "editor" of his own story).[15] In many cases, formally self-conscious editor figures sacrificed subjective immediacy, con-ducting autobiography as if it were biography. (Edward Bok, famously, spoke of himself in the third person.) McClure's account of the carefully devised formal strategies by which he negotiates the past raises an important question for Cather: Can such calculated formal approaches convincingly reconstitute something so powerful and subjective as our experience of the past? If the tropes of editorship can posit connections to alien histories, are they equally effective at intervening in beloved or despised histories? Can this quasi-professional estrangement from the past always be achieved—and should it even always be attempted? In other words, are the differences between autobiography (history of the self) and biography (history of an other) not worth respecting?

Melting-pot histories and autobiographies used a variety of devices to make the emotional and temporal distance evoked by biography and autobi-ography roughly equivalent. The publishers Thomas Y. Crowell introduced Annie Beard's *Our Foreign-Born Citizens: What They Have Done for America* (1922) by purposefully blurring the differences in feeling between biography and autobiography; the introduction argues that Beard's volume not only offers public, biographical recognition to immigrants but also offers affec-tively immediate accounts through which "aliens... will not be recognized as foreign, so closely have they entered into, and become identified with things American."[16] Texts such as this one share McClure's aim to evoke an emotional "middle distance"—the other's history drawn closer, the personal history pushed away. However, understanding McClure's aim (and its reso-nance with other melting-pot texts) is not the same thing as proclaiming his success.

Indeed, the immigrant autobiographer Edward Bok's awkward relation to his own past suggests that this middle distance was difficult to achieve, and that the editor figure is implicated in some autobiographies with serious emotional limitations in their relation to the past. While Mary Antin opens *The Promised Land* by announcing that she *could* write her autobiography in the third person, Bok actually does so, explaining in his preface:

> [The use of third person narration] came to me very naturally in dealing with Edward Bok, editor and publicist, whom I have tried to describe in this book, because, in many respects, he has been a personality apart from my private self.... Not that I ever considered myself bigger or broader than this Edward Bok: simply that he was different.... [Since his retirement,] There are no longer two personalities. The Edward Bok of whom I have written has passed out of my being as completely as if he had never been there, save for the records and files on my library shelves. It is easy, therefore, for me to write of him as a personality apart: in fact, I could not depict him from any other point of view. (vii–viii)

In Bok's account, the editor-self becomes a cipher for the doubling so often used to figure immigrant identities. Antin's autobiography proposed to split her self into the past (Russian-Jewish) self and the present (American) self, but much of her text undermined that schematic division. Bok, however, sticks to the plan, rhetorically and structurally separating the past (doubled, public and private) self from the present (unified, private) self. Bok's strategy smacks of containment (in the third person, in the professional realm, on the library shelves), and thus carries a tang of the tin cans from which Cather wanted to save the immigrant cook.

McClure's *Autobiography* makes some acknowledgment of the costs of this editorial approach to the past. McClure recalls a split second on the stoop outside his first magazine job, in which he paused before entering the path to editing:

> when you mounted the steps to enter the front door, you could not see the street down which you had come. It was just at that crook in the street that I said good-by to my youth. When I have passed that place in later years, I have fairly seen him standing there—a thin boy, with a face somewhat worn from wanting things he couldn't get, a little hurt at being left so unceremoniously. When I went up the steps, he stopped outside; and it now seems to me that I stopped on the steps and looked at him, and that when he looked at me I turned and never spoke to him and went into the building. I came out with a job, but I never saw him again, and now I have no sense of identity with that boy; he was simply one boy whom I knew better than other boys. (*SSM,* 151)

At the outset of the paragraph, McClure's colloquial form of address blurs the subject of his observation: neither he, nor someone else, but "you," his reader, seems to occupy this position. The past, "the street down which you had come," is obscured by the location he is about to enter. But though the location may seem cut off from the past, the narrative takes a Jamesian turn, and the step grows crowded: McClure sees "you," *and* the boy (his youth), *and* his job-seeking young self; at the moment of narration he also sees his self "of later years" in that space, sharing his vision. Yet McClure also disavows the possibility of any of these encounters by declaring "I never saw him again." The relationship that McClure envisions with his past must comprehend both the re-creation of this scene, in memory and narration, and the disavowal of any "origin" it may constitute.

A similar moment of reflection concludes Abraham Cahan's novel of assimilation and business success, *The Rise of David Levinsky,* which first appeared serially in *McClure's* shortly after Cather's resignation and in the same year as McClure's autobiography (1913). Cahan's Levinsky, however, mourns that he cannot leave the boy on the stoop as McClure did: "I cannot escape from my old self. My past and my present do not comport well. David, the poor lad swinging over a Talmud volume at the Preacher's Synagogue, seems to have more in common with my inner identity than David Levinsky, the well-known cloak-manufacturer."[17] Cahan's novel closely traces the suffering brought about by practical alienation from an emotionally compelling past. Levinsky experiences the "old self," the boy, the haunt, as more faithful to his "inner identity": the past is represented as private, intimate, "true," unlike the capitalistic dissimulations that make up Levinsky's public life.

Where Levinsky claims identity, or its close approximation, in the past, McClure shuts down the possibility of past-based identity: "now I have no sense of identity with that boy." "Now" and "that" make the critical distinctions of this sentence, marking McClure's estrangement as historical. "Now" McClure speaks from the position of a man with a "job"; he uses the language of value and circulation, and he is able to editorially manage his own and his public's relation to the past. On the other hand, the irretrievable boy suggests an important loss, a past form of value that has been sacrificed to serve current interests. In McClure's imagined interaction, the boy is hurt, rebuffed, abandoned—McClure describes him as he would a girl he had wronged, a cause to which he had been untrue. Does the treatment of the past troped in the figure of the editor entail a wrong to the past, a wrong that is somehow summed up in the sentimental language through which McClure narrates this split? How might the editor's relation to the past be made less bloodless, more "true"? After *My Autobiography* Cather explored a variety of means of resisting McClure's melting-pot instrumentalization of the past. The work that she produced through the rest of the decade, particularly her novel *My Ántonia* (1918), suggests that navigating the role of feeling in representations of "the precious, the incommunicable past" became central to her project.[18] While *My Ántonia* emphasizes the emotional value of the past, however, it opens up a series of questions about what system of valuation properly honors the past without freezing, misrepresenting, appropriating, or deforming its legacy.

"The Precious, The Incommunicable Past"

Cather's *My Ántonia* begins with two scenes that foreground the process of historical narration: a nameless writer and Jim Burden, old friends, spend a train ride west together and agree to set down their memories of "a Bohemian girl... [who] seemed to mean to us the country, the conditions, the whole adventure of our childhood" (*MA*, 5). Months later, Jim produces his account, self-consciously titling it "My" Ántonia to emphasize the passionate subjectivity of a history viewed "through myself" (5). This "my" echoes the title of McClure's *My Autobiography*. However, unlike McClure's autobiography, *My Ántonia* lingers agonizedly over the question of outside participants in histories; Jim Burden's name suggests that his mostly romantic narrative of immigrant life is a burden imposed upon Ántonia's figure. In his impetuous words to the nameless frame narrator, Jim articulates his problem: "I suppose it hasn't any form," he confesses of his account, both evoking and failing to practice McClure's attentiveness to form (6).

Of course, Jim's narrative has form, as anything does, but the gesture by which he rumples his hair when he determines to take on the project and the gulp with which he drinks his tea as he makes his confession of formlessness to the frame narrator effectively separate his style of action from a Henry Jamesian attentiveness to forms associated with the drawing-room. If we were to be generous, we might say that such form as Jim produces will be uncalculated, and that in its headlong enthusiasm it will archive the feeling generated by another's history in ways that the coldly self-conscious designs of the editor cannot. (Less generously, we might say that this willful blindness to form creates the "incommunicability" of the past, constituting it as a non-fungible object, and thus securing its value in the rapacious capitalist system that Jim has served so well.) When in the last moments of the novel Jim reflects on "the precious, the incommunicable past" that he and Ántonia share, he does so in the physical setting of his first transplantation to the prairie, along an old road where the "feelings of that night were so near that I could reach

out and touch them with my hand" (*MA,* 272). Feeling certainly constitutes
Jim's primary link to the past; the feelings that he associates with Ántonia are
those of a young boy faced with the obliteration of form, as the prairie night
taught him his own insignificance in time and space. Juxtaposed with Jim's
provocative comments of the introduction, these feeling-drenched recollections of the prairie suggest that the emotional immediacy of certain relations
to the past is bought at the cost of formal self-consciousness.

Certainly Jim is no formal or historical innovator, and he evinces little
interest in melting-pot ideas of historical indeterminacy: his concluding comments cast the old prairie road as "the road of Destiny," which "had taken
us to those early accidents of fortune which predetermined for us all that we
can ever be" (*MA,* 272). If Cahan's David Levinsky bemoans his inability
to become sufficiently alienated from his past self, Cather's Jim celebrates
a reductive vision of the past that keeps the old self in sight: "what a little
circle man's experience is," he reflects (272). The past, in this sense, remains
proximal because it is really just an early form of the present. Keeping it close
and intimate requires simplifying the ways in which it differs from the now.
This conceptually useful move turns out to have implications that extend far
beyond Jim's understanding of his relation to the past; as Jim's conversation
with the frame narrator on the train suggests, Ántonia has long served to figure
the past for him, and his relation with her bears the traces of his strategic simplifications. What Jim's narrative illuminates, in other words, are the effects of
using feeling to reduce temporal and subjective distance: *My Ántonia* explores
the troubling implications of collapsing biography into autobiography.

Jim Burden narrates a history of his childhood that is colored by passionate
response and exhibits some of the simplification that he later brings to bear
more forcefully upon Ántonia. However, Jim's version of his childhood history is less marked by determinism than his accounts of later life are; indeed,
the minimization of determinism as far as childhood is concerned is fundamental to the adult Jim's understanding of history. Jim sees childhood as a
unique stage of temporal and subjective flexibility, the beginning of personal
history, a time when fundamental patterns are established. As a child Jim
takes in the stories of those around him with such intensity that he practically
inhabits a version of their past. For example, after hearing two immigrants'
vivid account of being pursued through the Russian woods by wolves, he
experiences it as if it were his own: "At night, before I went to sleep, I often
found myself in a sledge drawn by three horses, dashing through a country
that looked something like Nebraska and something like Virginia" (*MA,* 50).
Jim and Ántonia share this intense response to the Russians' story of throwing
a wedding party to the wolves, and it penetrates their present experience: the

story is "never at an end" for them, never consigned to the past (50). McClure-like, the children renovate and refresh the past, as Jim's non-Russian setting for his dreamlike fusions suggests. Their passionate involvement in the story ensures that they guard Peter and Pavel's dark secret, keeping it for their own private use, preserving its intimately "painful and peculiar pleasure" (50).

Such painfully intimate fusions are nowhere in evidence in the more saccharine, nostalgic pleasures of Jim's adulthood, however. When Jim bids Ántonia goodbye before departing to embark on his Eastern law career, he does so wishing "I could be a little boy again" (238). Jim's adult yearning preserves his youthful tone of emotional intensity, but foregrounds his sense of temporal separation: in the farewell scene, he can "almost believe" that the shades of a boy and girl run parallel to his path (238). In the twilit scene he can barely see Ántonia's face, which he means to archive "under all the shadows of women's faces, at the very bottom of my memory" (238). Such an obscured Ántonia is figuratively buried, stifled into a premature grave. In other words, Jim's form of passionate preservation brings emotion back into the relation to the past, but seems to exact a toll from its object that is no less than the toll exacted by McClure's businesslike arrangements.

For Jim, Ántonia represents a means by which he aestheticizes the past, keeping it unfaded even as it remains separate from the present: "Ántonia had always been one to leave images in the mind that did not fade—that grew stronger with time. In my mind there was a succession of such pictures, fixed there like the old woodcuts of one's first primer" (*MA,* 258). Jim's historical determinism is reflected in the schematic representations of the woodcut. "Fixed" as a fundamental text of Jim's being, Ántonia continues to exert an emotional claim because Jim reinscribes her outside of history: "she lent herself to immemorial human attitudes which we recognize by instinct as universal and true," he reflects (258). Revealing the means by which Jim maintains the intensity of his connection to the past, the late sequences of Cather's novel also bare the conceptual clumsiness and anti-historicist fabrications that buttress that emotional intensity. Jim's approach is direct and affecting, but its faithfulness to the past is questionable. As a response to the problems of melting-pot history, it is just as inadequate as McClure's.

In *My Ántonia* the past suffers a fate comparable to that of the dried mushrooms that Ántonia's mother brought over from the old world: while it is not tossed mistrustfully into the fire (as Jim's grandmother deals with the mushrooms), neither is its dark pungency diffused, flavoring the broth (as Henry James would have it). Rather, the past is carefully contained by Jim's narrative. According to Jim's vision the immigrant brings new life to a brutal and unforgiving land, but she is encapsulated in her symbolic stance with her hand on a crab apple tree, as abstracted and circumscribed as the plough Jim earlier sees silhouetted within the disk of the setting sun. Jim favors aesthetic devices for this framing. While aesthetic containment may be preferable to the "tin cans" that Americanizers pressed on Bohemian housewives, it does not achieve the dissemination of the "penetrating" odor associated with old-world heritage (*MA*, 62).

Though Cather's novel represents Jim's strategy of historical containment as inadequate, it does not underestimate the formal and intellectual challenge of assimilating immigrant histories. Indeed, Jim's form of preservation is superior to his grandmother's quick rejection of the immigrant "gift"; and the privacy entailed in Jim and Ántonia's fusion with the story of Pavel and Peter suggests that some containment is needed to allow one's being to be "penetrated" by the past. (The figure of the melting *pot* makes this concession to containment, too.) If the Ántonia of the final section of the novel can be said to have successfully performed such an infusion of a treasured past into the contemporary United States, she has also accepted a certain degree of circumscription in order to do so. The adult Ántonia constructs a safe space for her Bohemian heritage on the American prairie: her farm produces both American commodities and Bohemian artisanal products, her brood of children speaks Bohemian at home and then English in the public school. Ántonia's family proudly and self-consciously shows off their fruit cave, which brims with barrels of pickles and rows of glass jars testifying to a successful act of preservation. If the "past" can be seen in spiced plums and kolaches, Bohemian newspapers and violin-playing, then it lives on at the Cuzak farm, fused with stories of the Harling children, the hired girls, Jim's family and the rest of historical Black Hawk, Nebraska. As if to signal her openness to such mixture, Ántonia has named one of her Bohemian-American daughters Nina, after a favored Harling daughter. But when Jim remarks on the "peace" in her orchard, he also notes that it has been maintained through "a triple enclosure; the wire fence, then the hedge of thorny locusts, then the mulberry hedge which kept out the hot winds of summer and held fast to the protecting snows of winter" (*MA*, 250). By 1918, when Cather's novel was published, Ántonia's farm represented one of the very last protected, peaceful corners of Bohemia; Cather's novel does not understate what is necessary to preserve and sustain this "incommunicable" past.

From the performance of cultural preservation on display at Ántonia's farm, Jim walks away with a narrative section entitled "Cuzak's Boys" and a plan to "play with" the boyish Cuzaks for many years to come (*MA*, 271). His final conclusions confirm the extent to which childhood is a touchstone for this novel, just as it was for McClure's autobiography. For Jim Burden childhood is the object of nostalgia because it represents a time of historical and temporal freedom, when he was capable of occupying the sleigh in Peter and Pavel's terrifying story, when emotional intensity promised full entry into the past and its extension into the future. In childhood the past is communicable; it can be caught like a cold, spread through talk. In contrast, the adult's emotions run in certain established grooves like tracks cut into the prairie, and are "incommunicable" because determined and natural-feeling. Maturation moves personal history to the center of emotional focus, such that Ántonia or Jim-the-child-imagining-himself-in-the-sleigh becomes the object of the adult Jim's emotional intensity: he glimpses his own boyishness in just these moments, as he trades away the freedom and openness to other positions that being a boy actually entailed. In *My Ántonia,* the story of maturation is the story of Jim's circumscription as well as Ántonia's, and historical, if not emotional, limitation commands center stage in this story.

Jim's passion for the past and his preserved boyishness emerge as versions of the same process that preserved Ántonia's Bohemian heritage; the fruit cellar proves that sugar and containment are powerful tools. But Cather's novel ends by exhibiting Jim's excess of sugar as if to suggest that, in Walter Lippmann's words from *Drift and Mastery* (1914), "Modern men are afraid of the past" because it "is a record of human achievement, but its other face is human defeat.... History is full of unbearable analogies which make enthusiasm cold and stale. It tells of the complications that are not foreseen, of the successes that caricature the vision."[19] Jim, like so many of Cather's characters, struggles with "the successes that caricature the vision." Indeed, quite aside from his own bittersweet professional success, which is relayed by the frame narrator, Jim's success in preserving Ántonia has resulted in a caricatured vision. Jim's mode of coping is enthusiasm, but such enthusiasm requires a comparative neglect of Lippmann's "unbearable analogies," the unforeseen complications lurking in the past. Cather never again goes in so heavily for enthusiasm, choosing instead to focus on more adult strategies for keeping passion and complexity intertwined. Her work continues to pursue the intensity of subjective response invested in the past, but it does so by attending to the past as what Lippmann, in the same essay, terms "a way to freedom":

An imagination fed on the past will come to see the present as a very temporary thing. Wherever routine and convention become unbearable weights, the abundance of the past is a source of liberty. Merely to realize that your way of living is not the only way, is to free yourself from its authority. It brings a kind of lucidity in which society is rocked by a devastating Why?[20]

Cather's work following *My Ántonia* focuses on a passionate lucidity, a commitment to the past that uses it to utter the "devastating Why." In these terms, her project speaks its continued investment in Progressive melting-pot thinking.

Only formally does *My Ántonia* ever advance toward the "devastating Why," and in this way it anticipates Cather's next steps in her engagement with the past. The frame narrator of *My Ántonia* assumes a kind of editorial position toward the past, silently inserting critical distance between the reader and the sentimental enthusiasms of Jim Burden. In *The Professor's House* (1925), as in *My Ántonia,* the past is an object of yearning; however, Cather's later novel escapes the saccharine excesses of Jim Burden's perspective by sampling the full cauldron of adult passions excited by the past. Resisting the false synthesis produced by Jim's nostalgia, *The Professor's House* is formally split between histories, using the friction and resistance between "Tom Outland's Story" and the surrounding novel to play out the problems faced by projects of historical fusion. As *The Professor's House* suggests, if histories cannot even be "shared" within the context of novelistic form, then the kinds of past-sharings theorized by melting-pot philosophers are little better than Jim Burden's illusions.

In *The Professor's House* Cather pursues Lippmann's "devastating Why" through multiple different engagements with the past, seeking an imaginative response to foreign possibilities that can inform a critique of contemporary insufficiencies. Of these engagements with the past, two emerge as "devastating": Tom Outland sacrifices his closest human relation to remain faithful to the Indian heritage he discovers on a deserted mesa, while Professor St. Peter submerges himself in feeling for his lost protégé, Tom Outland. A third form of engagement with the past is only sketchily traced in the novel: Louie Marsellus steps into Tom's place after the Great War, marrying his fiancée (St. Peter's daughter), marketing his invention (the "Outland vacuum"), and founding scholarships and memorials in his memory. Marsellus's relation to the past is represented as well-meaning and public-minded, but potentially devastating in its effects upon those with competing claims on the past he assimilates. All three of these figures register Cather's continued inquiry into the viability of assimilating different pasts.

"In the Face of Ourselves That Were"

The middle section of *The Professor's House* represents Tom Outland's fierce identification with an Indian past, a historical investment that resonated powerfully in the immigration debates of the twenties.[21] Even before the so-called tribal twenties, Horace Kallen's "Democracy *Versus* the Melting-Pot" used the figure of the Indian as an ironic proxy for old-stock ressentiment of the new melting-pot America; Kallen quotes Barrett Wendell's admission of feeling "as I should think an Indian might feel, in the face of ourselves that were."[22] In "Democracy *Versus* the Melting-Pot" Kallen worries at the disquieting relations of "ourselves that were," using the figures of both old-stock American and Indian to trope the challenges of pasts from which one is "externally...cut off" (*CD*, 86). Cather's *Professor's House* similarly uses Tom Outland's fiercely custodial relation to an extinct Indian civilization to conceptualize linkages to a past that is, in Kallen's terms, "Behind him in time" if not "tremendously in him in quality" (*CD*, 86).

At its crisis, "Tom Outland's Story" illustrates the way in which faithfulness to a heritage, even an adopted one, can distort social feeling. When Tom Outland fails to bring national attention to the Indian artifacts excavated on the Blue Mesa, his companion Roddy Blake sells them to a German collector. Learning of the sale, Tom explodes,

> But I never thought of selling them, because they weren't mine to sell—nor yours! They belonged to this country, to the State, and to all the people. They belonged to boys like you and me, that have no other ancestors to inherit from. You've gone and sold them to a country that's got plenty of relics of its own. You've gone and sold your country's secrets, like Dreyfus.[23]

Tom labels Roddy's failure to appreciate the national significance of the American Indian past as treason, the crime for which the Frenchman Alfred Dreyfus was convicted in 1894. In the very vocabulary of Tom Outland's explosion, Cather illustrates the danger of national identification with the Indian past. Too many critics have accepted Tom's assertion of his and his nation's inheritance of the mesa culture, without recognizing that the Dreyfus reference with which this claim is intertwined is, frankly, wrong.[24] Roddy, the novel has previously noted, believes that Dreyfus is innocent; by the time that Cather wrote the novel Dreyfus had been exonerated. Cather has Tom's claim on the mesa embrace the French nationalist discourse of Dreyfus's treason precisely *because,* by 1925, Dreyfus's innocence had been established. (There is little doubt that Cather believed in Dreyfus's innocence.[25]) The complication inherent in the Dreyfus reference in 1925 directly challenges both the simplified scenario of betrayal that Tom is attempting to assert and the simplified senses of national allegiance and history upon which it is predicated.

Tom articulates a clear but suspect formulation of his relation to an American Indian past here. The nation "owns" the Indian past (although among the individuals whom he imagines sharing this ownership, no Indians seem to figure). The cliff dwellings of the Blue Mesa were created by a now-vanished culture, and no living population has a greater claim to them than Tom. Does Tom's passionate response to these artifacts adequately justify his claim for himself and the nation? Or is his passion irrelevant? Does his claim violate the sanctity of something clearly separate—historically if not materially—from his world?[26] Cather had considered these questions in *The Song of the Lark* (1915), in which Thea Kronborg escapes her conventional life to southwestern cliff-dweller ruins that have a melting-pot effect, "like fetters that bound one to a long chain of human endeavour."[27] In this earlier novel, ancient ruins "lengthened her past," drawing Thea into "older and higher obligations" (*SL*, 282). Like Tom Outland, Thea is impassioned and strengthened by her contact with the cliff dwellings. However, Thea's language of fettering and of obligation conveys a lesser sense of her claim, personal or national. Rather than seeing the ancient Indian dwellings as hers by right, she feels herself "a guest," an honored visitor who feels the past deeply before moving on (*SL*, 279). In the ruins, Thea finds the basis for resistance—for uttering Lippmann's "devastating Why"—to the social conformity that formed the basis of so many Americanization campaigns. As her language of obligation indicates, she associates her passionate relation to the cliff dwellings with great responsibility. Her conscience specifically forbids her from separating the artifacts from their physical and cultural context, so dissemination of this material heritage is out of the question. (Cather herself also felt this responsibility, according to Elizabeth Sergeant: to her it "seemed a sacrilege to take anything for oneself from those cliff dwellings."[28]) Thea's response to cliff-dweller history is deeply personal, but it gives more than it takes for itself. In *The Professor's House,* Tom Outland's response to this past goes a step further, intertwining personal and public emotions. In its appeal to both public and private uses of history, the novel speaks to the "middle distance" that McClure's autobiography attempted to find between autobiographical and biographical approaches to the past. The Outland response proves a promising yet combustible mix of historical feeling, one that Cather ultimately judges as in danger of taking more than it gives.

By the time Cather began writing *The Professor's House,* a mix of personal and public emotions very similar to Tom Outland's had resulted in Southwestern Indian histories and cultures being claimed by sources as disparate as politicians, writers and artists, social activists, and marketers.[29] Anthropologist and Pueblo popularizer Edgar Lee Hewett, among others, promoted Indians as "the first Americans" and their culture as "original American culture."[30] By the 1920s, the *New York Times* responded to legislative threats to Pueblo land ownership with a reminder that these ancient peoples were particularly deserving of national respect, due to their status as perhaps "the oldest democracies on the face of the earth," positioning them as the spiritual forbears of the republic.[31] Tom Outland's passionate mesa-top declaration represents Cather's dramatization of this nationalist historical vision, with all its limitations.

Despite its element of cross-racial fantasy, this embrace of an Indian heritage often entailed emphasizing putatively biological histories: Teddy Roosevelt, for one, was said to regret not having "a strain of Indian blood" in his veins.[32] Mabel Dodge Luhan issued a "call" to writers like D. H. Lawrence "from across the world—to give him the truth about America: the false, new, external America in the east, and the true, primordial, undiscovered America that was preserved, living, in the Indian bloodstream."[33] Luhan's sentimentalization of the Indian past entailed an aesthetic program as well: she imagined gathering together artists to "transfuse," in James Weldon Johnson's words, a blood-borne heritage into disseminable culture. By releasing and giving new form to a past heretofore "preserved [in the] bloodstream," Luhan imagined, literature and culture would take the place of the archive biologically preserved in the twentieth-century Indian. These maneuvers all speak to the powerful presence of biological premises in even the culturally focused plans of melting-pot inheritance. Even more troublingly, these schemes of past-acquisition found their logic in contemporary living bodies, and yet cast those bodies as little more than "bloodstreams," curiously animate archives, as individually disposable as the "any living woman" Tom Outland discounts in his mesa-top declaration.

This past-romanticizing indifference to contemporary beings was met, at the beginning of the twentieth century, by a New, or Progressive, History, which saw itself as rescuing the study of history from its own antisocial tendencies. As historians the practitioners of this New History were as passionately committed to the past as any Cather character: "we are dependent on the past for our knowledge and ideals... it alone can explain why we are what we are, and why we do as we do," wrote James Harvey Robinson, one of the earliest articulators of this historical turn. Robinson's historical philosophy takes on a Deweyan aspect when it represents this dependence on the past not in deterministic terms, but in liberating ones:

History is what we know of the past. We may question it as we question our memory of our own personal acts and experiences.... We adjust our recollection to our needs and aspirations, and ask from it light on the particular problems that face us. History, too, is in this sense not fixed and immutable, but ever changing. Each age has a perfect right to select from the annals of mankind those facts that seem to have a particular bearing on the matters it has at heart.[34]

This philosophy posed unavoidable questions about the "matters at heart" of a culture that embraced conceptual pasts to the detriment of living agents. Unlike Tom Outland, who is "afraid [to] lose the whole in the parts," Progressive historians often focused their attention on the parts too often lost in the whole (*PH,* 227–28). Such parts—lives of everyday people, sites of economic conflict, laboring "cogs" in the wheel—promised to offer occasions for passionate contemporary response to newly relevant pasts.

In other words, like Samuel McClure, Progressive historians made use, contemporary social use, of history, and understood that usefulness as central to the value of history. Tom Outland is not totally at odds with such a motivation: he attempts to get experts from the Smithsonian involved in the excavation on the mesa, but to no avail. In the absence of such national sanction, he will not use the artifacts for personal gain. The matter of the mesa artifacts is different, as he tells Roddy, from "anything of our own, between you and me" (*PH,* 222). By virtue of attempting to elevate his bond with the past above the personal relation that proves so limiting for Jim Burden, Tom produces a historical outlook that is ruthlessly impersonal even as it is passionate.[35] When he finally leaves the mesa, he closes up his diary, a detailed record of his early days of excavation and discovery, in the cliff dwellings, immuring and abandoning the painstaking relation to the past that it represents. His peculiarly impersonal passion for this past means that if it cannot be put to the use he envisioned for it, he will resist its being released at all.

When Tom retreats from the cliffs to the land of human relations, he brings a past of great value into the orbit of the St. Peter family: from his first arrival in Hamilton he fills the St. Peter house with tales of exploring the ancient cliff dwellings of the American Southwest, and gifts of pottery and turquoises; years later, he continues to fill St. Peter's memories with his filial presence, his ease with the family, and his intellectual companionship. In the frame story of *The Professor's House,* Tom Outland died years ago in the Great War, but Professor St. Peter and his youngest daughter Kitty still like to reminisce about how "One seemed to catch glimpses of an unusual background behind his shoulders when he came into the room" (PH, 112). The middle section of the novel, "Tom Outland's Story" (the first-person account of Outland's time in the Southwest), is introduced into the frame narrative of *The Professor's House* through Professor St. Peter's nostalgic recollection. As Tom Outland felt about the past that the mesa represents, the professor feels about this precious heritage: access to it must be carefully controlled. The fragmented structure of the novel enacts the professor's resistance to dispersing that precious past, containing "Tom Outland's Story" just as Jim Burden imaginatively contained Ántonia's figure.

St. Peter, like the rest of his family, has a proprietary feeling about the past that Outland represents.[36] The professor is engaged in a particularly pointed play for Outland's historical legacy, for he is editing and annotating the diary in which Outland noted his mesa discoveries. He understands that for the published diary to "mean anything" he must write an introduction, contextualizing the text in the broader history of Outland's origins and his later accomplishments (*PH*, 150). Tom Outland once provided the professor with the context for his prize-winning history, *The Spanish Adventurers in North America*, compensating with his imagination and experience for the professor's "lack of early association": together they traced the paths of the early Spanish missionaries through the southwest and Mexico (*PH*, 234). Now the professor must return the favor, turning his own personal experience of Tom into sharable historical insight. However, he finds himself blocked, incapable of writing the introduction, incapable of guiding the dissemination of a precious history in the way that James Weldon Johnson's prefaces did.

Outland's diary is both a primary historical object and a secondary historical account; in its latter role, it parallels many of the historical practices at issue in melting-pot struggles over the past. The diary is a spare, minimalist account, made not for dissemination but for private use; it includes few interpretive cues or signals for how it ought to be used. In it Outland notes the details of his days' work, the changing weather and excavation routines; the tools, cloth, and pottery recovered in the ruins are attended to in minute detail, down to sketches and conjectures about the use and significance of the objects. St. Peter appreciates the "austerity" of the account, through which "one felt the kindling imagination, the ardour and excitement" (*PH*, 238). The professor senses that an introduction would violate that austerity, just as Outland's passionate nationalism violated the mesa's austerity—by asserting a new relation to the object, possibly even enabling multiple public relations to this precious past. As the professor resists that violation, he feels his own persona shifting to mirror the austerity and purity of the account: he feels himself to be rediscovering his own "original" self, a self that seems truer for its being unsullied by human relations. In a reflection reminiscent of the idealizations of childhood in *My Ántonia* and in Abraham Cahan's *Rise of David Levinsky*, the professor comes to feel that his life as a boy "was the realest of his lives, and that all the years between had been accidental and ordered from the outside" (*PH*, 240). To remain true to the insight he associates with

Outland's austere diary, he will submit to, and participate in, no more external and accidental relations for the moment. In this light his editorial relation to Outland and the Outland legacy must be terminated: he chooses the passionate preservationism of Jim Burden over the utilitarianism of McClure and Progressive History.

In *The Professor's House,* these divergent approaches to the past suddenly share a novel: they are less alternatives than they are competitors in a new, higher-stakes Catherian inquiry into the problem of the past. The professor's preservationist position is matched by the McClure-like utilitarianism of his son-in-law, Louie Marsellus. Louie, the Jewish parvenu, initially seems to be at a significant disadvantage to the professor; while he may have access to the Outland legacy, he has few supporters in his approach to it. The professor's other son-in-law, Scott, accuses Louie of having Outland's name "served up" at business and professional gatherings (*PH,* 94). Scott, the professor, and even Louie's wife, Rosamond, look askance at such "serving up," but that is precisely what Progressive-era melting-pot thinkers would recommend. Louie endows scholarships, spreads Outland's glory, and all the time reaps even greater financial rewards through this campaign: both he and society are made richer, not poorer, by "sharing" Outland. Louie does not require conformity with some idea of his own in order to be generous with what he possesses of Outland's legacy. His mode of relation is exquisitely responsive to differences of feeling: "It was to him that one appealed,—for Augusta, for Professor Crane, for the bruised feelings of people less fortunate," the professor grudgingly admires (*PH,* 141). Louie's summer home, "Outland," the name of which so violates the professor's sense of appropriate relations to the Outland legacy, doubles as a public memorial to Tom Outland. As Louie explains to the family:

> We are going to transfer his laboratory there, if the university will permit,—all the apparatus he worked with. We have a room for his library and pictures. When his brother scientists come to Hamilton to look him up, to get information about him, as they are doing now already, at Outland they will find his books and instruments, all the sources of his inspiration. (*PH,* 31)

Of course, the inaccuracy of this conception lies in Louie's belief that all of Outland's sources of inspiration can be gathered together at Louie's country home (even with Rosamond thrown in, as Scott jokes). Nonetheless, even the professor, as a scholar, must admit that this collection does justice to a certain part of Outland's legacy.[37] It is the best historicism in *The Professor's House,* committed to simultaneously protecting, contextualizing, and sharing its object. If he were not warded off by others' possessiveness, Louie might be able to assemble a collection that materially historicizes Outland as fully as possible.

Louie's impulses are in line not only with the kind of historical utilitarianism being advanced by Progressive figures such as James Harvey Robinson but also with the ethnographical display practices of museums, which were changing during precisely the years that Cather's novel spans.[38] Although museums by necessity displayed objects removed from their original contexts, by the turn of the century they did so with greater attentiveness to evoking something of the missing contexts. Jane Addams's Hull-House Labor Museum, for example, was designed to address immigration's troubling rending of objects, activities, and agents from their traditional contexts. Addams believed that the chasm between new-world children and old-world parents could be bridged through a form of public exhibit designed to "interest the young people working in the neighboring factories, in…older forms of industry, so that, through their own parents and grandparents, they would find a dramatic representation of the inherited resources of their daily occupation."[39] Addams's museum collected traditional spindles and spinning wheels from her neighbors, exhibiting these objects alongside a range of techniques in practice with Syrian, Greek, Italian, Russian, and Irish women. From these, she argued, attendees could easily see that "industry develops similarly and peacefully year by year among the workers of each nation, heedless of differences in language, religion, and political experiences."[40] Addams's museum is particularly provocative in the way it bridges old and new museum display practices (just as melting-pot thinking drew from old and new understandings of "culture"). She both displays a range of tools used for the same purpose, as nineteenth-century museums traditionally did, and builds a nuanced contextual portrait of one culture (that is, American industrial textile manufacture), as Franz Boas and others were prodding museums to do at the turn of the century. Through all of this, a passionately utilitarian approach to the past prevails.

Like Addams's museum, Louie's "Outland" memorial intends to allow a present generation, those untouched by Outland before his death, to connect to some substantive aspect of him. The collection is the ground on which Outland can be a historically relevant social factor, as opposed to a private memory. In *The New History* James Harvey Robinson argued that history and anthropology continually prove that "each new generation is indebted to the previous generation for very nearly all that it is and has."[41] "Outland" becomes the means by which Louie Marsellus recognizes his debt, registers his "fettering," in the language of *The Song of the Lark*. Unlike the other characters in the novel, Louie generously acquits himself of his debt to the past. While he is not an immigrant, as the lone Jewish character of the novel he faces the social exclusions and animosity that melting-pot thinkers aimed to overturn. In the face of resistance and hostility, he adopts, transfuses, and diffuses a valuable heritage.

Louie figures his relation to this past in language that makes it both intimate and contemporary: he thinks of Tom as "an adored and gifted brother" (*PH,* 145). Brothers represent generational proximity and shared inheritance (emotionally and biologically, if not always financially). By claiming Tom as a brother, Louie marshals figurative uses of biologically based language against the racist literalists who would balk at his Jewishness. Louie's rhetorical move represents not a repudiation of biological affiliation, but rather its incorporation and complication in melting-pot models. The assertion of brotherhood links figurative and biological modes of connecting across time: Louie's child will have Outland as uncle, while no child shall ever have Outland as a Kallen-style grandfather. In Louie's hands the family expansively incorporates both material and figurative bonds to the past, sampling from the passion and flexibility associated with each. The family becomes an extension of the memorial, rather than the memorial becoming the extension of the family.

Professor St. Peter so totally rejects this kind of relation to the past that by the end of the novel he retreats to the study of his abandoned house, living in an empty shell of the past, like Tom Outland on the mesa. His nostalgic embrace of his past relation with Tom and Tom's past has prevailed at the cost of his allegiance to all social bonds, and indeed, to the life of ideas as represented by the aborted editorial project. In this extremism the professor respects a logic articulated by Abraham Cahan's David Levinsky. According to Levinsky, certain faiths are incompatible with the melting pot's cut-and-paste approach to the past: the old-world Judaism of Levinsky's fathers "is exactly the same as it was a thousand years ago . . . absolutely inflexible. If you are a Jew of the type to which I belonged when I came to New York and you attempt to bend your religion to the spirit of your new surroundings, it breaks. It falls to pieces."[42] The realities of the professor's life threaten to shatter his inflexible vision of the past—particularly of Tom, but to some extent of his whole family. Retreat from the world seems the only option. It is an option that Cather's novel both represents sympathetically and implies is a failed form of custodianship of the past.

The Professor's House, itself broken into "pieces," addresses Levinsky's understanding of the paradox of historical orthodoxy through its distinctive form. The form of the novel has been described as "fragmentary and inconclusive" and marked by the "violence" with which the middle section, "Tom Outland's Story," fractures the narrative.[43] By shifting focus away from the front lines of immigrant assimilation and telegraphing a new level of abstraction through its insistence on form, the novel suggests that the problem of assimilating diverse heritages diffuses into the culture well beyond the "contact zones" of immigration. In its formal enactment of Cather's feeling that the "world broke in two in 1922 or thereabouts," *The Professor's House* aligns itself with Professor St. Peter's sense that the rift between past and present cannot be sutured without loss.[44] However, the novel does not follow St. Peter's retreat; indeed, it resists reduction to any single historical philosophy, any single mode of connecting past and present. The novel may mourn the loss of wholeness, but it also accepts that attempting to re-create such wholeness entails simply another form of violence. As its title implies, *The Professor's House* is more sympathetic to the professor's position than to that of Louie Marsellus; however, it also defies the professor's refusal by taking a form that looks like his aborted edition. (The frame narrative could be said to introduce and contextualize the central text.) The novel ambivalently, formally, integrates Louie's methodology with the professor's materials, producing that most melting-pot of texts, a synthesis ambivalent about the very idea of synthesis, a novel that enacts the kind of encounter with the past that might be possible if the professor were his "most human self" (*PH*, 142).

The professor pursues his repudiation of the broken, hostile, utilitarian world of the present so far as to constitute a direct contradiction to the imperatives of life, and *The Professor's House* does not shrink from representing St. Peter's intense attachment to a particular past as suicidal, even less sustainable than Outland's position on the mesa. The professor is saved, however, from the gas-filled study that represents his toxic attachment to the past. Thanks to the rescuing hand of a German immigrant, Augusta, the family seamstress, St. Peter returns to a world of individuals "with whom one was outward bound" (*PH*, 257). These outward bindings conjure up the "fetters" that Thea Kronborg felt in *The Song of the Lark,* and suggest that the professor has returned to a world of human responsibility. After Augusta's rescue, St. Peter feels that "He had let something go—and it was gone: something very precious, that he could not consciously have relinquished, probably" (*PH*, 258). Like Jim Burden, the professor values a truly precious past, one that extends beyond biological affiliation, into what Christopher Nealon terms "affect-genealogy."[45] The "seasoned and sound and on the solid earth" relations to which Augusta returns the professor may be social and "most human," but they are also "outward" in that they presume no passionate, devastating sense of connection (*PH*, 256). Indeed, compulsory middle-class heterosexuality and domesticity constitute the professor's future. His eldest daughter is expecting a child. Horace Kallen's grandfather-figure is in play again here: irrefutable biological ties extend across the generations at the end of this novel, both affirming the continuity of life and darkly suggesting the loss entailed in ceding life to mere brutal reproduction. Walter Lippmann's "devastating Why" seems to have had no liberating effect.

Cather's novel is not alone in suggesting that biological connection cannot be exorcised from the versions of affiliation proposed through the melting-pot metaphor. *My Mother and I* (1917), the autobiography of Elizabeth Stern, imagines the men and women who have culturally assimilated, like her, as figures always haunted by ghostly, loving, and yet alienated parents: "I shall never be able to see [the second generation] alone. I shall always see, behind them, two shadowy figures who will stand with questioning, puzzled eyes, eyes in which there will be love, but no understanding, and always an infinite loneliness."[46] Stern's vision infuses a realm of professional self-fashioning with familial inheritance. The puzzled parents, ironically, pose their own version of Lippmann's "devastating Why" to their culturally assimilated offspring. These historical ties always haunt and question.[47] Like Cather's novel, Stern's text reveals the extent to which biological and cultural understandings of selfhood remained messily and often contradictorily interwoven in melting-pot thinking. Louie's masterful performance of disseminated figurative brotherhood will always be haunted by more conventional understandings of biological belonging. Understandings of the past have their own pasts, in other words, which assert a kind of spectral continuity.

In *The Promised Land* Mary Antin represents cultural assimilation as a matter of having "thoroughly assimilated her past" in order to be free in the present; she both aspires to be rid of the "long past vividly remembered" that, "like a heavy garment . . . clings to your limbs when you would run," and ends her autobiography by claiming the "priceless heritage" of both America and the entire natural world.[48] Anzia Yezierska's immigration novel *Bread Givers* (1925) ends by evoking a "shadow still there, over me. It wasn't just my father, but the generations who made my father whose weight was still upon me."[49] The heaviness, the weight, the "clinging," haunting, shadowing presence of generations infuses these narratives even as they variously attempt to, in Antin's words, "take the hint from the Ancient Mariner, who told his tale in order to be rid of it."[50] By virtue of biologically based thinking, the histories represented by parents seem to have an unshakeable grasp, while the histories of consensual relations like those between the professor and Tom Outland seem ever-vulnerable to dissipation. Both forms of history can exert a tyrannical claim, but Augusta's intervention in the study suggests that the passions attached to an orphan past like Outland's can be dispelled in ways that St. Peter's grandchild will never be.

The specters of biological belonging, physical legacies, still potent even when deferred and denied, permeate Cather's texts, but (as Christopher Nealon argues) so do alternative visions of trans-generational connection: Jim Burden's adoptive Cuzak boys, St. Peter's idealized adoptive son, the celibate "Fathers" of *Death Comes for the Archbishop*. These figures are as lonely as the ghostly parents troped in Stern's autobiography, and they propose a queer, non-biological form of historical sharing again and again. Though *The Professor's House* painfully repudiates St. Peter's queer love for the past, replacing it with Louie Marsellus's triumphant reproduction, Cather returns to and renegotiates queer love as a model of relation to the past in *Death Comes for the Archbishop*. For Cather, queer love and affiliation exist as if in Jamesian excess of prescribed channels; this alternative, excessive, yet paradoxically restrained mode of connection takes shape as the fundamental formal principle at work in *Death Comes for the Archbishop*. Its vision permits a less bleak version of "broken time," a relation to the past resistant to the extremes of both preservationism and utilitarianism, and infused with the kinds of ideas that emerge from conjugating the verb "to love" in unexpected ways. It is, in this sense, Cather's fullest response to the problematic approach to the past that she saw in melting-pot models of assimilation.

"Soon to Have Done with the Calendared Time"

At the end of *Death Comes for the Archbishop*, Cather's archbishop of New Mexico, Father Latour, takes on an emblematic project. As he lies dying he attempts to dictate the unwritten history of the region to a young disciple. He finds that he lacks the strength to pursue this dictation "systematically"; his narration is haphazard, following no plan and observing no priorities.[51] He passes along a mixture of "facts he had come upon by chance" and "old legends and customs and superstitions," observations whose "flight" he can no longer arrest (*DCA*, 274). The old man seems surrounded by buzzing, fluttering elements of the past, which he plucks from the air in order to form his history. As Latour prepares for death, the "flightiness" of history also manifests itself in his relation to his personal past. His memories take new form; suddenly chronology seems as incidental as it did in McClure's autobiography, with the attendant effect of alienating him from his own subject position and historical placement:

> there was no longer any perspective in his memories. He remembered his winters with his cousins on the Mediterranean when he was a little boy, his student days in the Holy City, as clearly as he remembered the

arrival of M. Molny and the building of his Cathedral. He was soon
to have done with the calendared time, and it had already ceased to
count for him. He sat in the middle of his own consciousness; none of
his former states of mind were lost or outgrown. They were all within
reach of his hand, and all comprehensible. (*DCA,* 288)

Unlike McClure, or even Jim Burden or Professor St. Peter, Latour does
not lose his access to an earlier self. Instead, he loses "perspective," dispensing
with a European Enlightenment artistic convention that privileges the sight
lines of a single, dominant individual. The approach of death unsettles such
singularity, revealing to Latour the constructedness of conventional conceptions of the individual. Unlike the professor, who embraces a romantic conception of the self in his rediscovery of an "original, unmodified" identity,
the archbishop experiences a dizzying multiplicity, in which no moment
dominates, and alternate selves proliferate, much as they did with Henry
James in New York (*PH,* 239). Latour realizes that he has not outgrown any
of his past personas; rather than receding in a line away from him, they are
all mixed up—with each other and with him, forming a kind of halo, or, in
Latour's own word, a "constellation" (*DCA,* 260). The archbishop's pasts,
"All within reach of his hand," are no longer *past* in the strict sense of the
term, as they are rendered spatially rather than temporally. The "middle" that
Latour has found is not a midpoint in a time sequence, but rather more like a
position in the center of a circle, from which all other points are equidistant
and accessible (a "pivot," to use Edward Bok's term for the editor). This position represents the historical vision embedded in the form of *Death Comes for
the Archbishop:* even as it remains in dialogue with melting-pot ideas of the
past, it emends them in significant ways.

In the deathbed sequence, as the self multiplies and intermixes with others, Latour experiences a sense of access to, indeed envelopment by, temporal
difference. This scene translates Henry James's scenes of excess into explicitly
historical terms; it approaches Elizabeth Stern's 1917 description of autobiographical expression, in which the vivid pasts of others intersect in the self:
"In myself, as I write this record, I see the young girl whose father plucked
golden oranges in Italian gardens, the maiden whose mother worked on still
mornings in the wide fields of Poland, the young man whose grandmother
toiled in the peat-bogs of Ireland."[52] As with these other writers, in Cather's
novel temporal difference shades into other forms of difference, and suddenly
the self finds itself among others as among other moments.

Cather's novel, however, offers a less purely celebratory version of this mingling, lingering on the histories of violence, disadvantage, and exploitation

that the assimilative vision must do justice to. From Latour's deathbed position, "scenes from…bygone times, dark and bright, flashed back" to him: "the terrible faces of the Navajos waiting at the place on the Rio Grande where they were being ferried across into exile; the long streams of survivors going back to their own country…dark horsemen riding across the sands with orphan lambs in their arms—a young Navajo woman, giving a lamb her breast until a ewe was found for it" (*DCA*, 295). The Navajos are present to the archbishop at his death despite (or perhaps due to) their continued resistance to conversion and his complicity in their removal. As multiple historical positions become accessible to the dying man, he compiles a deeply felt archive of Navajo suffering and persistence in the face of persecution. His memories embrace a devastating dissonance—the American inability to accommodate the difference of the Navajo, counterpoised against a Navajo woman crossing the lines of species to offer a future to another creature. While his vision is, ultimately, as redemptive as Stern's immigrant-past mingling, it more explicitly traces that which must be redeemed, refusing to idealize the process it represents.

In Latour's vision "history" is made a present thing through figuration, which transforms the past as it transfuses it. Figuration, particularly the dense symbolism of the church in the guise of the lamb, transforms the breast, and thereby intervenes in the brutally biological and racial conceptions of history used to justify Navajo removal. Latour's memorializing figuration might be said to exceed his own familiar tradition in its willingness to infuse the body with a range of signifying capacities that extends to queer, unpredictable relations; however, even in this he is not entirely free from certain exegetic traditions. Like any interpreter, he invariably reshapes his material in his own image. Through these sequences Cather's novel suggests that particular traditions may, indeed, make important contributions to melting-pot theories of historical synthesis; the novel also insists, however, that the particular tradition from which these contributions emerge is never exceeded, and thus must be cited and examined in any historical project.

Latour's interpretive tradition makes a poor fit with the process-mindedness of most melting-pot forms of historical interpretation, for it predisposes him to imagine that history serves a certain end. Seizing on the redemptive figure of the Navajo woman and lamb, and reflecting on the privilege of having witnessed the Navajo return to their sacred ground in "a happy issue to those old wrongs," Latour imposes closure on the terrible scenes that flicker before him (*DCA*, 295–96). However, by figuring these images as part of the non-chronological being that Latour forges in the death sequence, Cather's novel suggests that both sin and redemption, both exile and return, might be kept simultaneous and contradictory. In this sense, *Death Comes for the Archbishop* introduces a messianic temporal simultaneity, in which end and endlessness cannot be distinguished, into melting-pot ideas of history. The novel uses such simultaneity to address the question of how histories of violence and exploitation should be accommodated within a melting-pot synthesis. Like the lynchings addressed by James Weldon Johnson and the pogroms at issue in Israel Zangwill's *The Melting-Pot,* the Navajo exile cannot be expunged through reference to any "happy issue to old wrongs." However, like lynching and the pogroms, the exile should be brought to an end, consigned to a certain kind of historical closure through termination. Cather's novel does not so much resolve this problem as suggest that the historical visions of melting-pot thinkers must take these challenges into account.

Of course, Cather cannot be expected to entirely resolve these problems; however, her anatomization of the historical challenges facing models of melting-pot fusion is made particularly stark by her skepticism about a device that many other melting-pot thinkers used to address the logical and ethical challenges of these models. Faced with the problem of eroded particularity brought on by submission to melting-pot fusion, James asserts agency: not that of the individual spectator, perhaps, but that of a thinly disguised person now located in the form of the text. Faced with the challenge of crafting an integrationist melting-pot that meets force without adopting its methods, Johnson asserts agency: the critical, self-conscious deployment of vernacular forms that imply a community behind the individual actor. Cather's work, however, more consistently damns the effects of human assertion and more consistently queries the value and relevance of agency. *Death Comes for the Archbishop* extends this skepticism: Latour spends his last seconds before death in an old memory, feeling himself once again "trying to forge a new Will" in his companion, Father Vaillant, in order that they may leave France together as missionaries to the New World (*DCA,* 297). Agency, the old question, is turned here into a component of the historical riddle. The will to which Latour so passionately returns is at once old and ever-new. In this novel it is the means by which the two men extract themselves from a certain, conventional, historical pattern, and enter an uncharted territory. This will is Jamesian in its self-undoing queerness. It enables Lippmann's "devastating Why," as in *The Professor's House;* however, it does so not by directing the repudiation of the world, but by requiring an immersion in it. The will is centrifugal, in other words, rather than centripetal; as a form of agency, it is about the diffusion and dissemination of energy, rather than its pointed concentration or its bounding.

Cather's limited endorsement of agency as a means of forging a responsible form of historical synthesis is best expressed, as in the cases of James and Johnson, in the form of her novel. The will asserted by *Death Comes for the Archbishop* is subtle, ever-alive to contingency, and fundamentally centrifugal. No grand trajectory unifies Cather's novel. In a published letter on the method of *Death Comes for the Archbishop,* Cather emphasized her novel's resistance to traditional modes of development and progression:

> I have wished that I could try something a little like [the Puvis de Chavannes frescoes of the life of Saint Geneviève] in prose; something *without accent,* with none of the artificial elements of composition. In the Golden Legend *the martyrdoms of the saints are no more dwelt upon than are the trivial incidents of their lives: it is as though all human experiences, measured against one supreme spiritual experience, were of about the same importance.*[53] (My emphasis.)

To abjure accent is to de-emphasize purposeful action in one's relation to the past, for accent works to advance particular ends, prioritizing certain elements or episodes in a way that anticipates progress. Accented elements in effect project forward in the narrative, toward conclusions that take what amounts to a historical stance: they look back, make sense of, or finally realize that intimated by earlier accented events. In the quoted matter above, the phrases accented through italicization project forward, anticipating, portending (and one hopes, preparing) the point in my argument that justifies their accenting. By withholding the accent, Cather's novel covers territory without a map. Without accent, episodes matter not for their justification of some ultimate agenda (saintliness), but can come to serve any number of different ends.

Death Comes for the Archbishop produces this effect by collapsing chronology into stark episodicity, producing a novel structured by clusterings, or constellations—of characters, events, and ideas. These clusterings sometimes center on an individual, as Latour's death scene does; however, reflecting Cather's skepticism about individual agency, they also often center on material objects rather than human agents. As if accepting that human agents bring with them not simply overweening attachments to purposeful movement through time, but also conventional life-patterns that stubbornly refuse the withholding of accent, Cather's novel lingers on objects. According to Cather, the material world provides a link to historical feelings that resist translation into other idioms:

> I used to wish there were some written account of the old times when those [old mission] churches were built; but I soon felt that no record of

them could be as real as they are themselves. They are their own story, and it is foolish convention that we must have everything interpreted for us in written language. There are other ways of telling what one feels, and the people who built and decorated those many, many little churches found their way and left their message. (*OW,* 5–6)

Death Comes for the Archbishop formally privileges "other ways of telling what one feels" by casting objects as eloquent historical witnesses, mediators of the thoughts and beliefs of the many populations interacting in Father Latour's diocese.[54] For Cather, objects become the means by which diverse histories meet and mingle without the single-mindedness of individualistic agendas; the novel formally adopts these means of materialistic mediation.

In an interview of 1921, Cather declared, "An old house built and furnished in miserable taste is more beautiful than a new house built and furnished in correct taste. The beauty lies in the associations that cluster around it, the way in which the house has fitted itself to the people" (*IP,* 46). For Cather the age of the old house, its past, is made manifest by present responses to it—by the William Jamesian "associations" that the interpreting mind finds there. According to this theory, objects offer eloquent testimony about the human energies invested in them. When they are used, examined, and interpreted, the traces of human investment that they bear disseminate and mingle. Objects also provide figurative sites for meeting; common objects link agents with different histories (in the Progressive era, for example, shared consumer objects were imagined to unite the immigrant masses).[55] In this way, the "clustering associations" of materiality represent a means of integrating difference, both temporal and cultural. Artifacts thus model the fusion of heritages that melting-pot thinkers envisioned, while avoiding the traps of human willfulness that Cather's earlier novels trace.

Death Comes for the Archbishop understands the material world as a palimpsest; like the onion soup that Father Latour and Father Vaillant share early in their time at Santa Fe, the broader world of objects is both result and evidence "of a constantly refined tradition... [with] nearly a thousand years of history in [it]," "not the work of one man," or even one culture, *pace* the priests' French nationalism (*DCA,* 38). The onion soup gives expression to a history, and by making soup of history, Vaillant makes the past quintessentially assimilable. In Cather's hands a nationalist discourse as potent as Tom Outland's on the mesa subtly morphs into a melting-pot figure, echoing the stews that permeate the discourse of cultural assimilation. Tasting the soup provides a moment in which those thousand years, those many men and cultures, come together with (and within) a contemporary cook and taster.

In Cather's novel the material world represents an archive that is distinctively open to a range of cultures and classes. As Brad Evans has shown, by the end of the nineteenth century the circulation of objects beyond the cultural boundaries that limited contact between peoples had become an object of ethnological fascination.[56] Objects teach Cather's priests about the cultural variety and syncretism that best expresses their southwestern diocese. Like the old silver bell of San Miguel that Father Vaillant unearths, these objects speak of generations of cultural interpenetration, sometimes violent and exploitative, and other times more openly collaborative. When Father Latour wakes to the silvery sound of the bell of San Miguel, he first hears the voice of Rome, and then a more "Eastern" tone. Later, speaking to Vaillant, Latour muses on the legacy of the silver bell: cast out of household silver and pledged to St. Joseph during the Spanish wars against the Moors, it, like all Spanish silverwork, draws upon the silver-working tradition of the Moors; imported to the New World, it inspired silver working in the Mexicans, who then passed the skill to the Navajos. The bell allows Latour to realize these interwoven histories; the persistence of the bell reminds him that through wars, enmities, and imperialisms, cultural intertwining and influence are always at work. Each culture has its own vibrant tradition of silver working, but it also, within these objects, carries the traces of countless other influences. Within the context of the object, histories are not incompatible; they coexist in multiplicity and disseminate with every multivocal peal of the bell. This bell is both pluralistic fable and melting-pot evidence: it registers the concatenation of distinct cultures, and within its form also mingles the "gifts" of those traditions. The bell suggests Cather's interest in cultural pluralism, even as it also demonstrates her ongoing exploration of melting-pot strategies of historical assimilation.

As if to drive home the peculiar kind of historical agency at work in the object world, the bell of San Miguel provokes a mini-version of the temporal mobility later experienced by Father Latour on his deathbed. In response to the peals of the bell, Latour begins making non-chronological mental connections: he imagines himself in Rome, which he has not visited for many years; he senses Jerusalem, projecting himself outward to a place and time unfamiliar to him; he remembers New Orleans, which he traveled through on his way to Santa Fe; he remembers the South of France of his childhood. These connections run the gamut from the personal to the abstract, the recent to the very remote past; the bell makes it possible for Latour to experience his impressions as a constellation, undoing strict chronology. Other versions of such materialist moments regularly punctuate *Death Comes for the Archbishop;* objects serve as fleeting narrative centers, offering a centrifugal richness of historical reference to the novel's form of non-chronological narrative constellation.

Death Comes for the Archbishop uses objects to propose a mode of historical encounter and exchange that is neither impersonal and professional (like that of McClure) nor deeply personal (like that of Jim Burden or Professor St. Peter). Indeed, objects allow Cather's novel (and her priest protagonists) to imagine a third mode of historical encounter and exchange, one whose sophistication James Weldon Johnson celebrated throughout the twenties: a vernacular tradition. Out of practical necessity given their proselytizing religion, the priests accept that interpretive histories, like the religious objects they find among their congregants, change over time: for example, faced with a carved wooden figure, Latour accepts the southwestern Santiago as the saint of horses (an identity that Santiago has acquired through local interpretations). Through the anonymous agents of Latour's and Cather's southwest, then, materiality becomes a metaphor for a vernacular communalism that spans many historical allegiances.

Through a combination of materialist moments and the final death scene, *Death Comes for the Archbishop* proposes Cather's most cogent alternative to the reductive and single-minded historical allegiances she critiqued in her earlier novels. In this late novel, historical synthesis is approached through an interrogation of the limited form of the individual. By focusing on the approach of death, the title of the novel seems to propose an account centered in the chronology of an individual life; however, at the moment of his death Latour realizes the inadequacy of the biographical model for comprehending the historical range that his experience has opened up to him. As a result, *Death Comes for the Archbishop* concludes that the answer to the historical questions posed by melting-pot ideas lies neither with autobiography and biography, nor with some "middle distance" between them, but with a total reframing of the question of historical experience. Cather's novel shows that the melting-pot dependence on individual actors in fact produces the model's problematic relations to the past; that is, a philosophical reliance on individual actors ends by limiting relations to the past to a natural but short-sighted preoccupation with the life course, or at the most with generations. Cather's pluralistic inclinations emerge in her rejection of individual-based models of conceiving of difference: like Horace Kallen, she seeks an expanded sphere of reference.

Cather's critique of biographical modes of historical understanding emerges most pointedly in contrast to her principal source for *Death Comes for the Archbishop,* a biography of Father Vaillant's historical counterpart (*Life of the Right Reverend Joseph P. Machebeuf,* by Reverend W. J. Howlett, 1908). Howlett celebrates biography as equivalent to the raising of a cathedral in Machebeuf's memory.[57] (Here Cather's novel concurs, insofar as it represents Latour's cathedral as monumental individualistic folly.) *Death Comes for the Archbishop* undoes the biographical narrative of the "great individual" by disseminating the focus of Howlett's biography (sharing it between Latour and Vaillant), implying that the individualist psychology then on the rise in American biography is as much a historical distortion as is traditional plot.[58] (Both are purged in the critical Latour deathbed scene.) *Death Comes for the Archbishop* does not imagine that individualistic approaches to the past can be totally eradicated: Father Latour is consistently vulnerable to their trap (especially as regards his cathedral). However, the novel connects the ends-directed individual narrative with crises of faith—Latour is most lost when he considers himself as a man with a biographical legacy. In one such crisis he feels that "he had nothing within himself to give his priests or his people. His work seemed superficial, a house built upon the sands" (*DCA*, 211). Only through a brief experience of vernacular materialism, shared with one of his lowliest congregants, is he reminded that his resources are not exclusively "within himself." Even as it repudiates the biographical model, then, the novel remains attuned to the difficulty of ignoring the call of the individualist life-course; even the man who has taken on a lifetime role of self-submission, of cultural mediator between traditions and cultures, can be undone by that call. In his individualist crisis Latour tropes his sense of failure through the figure of the "house built upon the sands," a non-monumental, historically evanescent structure.[59] In a less self-indulgent moment he realizes that this trope of individualist failure can also evoke the sense of historical contingency at the heart of his mission:

> Latour found his Navajo house favourable for reflection, for recalling the past and planning the future.... The hogan was isolated like a ship's cabin on the ocean, with the murmuring of great winds around it. There was no opening except the door, always open, and the air without had the turbid yellow light of sand-storms. All day long the sand came in through the cracks in the walls and formed little ridges on the earth floor. It rattled like sleet upon the dead leaves of the tree-branch roof. This house was so frail a shelter that one seemed to be sitting in the heart of a world made of dusty earth and moving air. (*DCA*, 229)

This house built on the sand offers a perspective similar to the one Latour gains in death. Its form privileges neither present, nor past, nor future, but enables consciousness about the relations connecting them. As a model for the self, the hogan promises continual communication with the outer world.

It is single, distinct, and isolated, but its door is open, its walls cracked, its roof thin, and its structure frail and permeable. The sand-storms emphasize the flux of the temporal medium in which the self finds itself. Sand writes upon the floor, leaving traces sometimes decipherable and sometimes indecipherable. This world of motion *is* the individual such as Cather's novel imagines him: engaged in constant reading and interpretation, faced with flux and erasure, this melting-pot agent never fully comprehends his place in time.

Cather's engagement with the formal and ethical problems entailed by melting-pot proposals to "share" cultural heritages culminates in the pluralistic, anti-individualistic form of *Death Comes for the Archbishop.* This melting-pot pluralism remains distinct from other twenties pluralisms: Cather remains adamant about the changeability of the past. Horace Kallen famously said of the immigrant that "externally he is cut off from the past. Not so internally: whatever else he changes, he cannot change his grandfather."[60] For Kallen the grandfather stands for a fixed cultural legacy, a past to which one can be either true or untrue, but which one cannot change and exchange. One may not be able to change one's grandfather, we might imagine Cather responding to Kallen. However, one rises above brutal biology through a passionate queerness that can, and does, change one's understanding of who one's grandfather is, what he represents, and what one's relation to other grandfathers might be. Most importantly, Cather envisions historical pluralism as a constellation of relations that make over the very nature of selfhood (rather than as a plurality of individuals anchored to distinct and different pasts). In addressing her concerns about the integrity of the past in the melting-pot model, Cather's late work devises an anti-individualist historical philosophy, one enacted through continual encounter and revision. It also performs its own act of historical preservation, embedding melting-pot concerns in mid-century modernist literary experiments.

✹ CHAPTER 5

Gertrude Stein and "Individual Anything"

Gertrude Stein's experimental text *The Making of Americans,* which she wrote intermittently from 1903 through 1911, firmly situates her within the immigration debates of the turn of the century (it was based on her own family's immigrant heritage). *The Making of Americans,* published in 1925, represents a paradigmatic melting-pot text: in it, a story of immigration becomes the occasion for Stein's radical modernist deformation of conventional narratives. The novel also takes on a central problem of melting-pot thinking: the indispensability of the individual to these theories of cultural mixture and merging. While James, Johnson, and Cather all touched on this problem, Stein focused more sustainedly on it. This chapter will trace her particular concern over the ways that the formal innovativeness of the melting pot was bound to the figure of the individual. Especially at the beginning of her career, Stein demonstrated a willingness to accept the individual as philosophical and aesthetic basis of melting-pot creativity; however, even from her earliest work she did not hesitate to query whether the philosophical and aesthetic promise of the melting pot justified such a reliance on the problematic figure of the individual. Her later work is far more damning about the ways individual being, to her mind, fetters melting-pot innovation.

The Making of Americans suggests some of the ways in which Stein's work puts special pressure on the individual-form. This early novel considers how

domesticity and the market serve as means to *make Americans,* or to incorpo-
rate individuals into systems putatively responsive to the independence and
mobility of those individuals. *The Making of Americans* finds the unspoken
logical basis of melting-pot ideas of mobility in the individual's freedom of
contract (both marital and economic). The conventional "plot" of *The Making
of Americans* (which is progressively submerged under Stein's formal experimentation) concerns financial success and marriage, the markers of individual assimilation in so many accounts of immigration. In Stein's hands,
however, narratives of market and middle-class home ineffectually punctuate
a relentless exercise in classification, one whose form evokes the isolation of
the individual in Progressive-era culture. This economic individual circulates
from *The Making of Americans* through much of Stein's literary production,
constituting her most enduring engagement with the aesthetic and philosophical problems of the melting pot.

A sense of the individual as necessarily, however uneasily, embedded within
the interlocking systems of market and domesticity was by no means peculiar
to the Progressive-era United States.[1] However, acceptance of this ideological
formation, however ambivalent, might be said to constitute the traditionalist
parameters for Progressive reform—that is, it separates reform from radical-
ism. Even the most socially conscious melting-pot Progressives, such as Jane
Addams and John Dewey, cast melting-pot assimilation as an individualized
process. In doing so, they firmly located the melting-pot paradigm within the
familiar intersecting systems of a modified free market and the home—for
individuality itself as imagined by Addams and Dewey was logically founded
in the economy. They were hardly alone in this. If the promise of labor and
the dream of financial independence drew immigrants to the United States,
the home was understood as the place where these individuals claimed intimate bonds and experiences that elevated them above industrial automatons:
the two spheres worked in concert to constitute melting-pot individuality.
Thus Dewey and Addams's practical, tempered, if not muted, support for radical interventions into contemporary labor conditions; thus Addams's influential adoption and remodeling of the form of the home in Hull-House.[2]

Even the most innovative melting-pot ideas of selfhood relied on economic tropes, drawing on William James's description of selfhood as a form
"ownership" in combination with more socialistic ideas of the self as contributor to a communal "fund."[3] Addams imagined that the self-interest characteristic of economic agents could drive assimilative social ethics: "If we
believe that the individual struggle for life may widen into a struggle for
the lives of all, surely the demand of an individual for decency and comfort,
for a chance to work and obtain the fullness of life may be widened until it

gradually embraces all the members of the community, and rises into a sense of the common weal."[4] Lesser-known melting-pot Progressives from Julius Drachsler to Mary Simkhovitch pointed out that the idea of contributions to a cultural fund required a private life that allowed a worker to "contribute his best to the whole" (which, in turn, depended on the kinds of wages that would permit some leisure).[5] These writers were all moderates, in that they accepted the premises of the industrial economy even as they attempted to make its operations less harsh. Yet C. B. Macpherson might as well have been talking about the Progressive era when he argued that liberal-democratic ideas of individuality (based in Hobbes's and Locke's ideas of possession) produced toxic effects in industrial economies, "when the development of the market society destroyed certain prerequisites for deriving a liberal theory from possessive assumptions, while yet the society conformed so closely to those assumptions that they could not be abandoned."[6] In other words, Stein was in good company when she constructed her melting-pot aesthetic experiments around the possessive individual.

This chapter begins by tracing the effects of both market and home in forming the "individual" of Stein's early immigration-oriented texts, *Three Lives* (1909) and *The Making of Americans.* In these works, Stein struggles with how to make good on melting-pot promises of individual assimilation as a form of self-realization. Her formal innovations position her as both diagnostician and healer of the melting pot's "individual problem"; revealing that neither market nor home provides adequate connection *between* melting-pot individuals, her early works test formal and expressive strategies by which that problem might be addressed. The chapter then follows these expressive strategies to their fullest implementation, in the more approachable autobiographical forms of Stein's mid- to late career (*The Autobiography of Alice B. Toklas,* 1933, and *Everybody's Autobiography,* 1937). Rather than representing a break in Stein's career, I show, these autobiographies extend Stein's interrogation of melting-pot individuality, attempting quasi-Jamesian balances of public "circulation" with private integrity. Stein's autobiographies represent a telling counterpoint to James's *American Scene,* however, for rather than representing the turn-of-the-century melting pot, they represent its continuing cultural effects, thirty years on.

Throughout her career, Stein matches "mixed-up" literary forms to the "mixed-up" logics she identifies in individuality: from the taxonomy of "ways of being" that *The Making of Americans* offers, to the atomized individual stories of *Three Lives,* to the expansive and welcoming ramble of *Alice B. Toklas* and the return to more obscure self-referentiality in *Everybody's Autobiography,* these texts insist on coming to grips with both the enabling and the deforming effects of the systems that structure individuality.[7] For Stein, this abiding critical impulse culminates not in the "democracy" or "social ethics" that the majority of melting-pot theorists used to de-center individualism, but in a surprising dismissal of the individual-form in favor of the more "interesting" problems of free-market circulation. Indeed, Stein's commitment to a formal experimentalism arrived at through melting-pot devices easily trumps her commitment to melting-pot social concerns. Faced by a 1930s America whose culture industry seemed unnervingly continuous and coherent, she reacted with animosity to mass movements, understanding them as fettering the free-market energy she associated with formal innovation. Thus, while her attention to the individual-form reveals her ongoing debt to melting-pot thinking, in the final instance Stein is the modernist who most fully exceeds her melting-pot origins—or, perhaps more troublingly, suggests how those Progressive origins translate not into the social programs of the Roosevelt era, but into a socially conservative attempt to save formal experimentalism from its own theoretical origins. Because her work alternately bares the incoherence of melting-pot fixations on the possessive individual and celebrates the freedom contingent upon that incoherence, Stein is indispensable to understanding the significance of melting-pot thinking at mid-century. She registers both the lingering effects and the dwindling force of this intellectual nexus over the first half of the century.

At the turn of the century, however, as Stein came of age, the challenge of making both individual and economy hospitable to melting-pot ideas of sharing galvanized the best minds of a generation. Because possessive individualism constituted the primary mode of conceiving of the self, many Americans understood individuality in terms of estrangement and oppositionality: Frederick Winslow Taylor used the term "individualizing" to refer to the process of convincing workers that they existed in a competitive, rather than cooperative, relation to each other.[8] Even Robert Park spoke of assimilation as shifting competition from the level of racial and ethnic blocs to that of their individual members.[9] Yet despite the difficulty of reconciling possessive individualism with the social ethics shared by many melting-pot thinkers, this market-based individual is everywhere in melting-pot discourse. This is so in large part because the melting pot was more force of ingenious recombination than it was deviser of radical interventions, and its very conception of recombinatory force depended on the logic of the market. As Mark Seltzer argues, "The generalized capacity of 'combining together' dissimilar powers and subjects, drawing into relation and into equivalence 'distant' orders of things such as bodies, capital, and artifacts: this *logic of equivalence* is the 'classic' logic of the market and of market culture."[10] Given the market allegiances of melting-pot thinking, we must be alert to the ways in which melting-pot thinkers attempted to evade, recraft, disguise, and emend the fundamentally capitalistic tropes they worked with.

Melting-pot Progressives attempted to dampen the competitive nature of market relations through figuring the melting pot as a *modified* market, one tempered by social ethics: both Addams and Dewey used the term "common fund" to evoke this sense of shared property.[11] Even Stein's early writings did not subscribe to such socialized visions, however. Stein's *Three Lives* (1909) exposes the raw, unmodified forces of the market at work, following them into the orbits of immigrant and African American working-class women. The three stories of *Three Lives* vividly exemplify the need for a "common fund," even as they point out its total absence from the scene.

The "Inside Connection"

The form of *Three Lives* starkly reflects the alienation of the possessive individual. (Testifying to that, Stein's friend and correspondent Mabel Weeks commended her "power of isolating [her] subject."[12]) *Three Lives* develops its critique of the isolation endemic to market society along three parallel but never intersecting narrative threads: the characters Anna, Melanctha, and Lena are as rigidly limited by their environments as they are by the short, repetitive narratives that chronicle their experiences. The blunt accounts of deaths that end the narratives suggest the extent to which the difference and dynamism of these women have been contained by a system that understands them as abstract, exchangeable units.

The unsatisfactory individual experiences of these three women are negotiated in constant reference to conventional domesticity.[13] Anna's story describes her running through a series of domestic employers and co-workers, just as Melanctha's charts her wandering through a series of romantic relationships and briefer hook-ups; neither forms a lasting relationship. Lena, even more troublingly, succeeds at securing a conventional domestic relationship and is profoundly alienated by it. Associated by nineteenth-century gender ideologies with the home, where the individualizing depth of intimate feeling was supposed to secure the abstract circulations of the market, these women in fact represent the living victims sacrificed to individualist ideology. (As Gillian Brown has shown, nineteenth-century American individualities were premised on the implied particularity of the affective ties of the domestic arena: because actors must be conceptually interchangeable in both democratic and marketplace structures, both democracy and the marketplace rely on domesticity to provide practical and philosophical support to the ideas of individual particularity upon which they depend. The domestic sphere promises a privacy that limits the tendencies of the public sphere to transform its participants into conceptual masses.[14]) Anna, Melanctha, and Lena reap none of the rewards of the logical relationship that structures their existences and their narratives.

Indeed, *Three Lives* centers on the steep price of market domesticity: for these women (but particularly Anna and Lena), buttressing individual particularity through service in the domestic sphere means forgoing opportunities to circulate more widely. Jane Addams conceded that the origins of domesticity lay in limitation, "the concentration of interest in one place, and... moral feeling... centered in a limited number of persons."[15] In *Three Lives* limitation does not lead to concentrated interest or moral feeling: indeed, Anna of "The Good Anna" deals with a series of under-servants ("cheerful Lizzies, the melancholy Mollies, the rough old Katies and the stupid Sallies") who, in their abstraction and evanescence, represent the domestic sphere as just as impersonal and unfeeling as the outside world, simply more circumscribed.[16] Similarly, Lena's relations—first with her aunt, then with her husband and child—are unemotional as well as limiting. Stein's flatly declarative prose style adeptly conveys the blank flatness of these relations that Addams and others looked to for depth and nuance.

But Stein herself continued to rely on melting-pot philosophies of individuality, as becomes clear in her *response* to the malaise she diagnoses in domestic individualism. *Three Lives* refuses to imagine Anna, Melanctha, and Lena liberated from domestic isolation at the cost of the theoretical foundations of individuality. Instead, Stein attempts to make domesticity more conceptually open to the marketplace (her focus on domestic laborers facilitates this maneuver). If those bound to the home are dehumanized by its constriction, then market circulation must simply be allowed to inform even the arenas of privacy. The form that can be tinkered with, that can be risked, is domesticity; the market-based individual remains peculiarly sacrosanct despite its place at the center of the problems Stein is confronting.

Stein's "Melanctha," the most experimental story of the collection, represents her fullest attempt to imagine circulation penetrating into domestic relations. The increasingly tortured and tortuous conversations between Melanctha Herbert and Jeff Campbell feel out how closely one may approximate the affective particularity of domesticity without succumbing to the limitations it imposes on circulation. "Melanctha" unsettles domestic stability, telegraphing Stein's interest in what Mary Antin's *Promised Land* (1912) describes as "that laxity of domestic organization, that inversion of normal relations... [that] sad process of disintegration of home life" that characterized the domestic sphere of the immigrant.[17] (Antin associates this domestic disarray with generational clashes, and imagines it as a passing phase rather than a permanent condition of the melting pot, but her own personal experience failed to bear out that optimism.) For Stein, laxity and disorganization likely seemed acceptable alternatives to what the Progressive social worker and settlement house founder Mary Simkhovitch saw in the domestic lives of industrial women: "a barrenness that is so striking as to be appalling."[18] Tortured and tortuous though it may be, the experimental fecundity of "Melanctha" bears out Stein's sense that prevailing domesticities (as represented in "The Good Anna" and "The Gentle Lena") could stand to be interrupted by a little "wandering."

In contrast to the striking barrenness of Simkhovitch's industrial domesticity, the clash between Melanctha's and Jeff's competing expectations of domestic intimacy produces the radical stylistic innovations constitutive of Stein's modernism. Melanctha's arguments reveal her desire to create a flexible but particular relation, while Jeff understands himself as interviewing for a position determined by convention.[19] The couple's conversations often revolve around Jeff's articulated desire for "just living regular and quiet and with my family, and doing my work, and taking care of people, and trying to understand it" (TL, 117). Domesticity as Jeff envisions it paradoxically bases intimate individual particularity on complacency within a conventional social system. Melanctha initially imagines Jeff as desiring "inside knowledge," or unconventional insight, just as she does, because he "ain't never ashamed to be with queer folks" (TL, 120). But partnerships based on respect for queerness are frail in "Melanctha," and Jeff is far more interested in working out systematic understandings than in joining Melanctha's queer wandering.[20] Melanctha's self-conscious circulation ends up ensuring her exclusion from marriage and domesticity. The melting pot's conceptual dominoes come crashing down: if there is domesticity, there cannot be full feminine circulation; if there is no feminine circulation, there cannot be full feminine individuality. In the context of Three Lives, this problem represents the limit for stylistic innovation. Like Melanctha, Stein's novel runs up against the problem but does not imagine how to challenge the limits of melting-pot individuality.

In the final instance, Stein's Melanctha is no counter-cultural rebel: she yearns for a "right position," and gropes for a form of domesticity that would simply allow the circulation valued by so many melting-pot intellectuals (TL, 86). In Melanctha's case this circulation, cast as "wandering," hardly amounts to even an exercise of agency; Stein's story represents it as an irrepressible impulse, an uncontrollable desire, which ultimately disqualifies Melanctha for "right positions." Melanctha's friend Rose even refuses to accommodate her as unpaid domestic labor, due to the unconventional implications of the arrangement. Rose's ejection of Melanctha from her domestic sphere leaves Melanctha "lost, and all the world went whirling in a mad weary dance around her" (*TL,* 232). In this scene the individual self is "lost" by virtue of its exclusion from this site of particular interior affirmation; the mobility that should be the prerogative of the melting-pot self is instead asserted as the privilege of the whirling "world." This late moment reinforces the primary discovery of Melanctha's early lesbian relationship with Jane Harden: even unconventional positions are structured by conventional patterns. The flexible, circulating selfhood that Melanctha earlier sampled ultimately depends on a conventional domestic sphere, that, ironically, bars women from any further circulation.

"The Gentle Lena" provides the text's most damning depiction of feminine domestic individuality. Unlike Anna and Melanctha, who at least cultivate eccentric relationships to the domestic sphere, Lena submits herself totally to domestic ideology. She plays a succession of feminine domestic roles—from daughter to servant to mother—never deriving any affirmation of her interior particularity from these roles, despite surrendering herself unquestioningly and without complaint to "maternal authority."[21] When she has children, her husband Herman's intense relationship with "his" babies edges her out of her own narrative. Lena never experiences what Mary Simkhovitch described as the half decade "of a more experimental nature, a wider range" in which young women might briefly enter an economy of circulation, display, and consumption; she never tastes "play, leisure, freedom," and as a result is, as Simkhovitch fears, made "a means to an end—the one unpardonable sin for a democracy."[22] Lena regularly sacrifices opportunities for individual mobility to the deindividuating labor required by the unappreciative domestic units to which she is assigned: when she is a hired girl she spends her days off with her aunt's family, although this family does not embrace her; once she is married she gives up visits to her friends from her days as a hired girl, for "it would not be right, now" (*TL,* 271). While Israel Zangwill's play *The Melting-Pot* imagines the domestic narrative as central to the mergings performed by the melting pot, domesticity in fact works to exclude Stein's Lena from true social combination. In "The Gentle Lena," domesticity acts as Americanization might, erasing Lena and imposing a template in place of what little self-awareness she had.

The brightest moment in Lena's dismal tale suggests a narrative strategy that Stein later uses to formalize resistance to individual limitation. Lena's husband-to-be fails to show up for their planned wedding, and Lena is sent home, in tears and in disgrace; her domestic scenario teeters on the brink. Her streetcar conductor guesses her trouble and responds to her more fully than any other character in the story. When he attempts to comfort her, Lena, constrained by convention and propriety, imagines her aunt scolding her for allowing a stranger that familiarity. However, the conductor presses on unfazed, airing the intimate domestic narrative in the public space of the streetcar. By disregarding "correct" behavior, the conductor forges a sympathetic connection with Lena, and then disseminates that connection:

> He chatted with the other passenger who had just come in, a very well dressed old man, and then with another who came in later, a good sort of a working man, and then another who came in, a nice lady, and he told them all about Lena's having trouble, and it was too bad there were men who treated a poor girl so badly. And everybody in the car was sorry for poor Lena and the workman tried to cheer her, and the old man looked sharply at her, and said she looked like a good girl, but she ought to be more careful and not to be so careless, and things like that would not happen to her, and the nice lady went and sat beside her and Lena liked it, though she shrank away from being near her. (*TL,* 258)

Lena is "feeling a little better when she got off the car" (*TL,* 258). Through their various expressions of support, from sternness bordering on censure to silent acknowledgment, the passengers absorb Lena's narrative: her "cultural material" circulates beyond her limited sphere for the first time. The *failure* of domesticity galvanizes fuller social access for Lena, more attention to her individual placement, needs, and contribution, than does its eventual success. The role of storyteller, played here by the conductor, is indispensable in crafting this glimpse of wider circulation. What the domestic sphere would keep private and unspoken, the conductor-storyteller gathers and shares.[23]

In many Progressive-era accounts of the immigrant domestic sphere, the settlement worker plays a role like that of the streetcar conductor in Lena's tale. In *Twenty Years at Hull-House* (1910), Jane Addams described herself as "perturbed in spirit,"

> because it seemed so difficult to come into genuine relations with the Italian women and because they themselves so often lost their hold upon their Americanized children. It seemed to me that Hull-House ought to be able to devise some educational enterprise, which should build a bridge between European and American experiences in such wise as to give them both more meaning and a sense of relation.[24]

Here Addams shares with Stein a sense that women laboring in the home suffered from a peculiar alienation. Addams's settlement organized evenings of song, history, and literature, forging a resolutely public domesticity to act as a bridge between individuals. Hull-House also established a series of expositions and lectures publicizing the traditional domestic crafts and industries of local immigrant populations; the success of these events resulted in a standing public exhibit in the Hull-House Labor Museum. In each of these cases, the songs, tales, and crafts that had been the cement of the domestic sphere in the old country were translated by the settlement into shared public culture. The domestic toil of the mother was emphatically connected to the industrial toil of her daughter; in Hull-House both were exposed to broader circulation. In each of these cases, the settlement worker—often Addams, here—serves a mediating and publicizing function similar to that of the streetcar conductor in Stein's "The Gentle Lena." Like so many settlement workers and immigrant autobiographers, Stein's *Three Lives* envisions representation as the primary response to the problem of individual alienation that dogs the melting-pot model.

Addams's Hull-House may have been among the most sympathetic and self-conscious of the settlement houses, but even so, it advanced an only slightly modified version of middle-class domesticity. A wide range of immigrant accounts—Anzia Yezierska's *Salome of the Tenements* (1922) and *Arrogant Beggar* (1927) represent the most vivid of these—rejected social workers' unwillingness to deviate from middle-class notions of home, work, and individualism. *Three Lives* represents a similar unwillingness to deviate from middle-class norms: the streetcar conductor offers to "publish" Lena's story, in a sense, but he requires her story to affirm that she is a "good girl," conventionally speaking, and so deserving of this inclusion in communal circuits of exchange. Ultimately, a moment of streetcar publicity no more offers Lena an escape from her domestic doom than settlement houses solved the intractable problems of industrial-era alienation. At the end of *Three Lives,* Stein's diagnosis of the exclusions constituting melting-pot individuality is clear; however, she offers no means, formal or otherwise, to extend cultural circulation to those required to invisibly tend to the melting-pot home.

The "Bottom Nature"

The text that Stein was working on both before and after *Three Lives* does, however, explore how formal innovation might move beyond diagnosis to intervention into the problematic exclusions at the base of melting-pot individuality. *The Making of Americans* begins *within* the paradigm of the melting-pot individual, fleshing out every nuance of the logic governing Progressive-era conceptions of being; it is based on the idea of a "bottom nature," an idea that is fundamentally consonant with melting-pot presuppositions of a particular and constant individuality capable of serving as the hanger, as it were, for the garments of cultural identification.[25] Even as a melting-pot individual changes through the process of assuming different forms, that individual must remain distinct from all others. Indeed, according to melting-pot logic even two individuals simultaneously adopting the same cultural material cannot fully share an identity; their different individual positions necessitate different experiences of, and relations to, the cultural material. In Stein's terms, this model of individuality presumes a "bottom nature" even as it claims that nothing (save its own distinctness) is *essential* to that bottom nature. Ironically, while the melting-pot model represents an attempt to create a sophisticated and flexible version of social selfhood, its premises dictate that even sharing is experienced as distinctly and separately as the stories of *Three Lives. The Making of Americans* remains alive to the alienation of the melting-pot individual, and particularly alert to the need for a system—any system more perfect than the claustrophobic domesticity of *Three Lives,* the novel implies—by which these units might be understood as correlated, or even just compatible.[26]

Ironically, melting-pot ideas of selfhood developed at least in part as interventions into the philosophical problem of individual isolation. John Dewey's *Democracy and Education* (1916) devotes a chapter to considering "The Individual and the World," addressing the philosophical error of imagining a "sharp demarcation of individual minds from the world"; he reminds his readers of the relative modernity of Cartesian dualism, and of pre-modern conceptions of the individual as a "channel" through which higher forces acted.[27] While wars and geographic expansion have reduced the physical space separating cultures by the beginning of the twentieth century, Dewey notes, concepts of individual identity have not fully absorbed the implications of these cultural contacts: "It remains for the most part to secure the intellectual and emotional significance of this physical annihilation of space" (*DE,* 86). Deweyan forms of education were conceived to "secure" this "intellectual and emotional . . . annihilation of space," along the lines of what Henry James experienced as he stood before the Rutgers Street tenements.

Stein's *Making of Americans* charts its own distinct course through these problems. The title of Stein's early masterpiece plays upon the titles of immigrant autobiographies; her text reverses their inexorable progression from individual account to communal significance, using its radically encyclopedic form to break communal formations down to their individual components. In a lecture given during her 1934–1935 visit to the United States,

Stein describes the intellectual and formal struggle that produced this literary experiment: she began to be concerned not simply with "types of people," but with "a whole human being felt at one and the same time," which she found much more difficult to "put into words."[28] In the process of expressing the complexity of the individual, Stein found herself continually expanding the scope of her text. As Dewey's philosophy did, Stein's text imagines the annihilation of intellectual and emotional space. Formally, however, such space was not so easily overcome: Stein's lengthening sentences and the monstrous size of *The Making of Americans* both reflect the enduring spaces that her language attempted to span.

The Making of Americans announces itself as an account of "the old people in a new world, the new people made out of the old" (*MAm*, 3). Enacting the new socially minded individuation of the melting-pot era, the novel takes the union of Julia Dehning and Alfred Hersland as an occasion to attend closely to the individual members of the two families joined by marriage. The twin impulses of individuation and social belonging serve as the Jamesian "germ" of the novel: indeed, the domestic pairing at the base of the novel's ever-expanding attentions is brought about by the intertwining of individuality and social belonging that the figure of Alfred Hersland seems to promise to Julia Dehning. "To a bourgeois mind that has within it a little of the fervor for diversity," the narrator explains, "there can be nothing more attractive than a strain of singularity that yet keeps well within the limits of conventional responsibility a singularity that is, so to speak, well dressed and well set up" (*MAm*, 21). Alfred Hersland represents such a figure, one whose "singularity" tropes "diversity" to Julia Dehning, since he is just beyond the limits of the Dehnings (who are proper in business and conservative at home). The novelty that Alfred Hersland introduces into the Dehnings' sphere is a "well dressed and well set up" singularity, an individuality that emerges from and collapses back into a resolutely "ordinary middle-class tradition," comfortingly affirming the familiar model even as it spices it up just a little bit (*MAm*, 34).

By yoking the "fervor for diversity" with "singularity," the narrator appeals to familiar melting-pot ideas, and then goes further to suggest their fundamental conservatism. Insistently locating her own and Julia Dehning's interest in singularity in the context of "a simple middle class monotonous tradition," the narrator proclaims:

> Middle-class, middle-class, I know no one of my friends who will admit it, one can find no one among you all to belong to it, I know that here we are to be democratic and aristocratic and not have it, for middle

class is sordid material unillusioned unaspiring and always monotonous for it is always there and always to be repeated, and yet I am strong, and I am right, and I know it, and I say it to you and you are to listen to it, yes here in the heart of a people who despise it, that a material middle class who know they are it, with their straightened bond of family to control it, is the one thing always human, vital, and worthy it—worthy that all shall monotonously repeat it,—and from which has always sprung, and all who really look can see it, the very best the world can ever know, and everywhere we always need it. (*MAm*, 34)

Despite its tongue-in-cheek tone, this paragraph unmasks the centrality of middle-class economic and domestic attitudes to even the "democrats" and "aristocrats" of the Progressive era. The sing-song cadence of Stein's narrator "monotonously" repeats the rhythms of her refrain. It also, however, suggests that such conservatism sometimes produces unexpected deviations and moments of creativity: peculiar deformations of conventional meaning pop up within the familiar refrain ("worthy it"?). The hanging "it" of this refrain suggests both the uncontrollable irruption of objectification in this paean to middle-class being, and the "vital and worthy" singularities produced by such irruptions. The "singularities" of Alfred Hersland's being and Stein's narrator's syntax are, in this context, merely the most recent manifestations of a middle-class counter-tradition of innovation. The narrator's later extensive quest for knowledge—what can be known about singular beings—is an equally "singular" elaboration of this counter-tradition, a radical attempt to represent conservative and continuous knowledge ("the very best the world can ever know") from within middle-class formations.

Much as Alfred Hersland represents the narratable occasion for *The Making of Americans,* the narrator also suggests that his "well dressed" amenable strain of middle-class individuality represents an attenuated version of singularity, "not with real singularity to be free in it" (*MAm,* 47). For the narrator such an observation is bittersweet, for well-dressed singularity signals the limits of current representation:

vital singularity is as yet an unknown product for us, we who in our habits, dress-suit cases, clothes and hats and ways of thinking, walking, making money, talking, having simple lines in decorating, in ways of reforming, all with a metallic clicking like the type-writing which is our only way of thinking, our way of educating, our way of learning, all always the same way of doing, all the way down as far as there is any way down inside to us. We all are the same all through us, we never have it to be free inside us. No brother singulars, it is sad here for us, there is no place in an adolescent world for anything eccentric like us, machine making does not turn out queer things like us, they can never make a world to let us be free each one inside us. (*MAm*, 47)

Here "product" emerges as the dominant idiom of middle-class consumerist individuality. The apparent fixity (producedness) of such an individual figure is destabilized, however, through the "we" produced here by the narrator. This "we": does it refer to an us "the same all through us," or to "brother singulars"? Or does even the narrator's identification with "brother singulars" in fact resonate with Progressive-era "ways of learning," "having simple lines in decorating"—that is, does the sadness that the narrator shares with her readers in fact mark "us" all as Julia Dehnings, with a (safe, manageable) "little of the fervor for diversity"? Alfred Hersland forms the occasion for *The Making of Americans* precisely because his passion for freedom inside him is lesser than that of his sister Martha, brother David, or even father David: the narrator's project coincides with Julia Dehning's attention, after all. By virtue of being amenable to the "metallic clicking like type-writing," the well-dressed singularity of Alfred Hersland paradoxically enables the narrator to open the door to ever-expanding visions of "queer" singularity.

Tracing the Alfred Hersland occasion for the representation of singularity back through the strains (and stains) of singularity in his middle-class antecedents, Stein's narrator begins penetrating and anatomizing the "mixtures" that make up these characters. This project embodies a profoundly melting-pot impulse, for it understands individuality as a container of historical material (and thus continuity) and of unexpected combination. Discussing the mixture constituting Alfred's father, David Hersland, prompts the narrator to explain why melting-pot genealogy must, characteristically, expand into a simultaneous exercise in philosophical definition:

> A man in his living has many things inside him. He has in him his feeling himself important to himself inside him, he has in him his way of beginning; this can come too from a mixture in him, from the bottom nature of him, from the nature or natures in him more or less mixed up with the bottom in him. ... Men in their living have many things inside them, they have in them, each one of them has it in him, his own way of feeling himself important inside in him. (*MAm*, 150)

Stein's narrator models the ability of critical investigation to collapse boundaries between apparently distinct fields of inquiry. In her hands the excavation of a middle-class genealogy of singularity (discussing Alfred Hersland requires discussing David Hersland, and so on) transitions naturally into an interrogation of the nature of individuality itself. What constitutes the individual, whether individuality is considered as ownership, actor, mixed-up nature, hanger for garments? Is it awareness of self ("feeling himself important inside"), or unique origin ("his way of beginning")? Is the individual the "him" with "things inside," or is it the "things inside"? Is individuality constituted by distinct mixture, or by a singular foundational "bottom nature"? The sequence quoted above toggles between singular "man" and comparative "men," suggesting that individuality is constituted both singularly and socially: the self is inextricably "mixed up" with that around it as well as that within it. The narrator's discussion mixes up modes just as more conventional melting-pot arguments did, combining specific historical and abstract philosophical modes of thought. This mixing of modes also conveys the mixedness of its objects, intimating that "historical" individuals such as the Herslands cannot be understood without reference to the logical parameters that define their being, while those logical parameters exist only in and through "historical" individuals. The seemingly inexorable progression of the narrator's inquiry from genealogy to speculative philosophy in fact *enacts* a kind of melting-pot acceptance of the impossibility of clearly demarcating boundaries between objects (be they "separate" individuals, or intellectual projects like genealogy and philosophical speculation).

The interrogation of individual being that initially fascinates the narrator of *The Making of Americans* gives way, therefore, to a Deweyesque insight into the social embeddedness of individuality: "The history of each one then is a history of that one and a piece of the history of their kind of men and women" (*MAm*, 191). Rather than stymieing the representational project, this insight into the multiply embedded nature of individuality translates into an imperative to expand the investigation: since "Every one then is like many others always living, there are many ways of thinking of every one. . . . There must then be a whole history of each one of them. There must then now be a description of all repeating" (*MAm*, 290). The isolated women of *Three Lives* represented a version of individuality with all-too-sharply demarcated boundaries (their domestic spheres, or even more baldly, their life courses). Here, the opposite problem manifests: an individuality conceived as endlessly porous and embedded requires a seemingly endless representational exercise. This problem provokes a Steinian excursion into melting-pot historicism, manifested through a presentism that resonates with Willa Cather's experiments in representing the past. The evolution of Stein's narrator's analysis—from being "a history of each one" to being "a description of all repeating"—is represented as not only philosophically and logically necessary, but *historically* so: "then" becomes "then now," "history" becomes "description." Action makes the past present, but it also suggests a loose boundary for an otherwise boundless exercise. The shift from recognizing that "there will be a history of every one" to presently *undertaking* that history aligns with a section break, in which the explicit narrative focus passes from the first generation (David and Fanny Hersland) to the contemporary or second generation, as represented by Martha Hersland, the sister of Alfred, our new well-dressed middle-class "singular." Presumably describing the repeating in this younger generation will accomplish what was intended by genealogy, but with the added benefit of recognizing contemporary individuals as socially connected *within* the melting-pot selves that contain these myriad repeatings.

As the narrator returns to the contested territory of "contemporary" individuality in the "Martha Hersland" section of *The Making of Americans*, she suddenly initiates a sustained sequence of self-referentiality; it is here, as Ulla Dydo has pointed out, that "the writer in the act of writing" takes over the text.[29] With the foregrounding of that "act of writing," a distinctly individual and presentist spirit infuses Stein's text. Through the narrator's reports of what she likes, what she feels, how she is excited or confused, how her intimates do not like reading her analyses of their beings, how she is beginning to enjoy conversation or certain new forms of reading, the epic fictional and intellectual exercise of *The Making of Americans* suddenly takes on a quasi-autobiographical, confessional tone. This tone evokes not so much a Steinian *continuous* present as a particular early twentieth-century present. The individual presentism of the "act of writing" suggests that "metallic clicking like the type-writing which is our only way of thinking" which the narrator associated with the middle-class celebration of safe ("well-dressed") singularity (*MAm,* 47).[30] In other words, the narrator is undoubtedly interested in continuity and difference over time, but the self-referentiality that marks "Martha Hersland" serves as a reminder that these investigations of individuality—genealogical, speculative, analytical, categorical—emerge from a particular context. "Middle-class, middle-class," the narrator effectively whispers throughout, but reminds us particularly clearly again here. The "singular" formal agenda that this narrator has brought to bear on the problem of melting-pot individuality—her insistence on "repeating," "beginning again and again," and most evidently, the grand system that she proposes (the "complete history of each one who ever is or was or will be living")—is nonetheless one that is articulated *in* and *through* a specific early twentieth-century context. Stein's syntax is singular, but it is still recognizable as syntax: so, too, are the visions of system and singularity that are elaborated by her narrator.

Indeed, the narrator herself—from her early assertion that "I am strong, and I am right, and I know it, and I say it to you and you are to listen to it" to her confession that "always in me really I am certain that it is an important thing in me and I am telling that"—increasingly figures her own singular being through the abstract form of her project, which is really not so different from what many melting-pot autobiographers did (*MAm,* 34, 584). She is of a piece with her characters of the younger (second) generation, of the new "adolescent" world of the early twentieth century. When, near the end of *The Making of Americans,* Stein kills off the promisingly singular junior David Hersland, leaving the narrative awash in the abstract "some ones," "any ones," "every ones," and "many ones" of its final sequence, the project of categorization stalls, but its director does not. The loss of the singular character, the individual *in* the text, coincides with the abandonment of the scientific ethos that Henry James's prefaces shared with so many Progressive-era reformers. The narrative foreshadows this abandonment much earlier, when the narrator muses that "Categories that once to some one had real meaning can later to that same one be all empty. It is queer that words that meant something in our thinking and in our feeling can later come to have in them in us not at all any meaning" (*MAm,* 440). "Categories," "lists," "diagrams," and systems fail to hold "our" (or the narrator's) attention. Individuals, even compelling ones like the younger David Hersland, die. But "that same one" to whom categories lose meaning, that "one" the maker and loser of meaning, is coextensive with the narrative; rather than the individuality *in* the text, we are left with the individuality *of* the text, a robust and puzzling enactment of the persistence of James's vision of the text as proto-melting-pot person.

The "queer" changeability of words that draws that "one" to the fore of Stein's text evokes her earlier "queer things like us," those singular beings that Stein's narrator understood to have no place in middle-class narrative (*MAm,* 47). "History of a Family's Progress," the final section of *The Making of Americans,* enacts the queer "losing-self sense" of words through repetition and abstraction, implying that so, too, can other forms of queer singularity find representation (*MAm,* 5).[31] In fact, this abstraction emerges directly from the repressive patterns of gender and class that so dominate the earlier history of a family's progress. The narrator has located a kind of queer individuality discernible *only* through middle-class habits of "always the same way of doing" (*MAm,* 47). A methodological reflection from the narrator-writer elaborates on this point:

> Sometimes I like it, almost always I like it when I am feeling many ways of using one word in writing. Sometimes I like it that different ways of

emphasising can make very different meanings in a phrase or sentence
I have made and am rereading. Always in writing it, it is in me only
one thing, a little I like it sometimes that there can be very different
ways of reading the thing I have been writing with only one feeling of
a meaning. (*MAm*, 539)

In taking this using and re-using of "one word" to its ultimate extension,
"History of a Family's Progress" suggests that both narrator and the individual singularity with which she has concerned herself can have "very different meanings," even when conceived with "only one feeling of a meaning."
Does this device secure a queer "vital singularity" in the face of (or even
out of) the repetitiveness of middle-class business and domesticity, formally
modeling a means to be "free each one inside us" (*MAm*, 47)? Lisa Ruddick
notes that the narrator's repetitive style of telling takes "a form of rhythmic
accumulation and release," a form that combines eroticism with the rhythms
of a consumer economy.[32] Beyond this queer eroticism, the novel offers little
response to the whispered chant of "middle-class, middle-class": at the most,
"a little I like it sometimes," readers may say with the narrator. But *The Making
of Americans* does, like Henry James's prefaces, strongly assert the independent, individual agency of a text that refuses to simply reproduce its narrator's "one feeling of a meaning." In a world of categories that seem to lose
meaning, the individuality of the text doggedly retains substance, even as it
registers "mixed" "feeling."[33]

Even with the limited success represented by the queer individuality of
the text, however, *The Making of Americans* cannot purge the alienation that
structured *Three Lives*. For example, it is not clear how the formal elaboration of modes of queer feeling addresses the terror of a once-singular Martha
Hersland, become "Mrs. Redfern," who finds herself trapped in a marriage
characterized by "great gulfs":

> Mrs. Redfern never understood what had happened to her. In a dazed
> blind way she tried all ways of breaking through the walls that con-
> fined her. She threw herself against them with impatient energy and
> again she tried to destroy them piece by piece. She was always thrown
> back bruised and dazed and never quite certain whence came the blow,
> how it was dealt or why. It was a long agony, she never became wiser
> or more indifferent, she struggled on always in the same dazed eager
> way. (*MAm*, 434)

Stein's later-life reflections on *The Making of Americans* take up the question
of how and why this excruciating scene does not exert the same claim in

The Making of Americans as it would have in *Three Lives*. In "The Gradual Making of *The Making of Americans,*" a lecture from the American tour, Stein recounts finding the form of her masterpiece as a process in which her "sentences grew longer and longer, my imaginary dependent clauses were constantly being dropped out" (*GSW,* 278). Stein's lecture reveals the stylistic abstraction pursued by her project as, paradoxically, succeeding at creating an abstractly inclusive system by excluding "dependent clauses." On the one hand, she has grammatically managed the problem of subordination by refusing it; on the other hand, by "dropping out" the dependent clauses, her style reinscribes the very exclusions that preoccupied her in *Three Lives*. The "dependent" beings here abstracted into grammatical clauses are disregarded in the ethnic, gendered, racial, and class particularity that they previously represented; they will not re-emerge until later, with particular forcefulness in Stein's post-American-tour writing, such as *Everybody's Autobiography*.

The years of high Steinian abstraction following the completion of *The Making of Americans* reveal a diffusion of the abstract, mobile individuality that emerges at the end of that great text. In them Stein achieves a literary version of the outlook that James Livingston associates with pragmatist proto-postmodernism: her texts "do not acknowledge an external or natural realm of objects, of things-in-themselves, which is ultimately impervious to, or fundamentally different than, thought or mind or consciousness."[34] *Tender Buttons* (1914) echoes the cadence and style of "History of a Family's Progress" to narrate everyday objects and spaces of consumer and domestic interest, as if to prove that the abstract, textual form of individuality can have similarly liberating effects upon "A Seltzer Bottle," "A Long Dress," "A Red Hat," "Mutton," "Breakfast," "Sugar," and the "Rooms" in which domestic business is transacted. The effect of this text, as with Stein's own domestic life as recounted in *The Autobiography of Alice B. Toklas,* is to suggest that the refrain "middle-class, middle-class" may be sung to very different tunes. Indeed, Stein's work and life did such an excellent job of suggesting the individual liberties possible within the still-conventional systems of market and home, that by 1932 Stein became willing to perform the ultimate melting-pot self-transformation: setting her own "singularity" aside, she would write a false autobiography, as the resolutely practical Alice Toklas. As Ulla E. Dydo suggests, this project was driven by Stein's need for greater market recognition; unwilling to consign herself to the limited audience of Lena's streetcar conductor, fixated on broader circulation, she resolved to write "a best-seller."[35] *The Autobiography of Alice B. Toklas* was serialized in the prestigious *Atlantic Monthly,* and its first American edition of 5,400 copies sold out nine days before the official date of publication.

The publication of *The Autobiography of Alice B. Toklas* transformed Stein from an obscure, parodied literary experimentalist to a central modernist public figure and cultural critic. And yet much of Stein's acutely self-conscious writing of the thirties reminds readers that *Alice B. Toklas* was specifically engineered as a means to fame that Stein planned to translate into publicity and circulation for her earlier, more experimental melting-pot texts. *The Autobiography of Alice B. Toklas* capitalizes on established melting-pot forms of self-dissemination, understanding Stein's experimental forms of the twenties to have "managed" the problems of melting-pot individuality. Only after visiting the United States in 1934–1935 would Stein begin to appreciate how different the problems posed by both individuality and self-dissemination were at mid-century, as opposed to in the Progressive era.

"A Mere Form, Really Everybody Could Come In"

In *The Autobiography of Alice B. Toklas,* "Alice Toklas" telling Gertrude Stein's story (and Stein telling Toklas's story) publicly shares another's cultural material, just like Lena's streetcar conductor. However, *Alice B. Toklas* locates both the autobiography and Stein's more avant-garde experiments squarely within the domestic sphere. (In this sense she returns to the unsolved problem of "Mrs. Redfern" in *The Making of Americans.*) The text positions the Stein-Toklas home at 27, rue de Fleurus as a queer domestic experiment, one driven by a logic parallel to that of settlement houses.[36] In *Alice B. Toklas* Stein demonstrates what *The Making of Americans* theorized: that the story of another can "repeat" one's own story—that individuals intersect and exchange through storytelling, *particularly* storytelling that is embedded in conventional middle-class domestic space.[37] This private space opens out into the public space of the market through the sophisticated forms of cultural barter that characterized Stein and Toklas's salon (as well as through book sales). The relatively untroubled play between public and private that *Alice B. Toklas* sites at 27, rue de Fleurus bespeaks Stein's continued investment in the basic logic of melting-pot individuality. This text models a "well-dressed" queerness—the kind of healthy, socially embedded individuality that melting-pot thinkers imagined emerging from unfettered circulation between market and home.

From the beginning of *The Autobiography of Alice B. Toklas,* 27, rue de Fleurus serves a multitude of functions: as a salon it affirms Gertrude Stein's social-circulatory range by including a wide variety of guests; as a domestic space dominated by the stove it affirms the intimate particularity of the individuals gathered; as an expressive venue it demonstrates Stein's flexibility, as she easily alternates between "talking and listening."[38] In Toklas's recollections,

Stein seems a model of the domestic circulation that Melanctha never fully achieves; further, Stein's exemplary success appears a matter of her innovative approach to *form*.[39] Toklas lingers over the famous ritual with which Stein played the role of hostess at the door of her home:

> She usually opened the door to the knock and the usual formula was, de la part de qui venez-vous, who is your introducer. The idea was that anybody could come but for form's sake and in Paris you have to have a formula, everybody was supposed to be able to mention the name of somebody who had told them about it. It was a mere form, really everybody could come in. (*ABT*, 13)

Stein transforms a ritual of exclusion by reconceiving of the form by which those exclusions were traditionally performed. The "mere form" that she institutes entails negotiating one's individual inclusion through the offering of another's name; it is "mere" form because the identity of the introducer (the content, as it were) is a matter of some indifference, since Stein does not admit based on any priority. One simply does not enter by means of one's own name, but rather by contributing a valued association to the "common fund" being assembled. Even at the doorway Stein has a market in action, exchanging access to the public brokered that evening for a promise of further extension and circulation. When Toklas later says that "Everybody brought somebody," she means it both literally and figuratively (*ABT*, 123). Under these circumstances, the network associated with the atelier extends far beyond the people who are physically present. Guests offer association with themselves and with others farther afield: they signify multiply, as do the objects and rooms that Stein unmoored from their traditional associations in *Tender Buttons*. Toklas's name-dropping disseminates the door-step ritual throughout *Alice B. Toklas,* turning the text into a hall of mirrors, in which names and relations are multiplied and refracted. The "mere form" of this ritual also serves as a reminder that forms, even those as apparently conventional and straightforward as the introduction, are always being recrafted and reperformed; in fact, it is this faith in the malleability of the most conventional and exclusionary of forms that best reflects the optimism of *Alice B. Toklas.*

Toklas's calculatedly accessible voice both depicts and enacts the hospitality of 27, rue de Fleurus; even her incessant name-dropping serves to initiate readers into an expansive social economy. Through what Mark Goble terms "cameos," Stein's text offers intimate access to a wide range of social and cultural contacts: Goble counts "four hundred individuals... mentioned by name."[40] *Alice B. Toklas* avoids the static and isolated individuality of *Three Lives* by putting these names into circulation. As in *The Making of Americans,* this text is structured around individuals, rather than plot; motion, development, emerges from characters. For example, when Toklas first visits the atelier, she is directed by Stein to sit with Fernande Picasso. Toklas's narration thus centers on Fernande: first, Toklas locates herself in the primary scene of her first time at the atelier and her visit with Fernande; then, from her later perspective, she contextualizes her interaction with Fernande as an early episode of sitting with "wives of geniuses," whom Fernande comes to represent; she then describes Fernande further; finally, because Fernande speaks of hats when Toklas first sits with her, Toklas recounts a later episode in which she and Fernande are noticed for their hats (*ABT,* 14). Like the constellation of impressions that forms Cather's *Death Comes for the Archbishop,* these impressions are organized by neither plot nor theme; narrative transitions are guided by the range of associations that Fernande provides for Toklas. In fact, Fernande's influence is so profound that, while her actual conversation with Toklas (about hats) goes unelaborated, its influence steers Toklas's narration toward the later hat episode. Such narrative movements seem no more necessary or overdetermined than the abrupt breaks and veerings of *The Making of Americans.* When the multiple time-frames and topics of the Fernande-centered meditation cede to Toklas's interaction with Matisse, Matisse then influences the direction of the narrative, until Toklas finds herself standing next to Picasso, and so on. The fluidly social form of the text still registers Toklas's distinct individuality, even as it (and she) samples the range and breadth of the cultural influences she circulates with.

As Toklas relates to these densely referential individuals, so *The Autobiography of Alice B. Toklas* relates to other texts; it makes frequent mention of Stein's own writings and those of her peers, without even pretending to exhaust the contents of those texts.[41] In fact, the contents of other texts are a matter of some indifference in *Alice B. Toklas,* for it is the form—of name-dropping, but also the form of the other text—that is at issue in this strategy. These other texts are, in a sense, cameo texts. They situate Stein's novel at the center of an economy of texts, drawing on the full range of reference available in the system. *Toklas* is also studded with unpublished cameo texts, using stories told from different perspectives to extend the circulatory area of its own system. (For example, Toklas recounts the Steins' purchase of the Matisse painting *La Femme au Chapeau* first from the Steins' point of view and then as told by the Matisses. Similarly, the battle of the Marne is described as recounted by both Nellie Jacot and Alfy Maurer, as well as in an unquoted letter from Mildred Aldrich.)

When an account becomes a matter of outright conflict—for example, when Wyndham Lewis and Roger Fry quarrel—Toklas's gloss on the conflict capably demonstrates the indispensable role played by domesticity in this fluid narrative economy. According to Toklas, Lewis and Fry "told exactly the same story only it was different, very different" (*ABT,* 123). Toklas's narration not only promises a space in which these views may be reconciled but also affirms the "different, very different" intimate particularity of the story whose abstract exact sameness emerges in extra-domestic circulatory systems. Throughout the text, Toklas's narration serves the function of pivot by whose action abstract exchangeability gives way to individual difference, and vice versa. In her description of the Lewis-Fry conflict, the different versions of the story merge into an individual, which insistently, and with strange effects upon syntax, is ("was") *singularly* different. In the words of *The Making of Americans,* Toklas's homey narration, her employment of the form of autobiography, pioneers a "singular" experiment by which conventional domestic privacies might admit "queer things like us" (*MAm,* 47).

After all, Toklas played a very traditional domestic role within this "endless variety" (*ABT,* 123). Indeed, one of the purposes of the novel is to insist that the "endless variety" associated with the market can, and must, circulate through the stuffiest middle-class homes. Toklas underlines this variety when she jokes that she has often considered writing a book, "The wives of geniuses I have sat with":

> I have sat with so many. I have sat with wives who were not wives, of geniuses who were real geniuses. I have sat with real wives of geniuses who were not real geniuses. I have sat with wives of geniuses, of near geniuses, of would be geniuses, in short I have sat very often and very long with many wives and wives of many geniuses. (*ABT,* 14)

Although the joke is a simple one, it prompts the kind of blossoming qualification and Steinian wordplay that characterized *The Making of Americans.* Through it, Toklas shows the multiplicity and variability of the people she has made to feel at home in her home. In other words, the very familiarity of Toklas's role within Steinian domesticity constitutes her nodal status. Stein and her geniuses have primary rapports of similarity and shared interests. Toklas's queer wifeliness consists instead of weaving social compatibility out of secondary relations. The riff quoted above elaborates on the many ways in which her "many wives and wives of geniuses" do not align perfectly with each other; ultimately, however, they all deal with her and, as a result, circulate and exchange through her. For this reason, the queer domestic partner forms the basis of the market-networked individuality proposed by *The Autobiography of Alice B. Toklas.* Because her relation to Stein is queer, Toklas has no, and so can offer no, "pure" and unmediated relation to those she entertains.

Indeed, even the Toklas–narrator's relation to Stein (and the reader's relation to Stein) is "singular." *The Autobiography of Alice B. Toklas* famously ends with Stein unmasking as narrator: the merged Stein-Toklas voice models the experimental nodal form proposed by the novel.[42]

The infectious optimism of *The Autobiography of Alice B. Toklas* translated into wide circulation for this most approachable Steinian experiment. (Even before, when the newspapers decried her writing as "appalling," she notes, her "sentences" did "get under their skin": she was quoted, circulating in all her queer singularity, while other writers were merely paraphrased [*ABT,* 70].) In the two years between September 1934 and October 1936, Stein saw her market vastly enlarged: she spoke on national radio, appeared in a newsreel, and published thirteen articles in *Vanity Fair, Cosmopolitan,* the *New York Herald Tribune,* and the *Saturday Evening Post.* In these public statements, as well as in the lectures delivered during her American tour of 1934–1935, Stein exploited her ever-increasing visibility just as anyone familiar with *Alice B. Toklas's* circuits of exchange would expect. However, as many critics have noted, Stein's reactions to popular culture and the mass media shifted as time passed.

As Stein chronicles in her newspaper writings of the 1930s and in *Everybody's Autobiography* (1937), thirties America offered new challenges for melting-pot thinkers. To one who had returned after a long absence, the culture seemed to have been unnervingly made over by just the kind of philosophy that melting-pot Progressives had been pushing at the turn of the century. The public range of the self had been expanded by opening up the private sphere to circulation, just as Stein had long proposed. Celebrities connected the masses, just as she had attempted to do in *The Autobiography of Alice B. Toklas.* Stein's opinion, however, began to resemble that of Walter Lippmann, who in *The Phantom Public* (1925) argued that by relying on "executive" functions Americans had disrupted "a most intricate mechanism of exchange, of contract, of custom and of implied promises."[43] She concluded that the culture of celebrity in fact demonstrated how displaying and circulating certain private selves would endanger both the individual-form and the market.

The U.S. tour initiates a dramatic shift in Stein's agenda, one in which she subjects her ideas, especially her inherited melting-pot premises, to intense scrutiny, and ruthlessly dispenses with anything that threatens to encroach upon the circulatory capacities that melting-pot thinkers had theorized through market metaphors. As I will argue below, this purge serves to preserve the formal innovativeness that Stein, along with other melting-pot thinkers, had long associated with cultural exchange and malleability. The purge also, however, dismantles and dispenses with many components of the traditional melting-pot model: Stein shrugs off the concerns about alienation and exclusion that color so many of her earlier texts, and ends by even proclaiming her indifference to the figure of the individual through which earlier melting-pot theories of formal innovation had been brokered. As a result, what emerges from Stein's American tour is a peculiarly maimed melting-pot modernism; it is also, however, an evocative example of how the particulate nature of the theory lent to its being taken apart and smuggled into the newer ideological and aesthetic formations of mid-century.

Knowing "Any One from the Outside"

According to *Everybody's Autobiography,* when Stein arrived in America there was every indication that she was well served by her visibility. *Everybody's Autobiography* describes Americans greeting Stein as she walks through the streets, suggesting to her "how pleasantly New York was like Bilignin where in the country everybody says how do you do in passing like they do in any country place" (*EA,* 149). In other words, a celebrity-obsessed New York may not be home, but it serves the same particularizing purposes as a home. In Stein's account, her fame transforms a large and alienating city into what John Dewey terms a "face-to-face" community, where beings circulate in individuated relation.[44] This New York is quite different from Henry James's. However, Stein produced two versions of this anecdote, and their differences telegraph her shifting feelings about the extent to which media celebrity could be trusted to solve the problems of melting-pot individuality. The first version, published as "I Came and Here I Am" in *Cosmopolitan* of February 1936, describes being recognized on the street as "comfortable," "comforting," "pleasant," and "natural," words which repeat several times in this version.[45] In *Everybody's Autobiography,* Stein drops the language of comfort and pleasure. The text draws a clear line from Stein's diminished ease and enthusiasm to her analysis of the American celebrity industry.[46]

The circulation-enhancing celebrity postulated by *The Autobiography of Alice B. Toklas* was, after all, still mostly theoretical (even if it was more referential than *The Making of Americans*). Following the melting-pot logic of an individuality particularized through the home and circulated through the market, celebrity culture seemed to promise to fuse domestic intimacy with market mobility. Stein's writings of the American tour do testify to the remarkably integrated public of thirties mass culture and mass consumption. However, these writings also articulate a new and unforeseen anxiety: privacy, that form of "vital singularity" traditionally grounded in the separate space of the home, seemed endangered by this public. Both *The Geographical History of America* (1936) and *Everybody's Autobiography* suggest that Stein began to understand even her own access to individuality as mediated through the persona she had assumed for mass circulation. This experience was, to say the least, alienating. As she approached her own person through the eyes of her public, she found it newly resistant to queer and innovative forms of representation: more straightforwardly, she suffered writer's block, for the first time in her life. Endangered privacy, it seems, also meant endangered formal experimentalism. The generally unremarkable *form* of *Everybody's Autobiography* follows from the incompatibility that Stein perceived between celebrity-selfhood and formal experimentation. Like so many of the texts we have considered here, this text embeds its engagement with melting-pot questions in its form—Stein's anxiety about the stalling of formal experimentalism simply results in a far less showy production than usual. *Everybody's Autobiography* samples from Stein's mass-media writings the way Johnson's prefaces sampled from one another, but in Stein's case this citation communicates the attenuated state of innovation in a celebrity culture.

Stein's American tour also confronted her with more practical questions about the viability of her earlier formal experiments. The queer domesticated market that she had postulated in *The Autobiography of Alice B. Toklas,* for example, did not perform as she had anticipated in her celebrity-hungry plans. The market for her individual image was robust, but the market for her more singular experiments remained flat (despite her best efforts she still couldn't really move *The Making of Americans*); the modes of media exchange for which she had such hopes in fact fiercely resisted the reformed individualities theorized in *The Making of Americans.*[47]

In the preface to *Everybody's Autobiography,* Stein describes an episode through which she began to grasp the limited nature of the media celebrity she had expected to use to advance her integrative program. At a party, Mary Pickford suggests that they be photographed together. There is general excitement over the idea, and then suddenly Pickford backs off. Stein, surprised,

> asked every one because I was interested just what it was that went on inside Mary Pickford. It was her idea and then when I was enthusiastic she melted away. They all said that what she thought was if I were enthusiastic it meant that I thought that it would do me more good than it would do her and so she melted away or others said perhaps after all it would not be good for her audiences that we should be photographed together, anyway I was very much interested to know just what they knew about what is good publicity and what is not. (*EA*, xxv)

Pickford is not just another Lena to have her story shared on the streetcar, it seems. The movie star's careful policing of her image suggests to Stein that publicity circuits of exchange can be just as constrictive, if not as obviously limited, as the old versions of the market and the household. Stein the amateur imagines that this photo would humorously underline the alignments and divergences of two famous individuals, reinforcing their particularity as it combines and extends their audiences. However, Pickford the professional has no more interest in combining her brand-persona with Stein's than Henry Cabot Lodge would have had in sharing cultural "gifts" with a turn-of-the-century immigrant. As an old hand at the celebrity game, Pickford teaches Stein about the way exclusion constitutes the individuals of the world of publicity just as surely as it did those of the melting pot and the immigrant labor market. Operating under traditional possessive-individualist assumptions, Pickford protects "her" market: no queer circulations wanted here.

Stein positions the Pickford incident in the preface to *Everybody's Autobiography* because it shows the ease with which markets can be manipulated and restricted; it suggests that the experience of celebrity will transform Stein's understandings of individuality and circulation. When she is freshly arrived in America, Stein's ideas of individuality still retain their turn-of-the-century melting-pot origins in marketplace metaphors: Stein imagines that under ideal conditions individuals and cultural material will circulate as freely as, in theory, money does.[48] (She is not totally alone in esteeming this form of circulation: the miser represents a powerfully corrupt figure in Cather's *Death Comes for the Archbishop* for just this reason.) The encounter with Pickford suggests to Stein that the economy may, in fact, easily segment, with individual exchanges confined to rigidly delimited circles. The Pickford scene stages an important choice for Stein: she may see this impulse toward segmentation as the nature of the market, and thus retain the importance of the individual-figure, while implying that valuing the market so highly may be a mistake; or she may see this impulse toward segmentation as the fault of the individual, and thus retain the importance of the market, while implying that valuing the individual-form so highly may be a mistake. Stein chooses the market over the individual. She interprets Pickford's behavior at the party as an inappropriate exercise of will, a form of market-tampering protectionism, a repudiation of the circulatory potential of a "free" market.

An interview conducted during the American tour suggests *why* Stein chooses the market over the individual, and it does so by demonstrating the continued relevance of melting-pot thinking to her literary and political imagination. In this interview, Stein associates her free-market ideology with formal experimentalism: "Building a Chinese wall is always bad," she explains to her interviewer. "Protection, paternalism and suppression of natural activity and competition lead to dullness and stagnation. It is true in politics, in literature, in art." "Chinese wall" acts here as the shorthand by which an ex-Californian refers simultaneously to economic protectionism and immigration restriction. Stein continues the interview by associating "competition" with the immigration question (which was, of course, by 1934, no longer really "the immigration question"):

> I do not approve of the stringent immigration laws in America today. We need the stimulation of new blood. It is best to favor healthy competition. There is no reason why we should not select our immigrants with greater care, nor why we should not bar certain peoples and preserve the color line, for instance. But if we shut down on immigration completely we shall become stagnant. The French may not like the competition of foreigners, but they let them in. They accept the challenge and derive the stimulus. I am surprised that there is not more discussion of immigration in the United States than there is.[49]

Some of Stein's priorities are holdovers from the melting-pot era, notably her defense of immigration and her association of "competition" with "stimulation," or, as we have seen, market circulation with formal innovativeness. In this interview Stein makes no indication that these melting-pot priorities might be incompatible with other propositions—"careful selection," or "bar[ring] certain peoples and preserv[ing] the color line," which resonate with particularly harsh restrictionism. The anxiety, the critique, the proposed emendations, from *Three Lives* to *Alice B. Toklas*—all fall aside in light of the lessons of 1930s America, in light of the imperative to craft a market that will not be distorted by individual tampering and opt-outs. What emerges here is a streamlined Steinian melting-pot modernism, and a cautionary example of the capacities and the limits of melting-pot thinking.

Stein's commitment to the melting-pot premise of free-market circulation is most clear in a series of essays on money published in the *Saturday Evening Post* in 1936; one can literally watch, here, as Stein determines to cast off the extraneous social commitments of melting-pot thinking.[50] The views articulated in these essays, which many critics justifiably considered reactionary, become more interesting when seen in light of Stein's ongoing negotiations of a melting-pot understanding of individuality: they affirm her belief that (in James Livingston's words) "money functions as mind or language functions under the sign of Enlightenment: it is strictly a medium of exchange, by which the correspondence between unlike things—the underlying unity of particular objects—is realized."[51] In "Money," Stein argues against government taxing and spending by declaring that such activity does not "know that money is money."[52] Her objection to such delegated spending is continuous with her sense of the problematic nature of Anna's use of her employer's name and purse in *Three Lives:* the delegate spender enters the economy not as a free individual constituted by market exchange, but as one pledged to represent the interests of another, thereby limiting the kinds of contact and exchange made possible by "money." Stein's essay attempts to restrict the legitimate spending of money to those who have earned it, reasoning that earners "really know that money is money," that is, know at first hand that money is a signifier as abstract and mobile as the phrases in *The Making of Americans* and the objects in *Tender Buttons.*[53] (*The Geographical History of America* confirms this association of money with words.) "All About Money" argues that consumer uses of money make visible the particularity of this abstract concept ("four dollars and fifty-five cents or four hundred and eighty-nine dollars"), while government spending never grasps that particularity ("when government votes money it is always even money. One or five or fifteen or thirty-six more or less does not make any difference").[54] In each of these cases, the government's status as a delegate spender distorts the operations of the market; in keeping with this theory, Stein repudiates welfare spending in defense of individual particularity and market circulation.

As Michael Szalay suggests, Stein's interest in money was bound up with her commitment to literary form.[55] The famous conclusion to her lecture "What Is English Literature," in which Stein invokes the writer's conflict between "serving god and mammon," nicely adumbrates the aesthetic politics behind the free-market rhetoric of her tour (*GSW,* 222). According to her, writing "the way writing has already been written" entails serving mammon, the false god of riches and avarice, "because you are living by something some one has already been earning or has earned"; far better, to her, is writing "as you are to be writing," which entails "serving as a writer god because you are not earning anything" (*GSW,* 223). Stein's notorious indifference to punctuation transforms the writer who does not earn into a kind of god ("a writer god"), here: a god faithful to her own free-market politics. To write conventionally is akin to taxing and spending as a government, for one draws on another's tropes and forms, and thus one is bound to represent that other's interests. The writer who writes "as you are to be writing" (in the present, that is) does not "know what earning is," for her writing is aimed at circulation rather than accumulation (*GSW,* 223).

Stein's essay "Still More About Money" introduces a bogey into her paeans to unfettered market operations, however. Here she targets organized unemployment, claiming that it cultivates an affective allegiance to the state of unemployment and thus creates a consensual group identity that limits the individual's willingness to circulate back into the labor market. Walter Lippmann had identified new consensual group identities as a phenomenon of the twenties, seeing in them a return to individualism following the failure of the "omnivorous state" in the First World War: this new individualism, Lippmann argued, was not "the atomic individualism of Adam Smith's economic man," but "a sort of molecular individualism of voluntary groups."[56] Stein is concerned with this "molecular individualism of voluntary groups" (which we might recognize as related to Kallen-style pluralism), seeing it as continuous with Mary Pickford's segmentation of audiences and kinds of publicity. Pickford's affect is invested in creating and maintaining separations that limit the circulatory potential of the market; at the other end of the social spectrum, the unemployed invest similar affect in what seems to Stein like their own separation from the market. How can the celebrity and the unemployed share this affect, this cultural value, when (according to Stein's formal scheme from *Toklas*) one is a nodal figure and the other excluded? Could this shared commitment to separate identities and limited circulation be the paradoxical legacy of melting-pot visions of cultural sharing? If so, then the parts of melting-pot thinking that Stein considered problematic or dispensable seemed to have become the basis for a shared culture. Stein saw the alienation she had represented in *Three Lives* reconfigured as affectively positive, as identity, something worth affirming and protecting from the recombinatory impulses of the market.

For Stein the miscarriage of the melting pot is finally an aesthetic issue, one born in and borne out by representation. Indeed, an article she published in the *New York Herald Tribune* in March 1935 elaborates on the representational toxicity of mass culture:

> in America they all learn to know any one from the outside, any one gets into the newspapers... there is practically no one who does not sometime find himself and his name printed in a paper. So many people's pictures are in the paper so many people talk through the radio or sing through it or do something in it and it all makes them know themselves as any one outside knows it.[57]

Stein acknowledges here that the media-celebrity circuits she discovered in the Pickford interaction give every indication of being inclusive. Great masses of people are "individualized" through these circuits; however, they circulate in conventional systems, learning to read themselves and others from the outside. They know individuality as an audience—or, as *The Geographical History of America* puts it, as a little dog—would, or as one looking in the mirror

would. The individual consciousness that Stein anatomizes in this essay falls
well short of the double-consciousness that melting-pot thinkers imagined.
The beings Stein decries, like little dogs, see *only* as audience members, *only*
from the outside, according to Stein: they do not experience "vital" singularity, or subjectivity as a site for conflicting, colliding, combining perspectives. The individual particularity theoretically afforded by the affective ties
of the domestic sphere has eroded in a culture of publicity: looking through
the eyes of others—of a passive audience, agreeably segmented into coherent blocks—now produces a coherent and bounded sense of self. The effect
of the melting-pot invitation of the masses into intimate spaces has simply
been the gutting of privacy and the attenuation of "vital singularity" in the
subjectively experienced self.

Stein's post-tour autobiography thus becomes an absurdist enactment of the
limiting nature of the individuality so central to melting-pot thinking. Stein
explains the changed artistic status of individuality in the following terms:

> now individual anything as related to every other individual is to me
> no longer interesting. At that time [the composition of *The Making of
> Americans*] I did not realise that the earth is completely covered over
> with every one. In a way it was not then because every one was in a
> group and a group was separated from every other one, and so the
> character of every one was interesting because they were in relation but
> now since the earth is all covered over with every one there is really no
> relation between any one and so if this Everybody's Autobiography is
> to be the autobiography of every one it is not to be of any connection
> between any one and any one because now there is none. (*EA*, 80)

To presume to translate Stein into the terms of my own argument, she dates
her concern with "individual anything" to the melting-pot era, when the
challenge faced by intellectuals was that of incorporating individual members
of "groups" (immigrants from different cultures, as well as African American migrants). Her tour reveals that the primary objective of melting-pot
Progressives seems to be accomplished: groupings seem for the most part
to be consensual, not coercive, and the mass culture of the thirties blankets
the earth, enabling her fans to recognize her as soon as she lands in New
York. Here she registers the "physical annihilation of space" that Dewey
associated—positively—with the modern era (*DE*, 86). However, in the
context of such complete assimilation, the old questions are suddenly revealed
as mistakes. Stein sees mass culture as creating a deadening experience of
personhood, one consonant, ironically, with melting-pot ideas of individuality; her text both exhibits and decries the effects of this culture. Individual

adjacency, even when it cites the circulatory individuality theorized by melt-ing-pot thinkers, is "really no relation," she argues, really not the kind of contact and exchange that interested her. An autobiography of "everybody" both reflects and performs the paradoxical effects of successful assimilation: selfhood understood from the "outside," limited circulation, attenuated for-mal experimentalism. Such a project cannot hold Stein's attention for long.

It is worth comparing Stein's thirties writings with John Dewey's late-twenties response to the post-Progressive crisis of individuality. Unlike Stein and Walter Lippmann, who in different ways conceded the defeat of turn-of-the-century conceptions of the democratic individual, Dewey contin-ued to criticize what he saw as corporate capitalism's false conflict between individual and society. His *Individualism Old and New* (1929) argues that at mid-century the Progressive version of the melting-pot individual had been compromised by an individual*ism* centered on negative liberties:

> It is difficult for us to conceive of individualism except in terms of stereotypes derived from former centuries. Individualism has been identified with ideas of initiative and invention that are bound up with private and exclusive economic gain. As long as this conception pos-sesses our minds, the ideal of harmonizing our thought and desire with the realities of present social conditions will be interpreted to mean accommodation and surrender. It will even be understood to signify rationalization of the evils of existing society. A stable recovery of indi-viduality waits upon an elimination of the older economic and politi-cal individualism, an elimination which will liberate imagination and endeavor for the task of making corporate society contribute to the free culture of its members. Only by economic revision can the sound ele-ment in the older individualism—equality of opportunity—be made a reality.[58]

Insisting on the "elimination" of old-fashioned individualism and commit-ting to "revision" and "free culture," Dewey sounds a lot like Stein of the American tour. However, he indicts laissez-faire economics along with indi-vidualism: the market is the form he proposes to revise most extensively. As I have shown, Stein's passionate commitment to the free operation of the markets can in large part be traced to her investment in their metaphorical capacities. Markets interest her because they trope her aesthetic and philo-sophical designs; for this reason, revising the market itself entails a boring and ultimately pointless project for her. (If one's aim is to "liberate imagi-nation and endeavor," why bother fussing with the market, if it was only ever a figure for the free circulation one aspired to?) Together, Dewey and

Stein adumbrate the thirties dissolution of the Progressives' Kantian bargain: aesthetic innovations no longer seem to offer solutions to the problems of liberal political theory. Dewey pursues innovation in social form, Stein pursues innovation in aesthetic form, and the strands of melting-pot synthesis are effectively uncoupled.[59]

By the late thirties, Stein salvages the ideals of formal contact and exchange only by purging her work of the individual-form that melting-pot thinking associated so closely with those ideals. Perhaps this utilitarian approach marks her as faithful to the relentlessly adaptive ethos embraced by melting-pot thinking. Certainly her radical late-career disassembly of melting-pot philosophy suggests how this cluster of Progressive ideas began to break down at mid-century, and how, fragmented and uncredited, it might still be traced in many late-century approaches to culture and aesthetics. We have felt that we might dismiss the melting pot as a benighted concept of the turn of the century, but it turns out that this nexus of ideas was both more sophisticated and more resilient than we might imagine. Even when we do not easily recognize their traces, melting-pot ideas often form the foundations of the intellectual and aesthetic movements of the mid- and late century.

Whether one traces one's intellectual lineage to Stein, as so many contemporary feminists do, to Franz Boas, as so many contemporary students of culture do, or even to Horace Kallen and Randolph Bourne, the ardent anti-assimilationists, as so many contemporary scholars of ethnicity do, there is much to be gained from recognizing the traces of melting-pot thinking that persist in these positions. To begin with, the intellectual struggles of the melting-pot generation can inform contemporary attempts to be open to difference and diversity. More specifically, attentiveness to the ways in which modernism and melting-pot thinking intertwine must produce a cultural criticism that is alive to the power of literary nuance. Stein's work shows us that the linguistic and often figural energies in melting-pot discourse account for its ability to self-transform and insinuate itself into cognate discourses, and therefore for its historical staying power. Until we become self-conscious about the ways in which these linguistic and figural energies continue to circulate, we will not only make mistakes when reading Stein, we will also make mistakes reading ourselves and our contemporary moment. The history we perform must be formal and literary as well as documentary, in other words. The aesthetic intensity of our objects often constitutes their intellectual and historical intensity; reading with an eye to that intensity, we will not find resolution, but rather a resistance to resolution that will compel us to keep our thinking supple.

Afterword

Melting-Pot Histories of the Present

> Instead of thoughts of concrete things patiently fol-
> lowing one another in a beaten track of habitual
> suggestion, we have the most abrupt cross-cuts and
> transitions from one idea to another, the most rarefied
> abstractions and discriminations, the most unheard-of
> combinations of elements, the subtlest associations
> of analogy; in a word, we seem suddenly introduced
> into a seething caldron of ideas, where everything is
> fizzing and bobbing about in a state of bewildering
> activity, where partnerships can be joined or loosened
> in an instant.
>
> —William James, "Great Men and Their
> Environment," 1880

      The majority of literary and historical studies today are influenced by a "cultural turn"—a turn that has reconfigured the academy over the course of the last twenty to thirty years and that uses a range of broadly conceived artistic materials to pursue a variety of intellectual projects. The melting pot represents an important early version of such a cultural turn, and though it is by no means the only origin-point of this contemporary cultural turn, it does instructively model some ways in which a cultural turn might offer access to "the most abrupt cross-cuts and transitions from one idea to another, the most rarefied abstractions and discriminations, the most unheard-of combinations of elements, the subtlest associations of analogy." In fact, melting-pot thinkers of the turn of the twentieth century offer an important methodological adjustment to much contemporary cultural criticism. Contemporary literary and historical studies with cultural bents too often slight the ideological flexibility most apparent through the fine grain of a text's aesthetic devices. The earlier cultural turn, by contrast, premised its ideological recombinations on an understanding that literary logics animate a wide range of cultural materials: as a result, melting-pot works from sociological treatises to Tin Pan Alley jingles reward careful, poetry-grade analysis. Work is already underway to re-infuse historically oriented scholarship with literary attentiveness (Marjorie Levenson's recent essay "What Is New Formalism?" provides an indispensable overview of such work).[1] *Melting-Pot Modernism* is meant to evoke one of the historical, political, and philosophical antecedents available to us as we attempt to create scholarship that is both methodologically and thematically "integrative."

In its openness to ideological flexibility, the early twentieth-century cultural turn carried within it the potential *undoing* of identitarian and nationalist logics. (This is not surprising, given its emergence from the relentlessly assimilative melting pot.) Far from defining boundaries of identity, nationality, culture, or text (as the contemporary cultural turn has too often been used to do), then, the earliest cultural turn was seen as a means of revealing the inconsistency of such boundaries, the possibility of James's "partnerships...joined or loosened in an instant." *Melting-Pot Modernism* begins the job of reacquainting us with earlier thinkers who conceived of nation, race, self, and text as constructs whose porosity was best revealed by "culture," and culture, in turn, as something operating according to the powerful, though inconsistent, associative logics of literature. Rather than reading literature as we might read another kind of text, in other words, the melting pot teaches us to extend literary reading skills as widely as possible, because these skills allow us to trace the unexpected links stretching across conceptual boundaries.

I do not mean to recommend that we should uncritically embrace the fusionism represented by the melting pot (even if—indeed, because—it does constitute an important antecedent for contemporary critical aspirations). As literary and historical scholarship increasingly turns to post-national themes, to hemispheric studies, to the study of transnationalism and trans-Atlantic movements, organizations, and contacts, to the critique of ideological investments in categories of nation or other neo-imperial categories, we must attend especially carefully to the cautionary lessons implicit in the voraciously assimilative outlooks of our melting-pot predecessors. To have the scholarly pendulum swing from a single-minded pursuit of difference to an equally single-minded pursuit of boundary-crossing serves no one. We must, in Wai Chee Dimock's terms, be alert to literature's capacity to intertwine "local circumstances" and "global circuits," but we must also look to past fusionist literary projects in order to separate what is valuable in this apparent intertwining from what is treacherous (in the sense of being imperialistic or even Pollyanna-ish).[2] Acknowledging the ways in which melting-pot ideas of fusion continue to haunt our current critical preoccupations represents a first step in that critical agenda.

William James used the figure of the caldron to underline the containment that enables our recognition of the most "unheard-of combinations" of ideas. Intellectual fusions are traced along certain lines, and pursued within certain spheres, whether the limits of those lines and spheres are acknowledged or not. The project of intellectual synthesis conducted here has been bounded by a national sphere within which the melting pot was conceptualized. Because the nation-state exercises legislative power in often coercive ways, it has recently received deserved critique from scholars. Many, if not most, melting-pot thinkers saw a nation-based outlook as a matter of intellectual, emotional, or legislative convenience: for them the nation was more a useful cultural construct than a natural or necessary boundary. Other melting-pot thinkers saw the nation-based aspect of legislation and the judiciary (especially as they regulated immigration and segregation), of public programs (such as education), and even of publishing media as enabling discursive fusions that would have been impossible in other contexts. Whether imagined as inessential or as essential, the nation was the enabling construct of the melting pot, as opposed to ethnicity, language, or hemisphere, and by virtue of that the fictions of the melting pot strengthen the fiction of the nation. The limitations of this·aspiration to exceed boundaries are more representative than exceptional, but for that very reason they merit our continued analysis.

In the final instance, I am not interested in either vindicating or condemning melting-pot thinking. On the one hand, I recognize melting-pot modernism as innovating in the kinds of boundary-troubling that current scholarship justifiably values; on the other hand, this history offers new cautions about the limits left untroubled by such an impulse. I cannot pretend to be able to resolve this conflict here, and not only because I value the ethos of non-resolution practiced by so many melting-pot thinkers. Any intellectual and aesthetic movement that resonates beyond its own moment does so because of its depth and complexity: the very elements that make for its long-term viability also militate against definitive judgment. Rather than providing intellectual prescriptions, therefore, *Melting-Pot Modernism* aims to illuminate the traps, blind spots, and opportunities that melting-pot thinking bequeathed to us. I understand this book as a critical beginning, an offering of new, if inconclusive, information about the surprising foundations of contemporary critical practice. In their willful resistance to the programmatic, to closure, to ideological certainty, melting-pot thinkers opened critical debates that we have not yet succeeded in concluding and that Edwidge Danticat, Junot Díaz, Aleksandar Hemon, and other contemporary writers continue to refine in our own moment.

That said, whether this project of boundary-destabilization extends beyond the realm of literature and into the world of pragmatic political effects (as both the melting-pot generation and our own critical generation seem to wish it to) is questionable: to make the logical bases of an activity (such as the practice of identity politics, say) incoherent is not the same thing as to make it impossible. History has shown the strategies of melting-pot modernism, at least, to be amenable to many subsequent projects that do not necessarily reconcile with their reformist origins. That is one price of an intellectual movement that values the fluidity of the literary so highly. It also, however, constitutes the endless surprise and reward of scholarship that attends to the nuances of the discursive realm.

❧ Notes

Introduction

1. To give a sense of the enormousness that this infusion represented, it should be noted that the population of the United States was just under 63 million in 1890. By 1910 more than 1 in 7 Americans were foreign-born. U.S. Bureau of the Census, *Historical Statistics of the United States, Colonial Times to 1970* (Washington, DC, 1975).

2. For a history of the immigration debates in the United States, see John Higham's *Strangers in the Land: Patterns of American Nativism, 1860–1925* (New Brunswick, NJ: Rutgers University Press, 1955).

3. Mary Antin, *They Who Knock at Our Gates: A Complete Gospel of Immigration* (Boston: Houghton Mifflin, 1914), 8–9.

4. Vida Scudder, *A Listener in Babel: Being a Series of Imaginary Conversations Held at the Close of the Last Century and Reported* (Boston: Houghton Mifflin, 1903), 80–81.

5. Israel Zangwill, *The Melting-Pot* (1914; New York: Macmillan, 1920), 203; further references will be cited as *MP.*

6. Robert E. Park, "Racial Assimilation in Secondary Groups With Particular Reference to the Negro," *American Journal of Sociology* 19 (March 1914), 606.

7. James Livingston, *Pragmatism and the Political Economy of Cultural Revolution, 1850–1940* (Chapel Hill: University of North Carolina Press, 1994), 176.

8. Walter Lippmann, *Drift and Mastery: An Attempt to Diagnose the Current Unrest* (Madison: University of Wisconsin Press, 1985), 118.

9. Philip Gleason, *Speaking of Diversity: Language and Ethnicity in Twentieth-Century America* (Baltimore: Johns Hopkins University Press, 1992); Werner Sollors, *Beyond Ethnicity: Consent and Descent in American Culture* (New York: Oxford University Press, 1986).

10. On this oscillation between the typical and the particular as constituting literary interest, see Steven Knapp, *Literary Interest: The Limits of Anti-Formalism* (Cambridge: Harvard University Press, 1993).

11. "The sense of the elements in the cauldron — the cauldron of the 'American' character — becomes thus about as vivid a thing as you can at all quietly manage, and the question settles into a form which makes the intelligible answer further and further recede." Henry James, *The American Scene* (1907; New York: Penguin, 1994), 92; further references will be cited as *AS.*

12. Matthew Jacobson, *Whiteness of a Different Color: European Immigrants and the Alchemy of Race* (Cambridge: Harvard University Press, 1998), and *Barbarian Virtues: The United States Encounters Foreign Peoples at Home and Abroad, 1876–1917* (New York: Hill and Wang, 2000); Gary Gerstle, *American Crucible: Race and Nation in the Twentieth Century* (Princeton: Princeton University Press, 2002).

13. James Livingston, *Pragmatism, Feminism, and Democracy: Rethinking the Politics of American History* (New York: Routledge, 2001), 11.

14. Here I'd like to echo George Hutchinson's argument that, "while acknowledging stereotypical views of African Americans [and, for my purposes, immigrants and "ethnic" Americans] as pervasive in even the most 'progressive' writing of the period (often by blacks as well as whites), [my method] necessarily shifts the focus of attention from these factors—which have received voluminous treatment in other important studies—in order to allow different, previously marginalized factors to emerge, factors that were of the first importance to everyone involved in the cultural drama being played out and that remain, I believe, of the first importance to understanding the politics of American cultural identity today. My partiality to intentionally egalitarian racial efforts, intimacies, and commitments in the United States, my belief in their efficacy and necessity, will be obvious to all and will be shared, perhaps, by only a few. That such relationships usually (and predictably) fall short of ideological purity, 'true' equality, and complete dialogue seems to me less significant than that they work at all in a culture so patently hostile to their existence... We must go beyond abstract judgment to validate *and* critique those active crossings that, however imperfect, open a path and create new opportunities for principled action." *The Harlem Renaissance in Black and White* (Cambridge: Harvard University Press, 1995), 27.

15. Philip J. Ethington, *The Public City: The Political Construction of Urban Life in San Francisco, 1850–1900* (Cambridge: Cambridge University Press, 1994), 288. That said, U.S. Progressives were mostly, but not exclusively, bourgeois, white, educated, from Protestant backgrounds, and born between the Civil War and the end of Reconstruction; responding to the rapid industrialization, urbanization, and national and transnational migrations of the end of the nineteenth century, they had grown unwilling to accept a society shaped by laissez-faire capitalism. For a fuller articulation of what Progressives shared (in terms of both background and beliefs), see Wilson Carey McWilliams, "Standing at Armageddon: Morality and Religion in Progressive Thought," in *Progressivism and the New Democracy,* ed. Sidney M. Milkis and Jerome M. Mileur (Amherst: University of Massachusetts Press, 1999), 103–25. Eldon J. Eisenach argues that American Progressive reforms reflected the "hegemonic" ambitions of a particular class, their desire to completely transform the "intellectual and moral culture" of the United States. In this sense, electoral reform, for example, was not so much its own end as it was a means of telegraphing an ideological message: that politics was not a game, bounded by an arbitrary set of rules, but was derived from and guided by certain principles. Eldon J. Eisenach, *The Lost Promise of Progressivism* (Lawrence: University Press of Kansas, 1994), 26–27.

16. Daniel T. Rodgers, "In Search of Progressivism," *Reviews in American History* 10.4 (December 1982), 114.

17. What has been called this group's revolt against formal*ism* entailed an insistence that mechanical, external reforms were of themselves inadequate; formal change remained critical, but it had to be associated with thoroughgoing change, just as the look in the face of Henry James's "sensitive citizen" was. See Morton White, *Social Thought in America: The Revolt against Formalism* (New York: Viking, 1949).

18. James T. Kloppenberg, *Uncertain Victory: Social Democracy and Progressivism in European and American Thought, 1870–1920* (New York: Oxford University Press, 1986), 6.

19. See "Towards a Definition of American Modernism," *American Quarterly* 39.1 (Spring 1987), 7–26.

20. "Ethnic writers, alerted to cultural clashes, may feel the need for new forms earlier or more intensely than mainstream authors. Furthermore, the rhetoric of ethnicity…has militated in favor of consent and the 'new' and thus supported drives toward formal innovation." Sollors also notes that some immigrants brought with them a familiarity with "modernist" aesthetic tendencies more developed on the continent. See *Beyond Ethnicity,* 247–48. See also Sollors's "Ethnic Modernism," in *The Cambridge History of American Literature,* Vol. 6, ed. Sacvan Bercovitch (Cambridge: Cambridge University Press, 2002), 353–556; or *Ethnic Modernism* (Cambridge: Harvard University Press, 2008).

21. Peter Nicholls, *Modernisms: A Literary Guide* (Berkeley: University of California Press, 1995), 4.

22. On this point, see Jonathan Freedman's argument that assimilation structures depictions of Jewishness in modernist fictions: "Lessons Out of School: T. S. Eliot's Jewish Problem and the Making of Modernism," *Modernism/Modernity* 10.3 (September 2003), 419–29, and *The Temple of Culture: Assimilation and Anti-Semitism in Literary Anglo-America* (New York: Oxford University Press, 2000).

23. Walter Benn Michaels, *Our America: Nativism, Modernism, and Pluralism* (Durham: Duke University Press, 1995); Michael North, *The Dialect of Modernism: Race, Language, and Twentieth-Century Literature* (New York: Oxford University Press, 1994); Ross Posnock, *Color and Culture: Black Writers and the Making of the Modern Intellectual* (Cambridge: Harvard University Press, 1998); Ann Douglas, *Terrible Honesty: Mongrel Manhattan in the 1920s* (Farrar, Straus and Giroux, 1995).

24. Priscilla Wald, *Constituting Americans: Cultural Anxiety and Narrative Form* (Durham: Duke University Press, 1995).

25. On the mutual imbrication of form and cultural history, see Elizabeth Maddock Dillon, "Fear of Formalism: Kant, Twain, and Cultural Studies in American Literature," *diacritics* 27.4 (1998), 46–69; Rita Felski, "Modernist Studies and Cultural Studies: Reflections on Method," *Modernism/Modernity* 10.3 (September 2003), 501–17; the special issue "Reading for Form," *MLQ* 61.1 (2000), ed. Susan Wolfson; and Marianne DeKoven, "The Politics of Modernist Form," *New Literary History* 23 (1992), 675–90.

26. Sara Blair, "Modernism and the Politics of Culture," in *The Cambridge Companion to Modernism,* ed. Michael Levenson (Cambridge: Cambridge University Press, 1999), 158.

27. Henry James, "Preface to *The Ambassadors*" in *The Art of the Novel: Critical Prefaces* (New York: Scribner's, 1934), 326; Jane Addams, *Twenty Years at Hull-House* (New York: Macmillan, 1910), 125–26, emphasis added.

28. Gertrude Stein, "Composition as Explanation," in *A Stein Reader,* ed. Ulla E. Dydo (Evanston: Northwestern University Press, 1993), 495.

29. Horace Kallen, "'Americanization' and the Cultural Prospect," in *Culture and Democracy in the United States* (New York: Boni & Liveright, 1924), 118. All subsequent references to this edition will be cited as *CD*.

30. Ezra Pound to Harriet Monroe, [July?] 1914, in *Dear Editor: A History of Poetry in Letters: The First Fifty Years, 1912–1962,* ed. Joseph Parisi and Stephen Young (New York: W. W. Norton, 2002), 176.

31. Gertrude Stein, *Everybody's Autobiography* (London: Virago, 1985), 266, 27.

32. Willa Cather, *Not Under Forty* (New York: Alfred A. Knopf, 1936), v.

33. See Linda Wagner-Martin, "The Hemingway-Stein Story," in Wagner-Martin, ed., *Ernest Hemingway: Seven Decades of Criticism* (East Lansing: Michigan State University Press, 1998), 389–401.

34. Eric J. Sundquist, "In the Lion's Mouth," *American Literary History* 15.1 (Spring 2003), 38.

Chapter 1. The Melting Pot

1. John Dewey to Horace M. Kallen, 31 March 1915, Kallen Papers (American Jewish Archives, Cincinnati); qtd. in Rivka Shpak Lissak, *Pluralism and Progressives: Hull House and the New Immigrants, 1890–1919* (Chicago: University of Chicago Press, 1989), 175.

2. Kallen, "Democracy *Versus* the Melting-Pot" (1915), *CD*, 116.

3. See Russell A. Kazal, "Revisiting Assimilation: The Rise, Fall, and Reappraisal of a Concept in American Ethnic History," *American Historical Review* 100.2 (April 1995), 437–71; John Higham, *Send These to Me: Immigrants in Urban America* (Baltimore: Johns Hopkins University Press, 1984); Laurence Fuchs, *The American Kaleidoscope: Race, Ethnicity, and the Civic Culture* (Hanover: University Press of New England, 1990).

4. Just a year later, Milton Gordon's academic study of assimilation, *Assimilation in American Life*, distinguished between "Anglo-conformity" models of assimilation and the "true" melting pot. Nonetheless, in the years following Gordon's study, Glazer and Moynihan's characterization of assimilation has stuck. Milton Gordon, *Assimilation in American Life* (New York: Oxford University Press, 1964), 72. For the comparison of this popular version of assimilation to the "true" melting pot, see Gordon, 88–114.

5. See Sollors, *Beyond Ethnicity,* 189–91; Philip Gleason, "The Melting Pot: Symbol of Fusion or Confusion?" *American Quarterly* 16.1 (Spring 1964), 20–46, and *Speaking of Diversity.*

6. James Kloppenberg describes American Progressivism as entailing "several progressive factions," of which only one advocated "a new spirit of 'social consciousness,' a heightened awareness of the individual's 'social duty,' and a new conception of the government's central role in securing the 'common good'" (*Uncertain Victory,* 311).

7. Henry Pratt Fairchild, *The Melting-Pot Mistake* (Boston: Little, Brown, 1926), 10.

8. As Philip Gleason argues, "The melting pot provided a large symbol, a comprehensive figurative framework, which subsumed into itself many metaphoric terms already in common use; it seemed to conform in some way to the process that was going on, and it lent itself to picturesque elaboration that made it ideal for colorful use by journalists. Consequently, the symbol became extremely popular and entered deeply into the whole thought process respecting immigration; for many people, no doubt, it was the basic piece of intellectual equipment where immigration was concerned. But considering the lack of precise understanding of the subject and the very loose use of the symbol, it was bound to be ambiguous; it could not convey anything

univocal because what it stood for was neither clearly nor univocally understood" (*Speaking of Diversity,* 23).

9. Ralph Ellison, "The Little Man at Chehaw Station," [1977] from *Going to the Territory,* in *The Collected Essays of Ralph Ellison,* ed. John F. Callahan (New York: Modern Library, 1995), 508–9.

10. Herbert Croly, *The Promise of American Life* (1909; ed. John William Ward [Indianapolis: Bobbs-Merrill, 1965]), 315–16.

11. See Jonathan M. Hansen, on "cosmopolitan patriots" and ideas of reciprocity: *The Lost Promise of Patriotism: Debating American Identity, 1890–1920* (Chicago: University of Chicago Press, 2003).

12. Here I draw on James Livingston's use of Kenneth Burke's "comic frame of acceptance" in *Pragmatism and the Political Economy of Cultural Revolution,* xix.

13. Henry Pratt Fairchild, *Immigration: A World Movement and Its American Significance* (New York: Macmillan, 1913), 398–404.

14. Julius Drachsler, *Democracy and Assimilation* (New York: Macmillan, 1920), 171, 173. Further references to this edition will be cited as *DA.*

15. Matthew Arnold, *Culture and Anarchy,* ed. Samuel Lipman (New Haven: Yale University Press, 1994), 33.

16. Franz Boas, "Instability of Human Types" (1911), in Franz Boas, *The Shaping of American Anthropology, 1883–1911: A Franz Boas Reader,* ed. George W. Stocking, Jr. (New York: Basic Books, 1974), 217.

17. Franz Boas, "The Mythologies of the Indians" (1905), in *The Shaping of American Anthropology,* 145.

18. On this see Susan Hegeman, *Patterns for America: Modernism and the Concept of Culture* (Princeton: Princeton University Press, 1999), 35–58; Brad Evans, "Where Was Boas During the Renaissance in Harlem? Diffusion, Race, and the Culture Paradigm in the History of Anthropology," in *Central Sites, Peripheral Visions: Cultural and Institutional Crossing in the History of Anthropology,* ed. Richard Handler (Madison: University of Wisconsin Press, 2006), 69–98. See also Michael Elliott, *The Culture Concept: Writing and Difference in the Age of Realism* (Minneapolis: University of Minnesota Press, 2002); and Scott Michaelsen, *The Limits of Multiculturalism: Interrogating the Origins of American Anthropology* (Minneapolis: University of Minnesota Press, 1999).

19. Robert F. Zeidel, *Immigrants, Progressives, and Exclusion Politics: The Dillingham Commission, 1900–1927* (DeKalb: Northern Illinois University Press, 2004), 86–100, 89, 98.

20. John Dewey, "Nationalizing Education" (1916), *The Essential Dewey, Volume I: Pragmatism, Education, Democracy,* ed. Larry A. Hickman and Thomas M. Alexander (Bloomington: Indiana University Press, 1998), 267. All subsequent references will be to this edition and will be cited as NE.

21. Dewey, NE, 267.

22. Elsewhere in this same essay Dewey does address the "common struggle of native born, African, Jew, Italian and perhaps a score of other peoples" (267).

23. Sarah E. Simons, "Social Assimilation. I," *American Journal of Sociology* 6.6 (May 1901), 791. Quoting Franklin H. Giddings, *Elements of Sociology.*

24. It is also relevant, of course, that several influential figures in this stage of sociology came from "literary" backgrounds—Park was a reporter and W. I. Thomas, who is most famous for *The Polish Peasant,* was a professor of English.

25. Robert E. Park and Herbert A. Miller, *Old World Traits Transplanted* (New York: Harper & Bros., 1921), 280, 260. Further references are to this edition and will be cited as *OWT.*

26. William James, "Great Men and Their Environment," in *The Will to Believe and Other Essays in Popular Philosophy* (New York: Longmans, Green, 1897), 248. On William James and figuration, see Charlene Haddock Seigfried, *William James's Radical Reconstruction of Philosophy* (Albany: State University of New York Press, 1990), 209–35.

27. Jane Addams, *Democracy and Social Ethics* (1902; New York: Macmillan, 1907), 273.

28. Horace Kallen, "A Meaning of Americanism," *CD,* 36.

29. Abraham Cahan, *Yekl: A Tale of the New York Ghetto* (New York: D. Appleton, 1896), 44; further references are to this edition and will be cited as *Y.* On this play, as well as the more general politics of dialect at the turn of the century, see Hana Wirth-Nesher, *Call It 'English': The Languages of Jewish American Literature* (Princeton: Princeton University Press, 2006); Gavin Jones, *Strange Talk: The Politics of Dialect Literature in Gilded Age America* (Berkeley: University of California Press, 1999), 134–81.

30. See Barbara Ballis Lal, *The Romance of Culture in an Urban Civilization: Robert Park on Race and Ethnic Relations in Cities* (London: Routledge, 1990), 72; also Mary Jo Deegan, *Race, Hull-House, and the University of Chicago: A New Conscience against Ancient Evils* (Westport, CT: Praeger, 2002).

31. For a fuller theorization of this model of reading, see Steven Knapp, *Literary Interest: The Limits of Anti-Formalism* (Cambridge: Harvard University Press, 1993).

32. Versions of this theory have been advanced more recently by the philosopher Martha Nussbaum [*Poetic Justice: The Literary Imagination and Public Life* (Boston: Beacon Press, 1995)], and the historian Carroll Smith-Rosenberg ["Domesticating Virtue: Coquettes and Revolutionaries in Young America," in *Literature and the Body: Essays on Populations and Persons: Selected Papers from the English Institute,* ed. Elaine Scarry (Baltimore: Johns Hopkins University Press, 1988), 160–84].

33. Lillian D. Wald, *The House on Henry Street* (1915; New York: Dover, 1971), 290. Further references to this edition will be cited as *HS.*

34. E. G. Stern, *My Mother and I* (New York: Macmillan, 1917), 32. On Stern's problematic status as immigrant autobiographer, see Laura Browder, *Slippery Characters: Ethnic Impersonators and American Identities* (Chapel Hill: University of North Carolina Press, 2000).

35. See Henry Adams, *The Education of Henry Adams* (1918; New York: Penguin, 1995), 360–70 ("The Dynamo and the Virgin [1900]").

36. Kallen, "'Americanization' and the Cultural Prospect," *CD,* 148.

37. Robert Park and Ernest Burgess, *Introduction to the Science of Sociology,* 2nd ed. (Chicago: University of Chicago Press, 1924), 735. Further references are to this edition and will be cited as *ISS*

38. Israel Zangwill, *MP,* "Afterword," 203.

39. Mary Antin, *The Promised Land* (1912; New York: Penguin, 1997), 3. Further references are to this edition and will be cited as *PL.* On garments and immigrant assimilation, see Andrew Heinze, *Adapting to Abundance: Jewish Immigrants, Mass Consumption, and the Search for American Identity* (New York: Columbia University Press, 1990), chap. 5: "The Clothing of an American."

40. Jane Addams, *Twenty Years at Hull-House,* 125; further references will be cited as *HH.*

41. Jane Addams, *Democracy and Social Ethics,* 5–6.

42. Leah Morton (Elizabeth Stern), *I Am a Woman—and a Jew* (New York: J. H. Sears, 1926), 315.

43. Constantine Panunzio, *The Soul of an Immigrant* (New York: Macmillan, 1921), 169. Other references will be to this edition and will be cited in the text as *SI.*

44. See Andrew R. Heinze, "*Schizophrenia Americana:* Aliens, Alienists, and the 'Personality Shift' of Twentieth-Century Culture," *American Quarterly* 55.2 (2003), 227–56.

45. Park, *OWT,* 38–39.

46. Kallen, "Democracy *Versus* the Melting-Pot," *CD,* 78.

47. Stern, *My Mother and I,* 11.

48. On the theatricality of assimilation, see Andrea Most, *Making Americans: Jews and the Broadway Musical* (Cambridge: Harvard University Press, 2004). See also Sabine Haenni, "Visual and Theatrical Culture, Tenement Fiction, and the Immigrant Subject in Abraham Cahan's *Yekl,*" *American Literature* 71.3 (September 1999), 493–527.

49. Quoted in Jacobson, *Whiteness of a Different Color,* 78.

50. See, in this direction, Mary C. Waters, *Ethnic Options: Choosing Identities in America* (Berkeley: University of California Press, 1990), and Herbert J. Gans, "Symbolic Ethnicity: The Future of Ethnic Groups and Cultures in America" in *On the Making of Americans: Essays in Honor of David Riesman,* ed. Herbert J. Gans, Nathan Glazer, Joseph R. Gusfield, Christopher Jenks (Philadelphia: University of Pennsylvania Press, 1979).

51. Or, as K. Anthony Appiah puts it in another context, "We make up selves from a tool kit of options made available by our culture and society.... We do make choices, but we don't determine the options among which we choose" (K. Anthony Appiah and Amy Gutmann, *Color Conscious: The Political Morality of Race* [Princeton: Princeton University Press, 1996], 96).

52. For William James's use of post-Darwinian graft theory, see David Kadlec, *Mosaic Modernism: Anarchism, Pragmatism, Culture* (Baltimore: John Hopkins University Press, 2000), 28.

53. The distinctions that Park makes between "accommodation" and "assimilation" are instructive here; according to him, "In accommodation the person or the group is generally, though not always, highly conscious of the occasion, as in the peace treaty that ends the war, in the arbitration of an industrial controversy, in the adjustment of the person to the formal requirements of life in a new social world. In assimilation the process is typically unconscious; the person is incorporated into the common life of the group before he is aware and with little conception of the course of events which brought this incorporation about" (*ISS,* 736).

54. Many of the most compelling accounts of fluidity of identity were fashioned by Jews. Unlike members of other ethnic groups, most Jewish immigrants had no plans to return to the countries from which they emigrated, and so their imaginative energy was more focused on the American scene.

55. W. E. B. Du Bois, *Dusk of Dawn: An Essay toward an Autobiography of a Race Concept* (1940), in *W. E. B. Du Bois: Writings,* ed. Nathan Huggins (New York: Library of America, 1986), 640.

56. Abraham Cahan, *The Rise of David Levinsky* (New York: Penguin, 1993), 94.

57. Jacobson, *Whiteness of a Different Color;* David Roediger, *The Wages of Whiteness: Race and the Making of the American Working Class* (London: Verso, 1991); Noel Ignatiev, *How the Irish Became White* (New York: Routledge, 1995). On Levinsky's parallel trajectory, see Michael Rogin, *Blackface, White Noise: Jewish Immigrants in the Hollywood Melting Pot* (Berkeley: University of California Press, 1996), and Karen Brodkin, *How Jews Became White Folks and What That Says about Race in America* (New Brunswick: Rutgers University Press, 1999).

58. See Eric Lott, *Love and Theft: Blackface Minstrelsy and the American Working Class* (New York: Oxford University Press, 1993); Rogin, *Blackface, White Noise.* On the other hand, see W. T. Lhamon, *Raising Cain: Blackface Performance from Jim Crow to Hip Hop* (Cambridge: Harvard University Press, 1998), and Browder, *Slippery Characters.*

59. William James, Letter to *Boston Evening Transcript,* 4 March 1899; qtd. Carrie Tirado Bramen, *The Uses of Variety: Modern Americanism and the Quest for National Distinctiveness* (Cambridge: Harvard University Press, 2000), 61–62.

60. Robert Park, "Racial Assimilation in Secondary Groups with Particular Reference to the Negro," *American Journal of Sociology* 19.5 (March 1914), 610–11. Further references to this essay will be cited in the text as RA.

61. See Dorothy Ross, *The Origins of American Social Science* (Cambridge: Cambridge University Press, 1991) for an account of Park's later extension of his theory of assimilation to racialized minorities. James and Park anticipate the connection Lauren Berlant makes between the full privileges of democratic citizenship and unequally available disembodied abstraction. See "National Brands/National Body: *Imitation of Life,*" in *The Phantom Public Sphere,* ed. Bruce Robbins (Minneapolis: University of Minnesota Press, 1993), 173–208. On the role played by vision and the visible as "the primary vehicle for making race 'real' in the United States," see Robyn Wiegman, *American Anatomies: Theorizing Race and Gender* (Durham: Duke University Press, 1995), 21.

62. The "ethnic model" of racial identity that ideas of assimilation often presuppose was critiqued most famously by Michael Omi and Howard Winant in *Racial Formation in the United States: From the 1960s to the 1980s* (New York: Routledge, 1986). As Omi and Winant note, the ethnicity paradigm does not adequately take into account "race *per se,*" and thus tends to slight "a qualitatively different historical experience"; since its tendency is to explain racial groups' success or failure by their "norms," "ongoing processes of discrimination" are inadequately considered; most important, ethnicity theory tends to overlook cultural variation (that is, ethnicity) within racial groups (21–24). To some extent the melting-pot model does anticipate and attempt to address this critique: it does so by opening up previously "distinct" histories to broader investments, by undercutting the notion of stable norms, and by multiplying the sites of access to cultures.

63. E. Franklin Frazier, "Sociological Theory and Race Relations," *American Sociological Review* 12.3 (June 1947), 270. See also James B. McKee, *Sociology and the Race Problem: The Failure of a Perspective* (Urbana: University of Illinois Press, 1993).

64. See Jacobson, *Whiteness of a Different Color;* Ignatiev, *How the Irish Became White.*

65. For some sense of this range see George W. Stocking, Jr., *Race, Culture and Evolution: Essays in the History of Anthropology* (Chicago: University of Chicago Press,

1968); Carl Degler, *In Search of Human Nature: The Decline and Revival of Darwinism in American Social Thought* (New York: Oxford University Press, 1992); and Sandra Harding, ed., *The 'Racial' Economy of Science: Toward a Democratic Future* (Bloomington, Ind.: *Indiana University Press,*1993). For considerations of the way literary production was implicated in these debates, see Daylanne English, *Unnatural Selections: Eugenics in American Modernism and the Harlem Renaissance* (Chapel Hill: University of North Carolina Press, 2004); Maria Farland, "W. E. B. Du Bois, Anthropometric Science, and the Limits of Racial Uplift," *American Quarterly* 58.4 (December 2006), 1017–45, and "Gertrude Stein's Brain Work," *American Literature* 76.1 (March 2004), 117–48.

66. Charles W. Chesnutt, *The Marrow of Tradition* (1901; New York: Penguin, 1993), 168.

67. Paul Gilroy, *The Black Atlantic: Modernity and Double Consciousness* (New York: Verso, 1993).

68. James Weldon Johnson, "Speech Given at State Industrial School for Negroes," 1915, in *The Selected Writings of James Weldon Johnson,* Vol. II, ed. Sondra Kathryn Wilson (New York: Oxford University Press, 1995), 15–16.

69. *Souls* sold well—almost 10,000 copies over five years—and David Levering Lewis counts William James, the well-known social worker Robert Hunter, and reviewers for the New York *Evening Post,* the *Nation,* and the *Independent* among the book's enthusiasts. Lewis also quotes at some length from correspondence Du Bois received from D. Tabak, an immigrant resident of New York's Lower East Side who "thanked Du Bois for the greatly heightened sense of humanity and 'sympathy to all nature's children' he had derived from *The Souls of Black Folk.*" *W. E. B. Du Bois: Biography of a Race* (New York: Henry Holt, 1993), 294.

70. W. E. B. Du Bois, *The Souls of Black Folk* (1903; New York: Knopf, 1993), 9. Further references to this edition will be cited as *SBF.*

71. See Barbara Johnson, "Thresholds of Difference: Structures of Address in Zora Neale Hurston," in *"Race," Writing, and Difference,* ed. Henry Louis Gates, Jr. (Chicago: University of Chicago Press, 1986), 317–28.

72. However, *Souls* represents only a particular phase of Du Bois's thought. Its complicated mixture of impulses is sandwiched between the more straightforwardly anti-assimilationist sociology of *The Conservation of Races* (1897) and the racial nationalism of the later pan-Africanism. On Du Bois and "cosmopolitan universalism," see Ross Posnock, *Color and Culture.*

73. Kallen, "Democracy *Versus* the Melting-Pot," *CD,* 78.

74. She is not alone in this position; figures of resistance, often female, appear in much of the literature of assimilation. In Sui Sin Far's short story "The Wisdom of the New" (1912), Pau Lin poisons her son Yen to save him from assimilation. See also Katrina Irving, *Immigrant Mothers: Narratives of Race and Maternity, 1890–1925* (Urbana: University of Illinois Press, 2000).

75. Dewey, NE, 267.

76. Kallen, "Democracy *Versus* the Melting-Pot," *CD,* 87.

77. Marcus Eli Ravage, *The Making of an American* (New York: Harper & Bros., 1917), Introduction, n. pg.

78. Addams, "The Play Instinct and the Arts," in *The Second Twenty Years at Hull-House* (New York: Macmillan, 1930), 345.

79. John Dewey, *Democracy and Education: An Introduction to the Philosophy of Education* (1916; New York: Free Press, 1997), 30–31.

80. Addams, *Democracy and Social Ethics,* 8. On the ways in which definite and indefinite intersect in literature, in contrast to the limitations of more abstract forms of representation, see Wai Chee Dimock, *Residues of Justice: Literature, Law, Philosophy* (Berkeley: University of California Press, 1996).

81. Frances Ferguson, *Solitude and the Sublime: Romanticism and the Aesthetics of Individuation* (New York: Routledge, 1992), viii.

82. See Amy Hungerford, *The Holocaust of Texts: Genocide, Literature, and Personification* (Chicago: University of Chicago Press, 2003).

83. On fiction and the writing of the self, see Paul John Eakin, *Fictions in Autobiography* (Princeton: Princeton University Press, 1985); alternatively, James Olney, ed., *Autobiography: Essays Theoretical and Critical* (Princeton: Princeton University Press, 1980).

84. Dorothy J. Hale, *Social Formalism: The Novel in Theory from Henry James to the Present* (Stanford: Stanford University Press, 1998), 14. The critical implications of this imagining of the text along the lines of a person resonate through the twentieth century. The melting-pot modernists laid the foundation for I. A. Richards's 1926 elevation of "what [a poem] is" over what it "says." Melting-pot ideas of textual being also anticipate the late-modernist version of the text as "organic" being, a formal expression of a complex system of relations, as postulated by Cleanth Brooks and Robert Penn Warren in *Understanding Poetry* (1938). This emphasis on being opens the door, later in the century, to understanding texts as instantiating identity positions, or to applying psychoanalytic approaches to literary texts, or to theorizing ethical relations to literary texts. See I. A. Richards, *Science and Poetry* (New York: W. W. Norton, 1962), 34–35.

Chapter 2. Henry James in the "Intellectual *Pot-au-feu*"

1. Henry James to George Harvey, 21 October 1904. In Leon Edel, ed. *Henry James Letters,* vol. IV (Cambridge: Harvard University Press, 1984), 327. All subsequent references to this edition will be cited as Edel.

2. Ross Posnock, *The Trial of Curiosity: Henry James, William James, and the Challenge of Modernity* (New York: Oxford University Press, 1991), 16.

3. David McWhirter, "'A Provision of Responsibilities': Senses of the Past in Henry James's Fourth Phase," in *Enacting History in Henry James: Narrative, Power, and Ethics,* ed. Gert Buelens (Cambridge: Cambridge University Press, 1997), 148–65.

4. Henry James to William James, 24 May 1903. Edel, 271.

5. Leon Edel, ed., *Henry James Letters,* vol. I (Cambridge: Belknap Press of Harvard University, 1974), 77.

6. Henry James, Review of Theodore Roosevelt, *American Ideals and Other Essays Social and Political* (1898), in *Literary Criticism: Essays on Literature, American Writers, English Writers* (New York: Library of America, 1985), 664.

7. Henry James to George Harvey, 21 October 1904. Edel, 328.

8. Henry James, *AS,* 50, 89, 92.

9. Mary Antin, *PL,* 1.

10. See James to George Harvey, 21 October 1904. Edel 328.

11. Ernest Poole, *The Voice of the Street* (New York: A. S. Barnes, 1906), 2.

12. Henry James, "The Art of Fiction," in *Literary Criticism: French Writers, Other European Writers, The Prefaces to the New York Edition,* ed. Leon Edel (New York: Library of America, 1984), 1107.

13. William James's "unclassified residuum" represents that which is not already comprehended (assimilated) by scientific theory. William James, "What Psychical Research Has Accomplished," in *The Will to Believe and Other Essays in Popular Philosophy* (New York: Longmans, Green, 1897), 299.

14. See Beverly Haviland, *Henry James's Last Romance: Making Sense of the Past and the American Scene* (New York: Cambridge University Press, 1997), 135.

15. Henry James, "The Jolly Corner," in *Eight Tales from the Major Phase* (New York: Norton, 1969), 336. Further references to this edition will be cited as JC. See also Deborah Esch, "A Jamesian About-Face: Notes on 'The Jolly Corner,'" *ELH* 50 (Fall 1983): 587–605.

16. As this sequence suggests, the "luxury of some such close and sweet and *whole* national consciousness as that of the Switzer and the Scot" (*AS,* 67), with which James closes the Ellis Island segment (first published in *Harper's* of February 1906), is an unconsidered position, impossible for him. (Elsewhere he labels Switzerland and Scotland the "'show' sections of the earth" [*AS,* 20].) The book form of *The American Scene* complicates the false closure represented by this idea.

17. I understand Jamesian sympathy more along the lines of Rousseau than of Adam Smith, and in keeping with Cindy Weinstein's important recent reevaluation of nineteenth-century U.S. sympathy (as a varied and multifaceted process, in distinction to the critical tradition that understands sympathy principally as appropriation). See Cindy Weinstein, *Family, Kinship, and Sympathy in Nineteenth-Century American Literature* (New York: Cambridge University Press, 2004).

18. For discussions of this connection, see John F. Sears, "Introduction," *The American Scene* (New York: Penguin, 1994), xiii; Haviland, 139, 161; Gert Buelens, *Henry James and the "Aliens" in Possession of the American Scene* (Amsterdam: Rodopi, 2003), 95–97.

19. Eldon J. Eisenach, *The Lost Promise of Progressivism,* 26.

20. This, from James's preface to Volume XII of the New York Edition, establishes a *typical* ghostliness that "The Turn of the Screw" violates.

21. This resistance to reproduction is particularly significant just as James's contemporary and friend, the ardent nativist Henry Cabot Lodge, was reminding white native-born Americans of their duty to reproduce in order to maintain the existing American racial composition.

22. W. E. B. Du Bois, "The Evolution of the Race Problem" (1909), in *W. E. B. Du Bois Speaks: Speeches and Addresses, 1890–1919,* ed. Philip S. Foner (New York: Pathfinder, 1970), 205.

23. William James, *A Pluralistic Universe* (London: Longmans, Green: 1909), 321, 325.

24. James, *A Pluralistic Universe,* 324.

25. As John Carlos Rowe notes, "It is clear enough that James feared 'the masses,' especially the immigrants to America" (*The Other Henry James* [Durham: Duke University Press, 1998], 30). However, most recent critiques of James's response to racial and ethnic difference are not attacks along the lines of Maxwell Geismar (*Henry*

James and the Jacobites [Boston: Houghton Mifflin, 1963]). Instead, they identify the troublingly nuanced forms of intellectual and affective rejection that James's analyses often combine with interest and bewilderment. See, for example, Kenneth Warren, *Black and White Strangers: Race and American Literary Realism* (Chicago: University of Chicago Press, 1993); Sara Blair, *Henry James and the Writing of Race and Nation* (New York: Cambridge University Press, 1996); Jonathan Freedman, *The Temple of Culture;* Gert Buelens, *Henry James and the 'Aliens' in Possession of the American Scene.* My purpose here cannot be to advance what is by now a well-established critique; instead I aim to show the ways in which this fearful James nonetheless admitted and enacted forms of melting-pot selfhood and fellowship.

26. James's autobiography *A Small Boy and Others* (1913) deploys similar terms to describe his own past; under his gaze, "aspects began to multiply and images to swarm": *A Small Boy and Others* (New York: Scribner's, 1913), 2. Subsequent references to this edition will be cited in the text as *SB.* As Jonathan Freedman has argued, "merely noting the similarities between James's language and perceptions and those of his anti-Semitic contemporaries is not, in my view, sufficient. Indeed, it errs in precisely the same way that anti-Semitism does, by mistaking metonymies for identities, confusing similarity and same." *The Temple of Culture,* 121.

27. William Boelhower, *Through a Glass Darkly: Ethnic Semiosis in American Literature* (New York: Oxford University Press, 1987), 24.

28. Charles Baudelaire, "The Painter of Modern Life," in *The Painter of Modern Life and Other Essays,* trans. and ed. Jonathan Mayne (New York: Phaidon, 1970), 9. See Tom Gunning, "From the Kaleidoscope to the X-Ray: Urban Spectatorship, Poe, Benjamin, and *Traffic in Souls* (1913)," *Wide Angle* 19.4 (1997), 32–33.

29. On James's use of this term, see Blair, *Henry James and the Making of Race and Nation,* 158–210.

30. The *Oxford English Dictionary* notes the unclear origin of the term and suggests that it may have been coined simply as a "mouth-filling and startling term."

31. See Terry Castle, "Phantasmagoria: Spectral Technology and the Metaphorics of Modern Reverie," *Critical Inquiry* 15.1 (Fall 1988), 26–61; see also Tom Gunning's work on early cinema and visual culture.

32. Jacob A. Riis, *The Making of an American* (New York: Macmillan, 1901), 306–7.

33. Henry James to Edith Wharton, 8 November 1905. Edel, 375.

34. Volitional conversion is imperfect because it does not involve self-surrender, William James explained; only by *relinquishing* the personal will can one overcome the "imperfect self." William James, *The Varieties of Religious Experience* (1902; New York: Penguin, 1985), 206, 209. Further references to this edition will be cited as *VR.*

35. Henry James to Paul Bourget, 21 December 1905. Edel, 388.

36. George Herbert Mead, "The Social Self," *Journal of Philosophy, Psychology, and Scientific Methods* 10 (1913), 378.

37. Jane Addams, *Democracy and Social Ethics,* 5.

38. Henry James to Sarah Butler Wister, 21 December 1902. Edel, 259.

39. Abraham Cahan, *Yekl: A Tale of the New York Ghetto,* 30.

40. Henry James to Edmund Gosse, 27 October 1904. Edel, 332.

41. On coercive uses of leisure in the immigrant scene, see William Gleason, *The Leisure Ethic: Work and Play in American Literature, 1840–1940* (Stanford: Stanford University Press, 1999), especially chap. 3, "Resistance to Play Progressivism"; and

Bill Brown, *The Material Unconscious: American Amusement, Stephen Crane, and the Economics of Play* (Cambridge: Harvard University Press, 1996).

42. Walter Lippmann, *Drift and Mastery,* 130.

43. Frederick Law Olmsted, "Public Parks and the Enlargement of Towns" (1870), quoted in Alan Trachtenberg, *The Incorporation of America: Culture and Society in the Gilded Age* (New York: Hill and Wang, 1982), 110.

44. On Central Park see Trachtenberg, *The Incorporation of America,* 101—47; Lawrence W. Levine, *Highbrow/Lowbrow: The Emergence of Cultural Hierarchy in America* (Cambridge: Harvard University Press, 1988), 200—219; and Thomas Bender, *Toward an Urban Vision: Ideas and Institutions in Nineteenth-Century America* (Lexington: University of Kentucky Press, 1975), 159—88.

45. Roy Rosenzweig and Elizabeth Blackmar, *The Park and the People: A History of Central Park* (Ithaca: Cornell University Press, 1992), 308. However, in *How the Other Half Lives* (New York: Scribner, 1917), Jacob Riis notes that in one downtown public school only three of forty-eight boys had ever been to the park (140).

46. J. Crawford Hamilton, "Snap Shots in Central Park," *Munsey's Magazine* (October 1891), 5—6.

47. Rosenzweig and Blackmar, *The Park and the People,* 337, 338, 390.

48. Olmsted to Henry Van Brunt, 22 January 1891, Olmsted Papers, Reel 22; qtd. in Erik Larson, *The Devil in the White City* (New York: Random House, 2003), 50—51.

49. Henry James, *The Tragic Muse* (New York: Penguin, 1995), 126. Further references will be cited as *TM.*

50. Rosenzweig and Blackmar, *The Park and the People,* 314.

51. See Constantine Panunzio, *The Soul of an Immigrant.*

52. See Alan Ackerman on the Jamesian reconception of the role of the audience in the drama: *The Portable Theater: American Literature and the Nineteenth-Century Stage* (Baltimore: Johns Hopkins University Press, 1999), 211—20.

53. Mead, "The Social Self," 377—78. See Posnock, *The Trial of Curiosity,* on the theatricality of the social self (141—92).

54. Henry James, "Preface to *The Golden Bowl,*" *The Art of the Novel,* 337. Subsequent references to this work will be cited in the text as *AN.*

55. "Preface to *The Princess Casamassima.*"

56. On the question of market-driven (i.e., copyright) determinations of formal outcomes, as in the case of *The Bostonians,* see David McWhirter, ed., *Henry James's New York Edition: The Construction of Authorship* (Stanford: Stanford University Press, 1995), esp. McWhirter's "'The Whole Chain of Relation and Responsibility': Henry James and the New York Edition," 1—22, and Michael Anesko, "Ambiguous Alliances: Conflicts of Culture and Ideology in the making of the New York Edition," 77—89.

57. *The American Scene* is amputated in the sense that James abandoned the project of a second volume of American impressions, which "would have attacked the subject (and my general mass of impression) at various *other* angles, thrown off various other pictures, in short *contributed* much more" (Henry James to William James, 17 October 1907; Edel, 466).

58. Edel, 327.

59. See Warren, *Black and White Strangers,* 111—16, 120—24.

60. On the persistently entwined nature of art and power in James's work, see Mark Seltzer, *Henry James and the Art of Power* (Ithaca: Cornell University Press,1984).

61. Lippmann, *Drift and Mastery,* 161.

62. Lippmann, 173.

63. As Julie Rivkin argues in *False Positions: The Representational Logics of Henry James's Fiction* (Stanford: Stanford University Press, 1996), the succession of delegations undertaken by *The Ambassadors* serves ultimately to empty out the idea of any originary authority; figuration, and the mode of exchange it represents, can never be as faithful as the logic of delegation would have it (58).

64. On history and the past in James's work, see Beverly Haviland, *Henry James's Last Romance;* Roslyn Jolly, *Henry James: History, Narrative, Fiction* (Oxford: Clarendon Press, 1993); and Ian F. A. Bell, *Henry James and the Past: Readings into Time* (London: Macmillan, 1991).

65. Michael Pupin, *From Immigrant to Inventor* (New York: Scribner's, 1924), 281. Emphasis in original.

66. Hale, *Social Formalism,* 37–38.

67. Henry James to Henry James III, 15–18 November 1913. Edel, 802. See Adeline Tintner, "Autobiography as Fiction: The 'Usurping Consciousness' as Hero of Henry James's Memoirs," *Twentieth Century Literature* 23.2 (May 1977), 239–60.

68. Henry James, *Notes of a Son and Brother* (New York: Scribner's, 1914), 15. All subsequent references will be to this edition and will be cited as *NS.*

69. For a fuller account of these liberties, see Michael Millgate, *Testamentary Acts: Browning, Tennyson, James, Hardy* (New York: Oxford University Press, 1992), 73–109.

70. Henry James to Henry James III, 15–18 November 1913. Edel, 802.

71. Henry James to Henry James III, 15–18 November 1913. Edel, 803.

Chapter 3. James Weldon Johnson's Integrationist Chameleonism

1. See Harold Cruse, *The Crisis of the Negro Intellectual* (New York: William Morrow, 1967); David Levering Lewis, *When Harlem Was in Vogue* (New York: Alfred A. Knopf, 1981); and Henry Louis Gates, Jr., "The Trope of a New Negro and the Reconstruction of the Image of the Black," *Representations* 24 (1988), 129–55.

2. George Hutchinson, *The Harlem Renaissance in Black and White,* 26.

3. Johnson, "The Larger Success" (1923), in *The Selected Writings of James Weldon Johnson, Volume II: Social, Political, and Literary Essays,* ed. Sondra Kathryn Wilson (New York: Oxford University Press, 1995), 56. Further references to this edition will be cited as *Writings II.* Johnson silently cites W. E. B. Du Bois's conclusion to "The Sorrow Songs," in *The Souls of Black Folk.*

4. James Weldon Johnson, "The Dilemma of the Negro Author" [*American Mercury,* 1928], in *James Weldon Johnson: Selected Writings,* ed. Sondra Kathryn Wilson (New York: Library of America, 2004), 751, 752 (my emphasis). For more on Chesnutt's "The Future American," see *MELUS* 15.3 (Fall 1988) for a special forum on this topic.

5. James Weldon Johnson, "African Colonization Schemes" (*New York Age,* 12 August 1922), in *The Selected Writings of James Weldon Johnson, Volume I: The New York Age Editorials (1914–1923),* ed. Sondra Kathryn Wilson (New York: Oxford University Press, 1995), 132. Further references to this edition will be cited as *Writings I.*

6. Eric J. Sundquist, *To Wake the Nations: Race in the Making of American Literature* (Cambridge: The Belknap Press of Harvard University Press, 1993), 538.

7. *Negro Americans, What Now?* (1934), for example, calls for equal rights while vowing that they "would not, of course, have the effect of suddenly doing away with voluntary grouping in religious or secular organizations or of abolishing group enterprises—for example, Negro newspapers" (*Writings II*, 145).

8. However, Johnson's position differs from Bourne's in its embrace of the "cultural half-breeds" that Bourne decried, and in Johnson's support for integrationist programs that Bourne repudiated as statist engines of homogenization.

9. James Weldon Johnson, *Along This Way* (1933; New York: Da Capo, 2000), 328. Further references to this edition will be cited as *ATW.*

10. Bob Cole, J. Rosamond Johnson, James Weldon Johnson, "Under the Bamboo Tree" (New York: Jos. W. Stern, 1902).

11. Israel Zangwill, *MP,* 204. W. E. B. Du Bois, *SBF,* 15.

12. James Weldon Johnson to Sherman, French, and Co., 17 February 1912. James Weldon Johnson Collection in the Yale Collection of American Literature, Beinecke Rare Book and Manuscript Library, Yale University. MSS Johnson, Series I, Box 18, Folder 435.

13. Werner Sollors notes that Johnson's text "represents a perfect *formal* answer to the theme of passing": *Neither White Nor Black Yet Both* (New York: Oxford University Press, 1997, 264.

14. On autobiographical challenges to authentic identities, see Laura Browder, *Slippery Characters.*

15. William M. Tuttle, Jr., "W. E. B. DuBois' Confrontation with White Liberalism during the Progressive Era: A Phylon Document," *Phylon* 35.3 (1974), 241–58.

16. James Weldon Johnson, *The Autobiography of an Ex-Coloured Man* (New York: Vintage, 1989), xxxix. Further references will be cited as *Ex.*

17. Robert Stepto calls the *Autobiography* an "aborted narrative of immersion": *From Behind the Veil: A Study of Afro-American Narrative* (Urbana: University of Illinois Press, 1979), 128.

18. On the conservative politics of exposure in early twentieth-century American writing, see Amy Kaplan, *The Social Construction of American Realism* (Chicago: University of Chicago Press, 1988); Mark Pittenger, "A World of Difference: Constructing the 'Underclass' in Progressive America," *American Quarterly* 49.1 (March 1997), 32–33; and Keith Gandal, *The Virtues of the Vicious: Jacob Riis, Stephen Crane, and the Spectacle of the Slum* (New York: Oxford University Press, 1997).

19. Donald Goellnicht connects the Preface's use of ethnography to pornography: "Passing as Autobiography: James Weldon Johnson's *The Autobiography of an Ex-Coloured Man,*" *African American Review* 30.1 (Spring 1996), 20.

20. Sollors connects mirrors and reflections with racial and ethnic double consciousness in *Beyond Ethnicity* (249). See also Judith Oster, "See(k)ing the Self: Mirrors and Mirroring in Bicultural Texts," *MELUS* 23.4 (Winter 1998), 59–83.

21. As E. Franklin Frazier pointed out, Cooley's beliefs about race were problematic: while, on the one hand, he recognized that race as observed in the United States was more of a caste system than any reflection of a natural order, he also conjectured that such a caste system might produce differences in intelligence over time. He did not believe that race ought to be isolated and studied as a separate factor, and he

did believe in Asian exclusion, on the theory that whites and Asians could never be expected to integrate. E. Franklin Frazier, "Sociological Theory and Race Relations," *American Sociological Review* 12.3 (June 1947), 267.

22. Charles Horton Cooley, *Human Nature and the Social Order* (New York: Charles Scribner's Sons, 1902), 152.

23. The narrative is punctuated by thresholds: when the narrator's racial background is revealed to him by a school teacher, he describes a psychological "transition from one world into another" (*Ex,* 20). His passages into figurative inner sanctums are matched by many more literal instances of boundary-crossing, physical and linguistic (in the New York Tenderloin, among Cuban cigar workers, etc.).

24. JWJ to Carl Van Doren, 28 December 1922. Johnson Collection, YCAL. MSS Johnson, Series I, Box 21, folder 493.

25. See Eric Sundquist's *The Hammers of Creation: Folk Culture in Modern African-American Fiction* (Athens: University of Georgia Press, 1992), on cultural "forgetting" and the narrator's unsignaled shuttling back and forth across the color line.

26. Edwin E. Slosson, "Introduction" (1906), *The Life Stories of Undistinguished Americans as Told by Themselves,* ed. Hamilton Holt, introd. Werner Sollors (New York: Routledge, 1999), 2.

27. Michael Pupin, *From Immigrant to Inventor,* 281.

28. See Joseph Entin on the modernist deployment of shocking scenes as "convulsive emblems of political protest, epistemological rupture, and formal innovation": *Sensational Modernism: Experimental Fiction and Photography in Thirties America* (Chapel Hill: University of North Carolina Press, 2007), 20.

29. The narrator does not find himself entirely without words, for after his wave of shame he engages in an extended analysis of racial violence in the South. That analysis, which I will consider shortly, substitutes for the fuller documentation that is missing here.

30. Eugene Levy, *James Weldon Johnson: Black Leader, Black Voice* (Chicago: University of Chicago Press, 1973), 110.

31. Jane Addams, "Respect for Law," *New York Independent* 53 (3 January 1901); Ida B. Wells, "Lynching and the Excuse for It," *New York Independent* 53 (16 May 1901); see Maurice Hamington, "Public Pragmatism: Jane Addams and Ida B. Wells on Lynching," *Journal of Speculative Philosophy* 19.2 (2005), 167–74.

32. Wells was exceptional among reporters covering lynching in her resistance to using anonymous reportage. See Jean Lutes, "Lynching Coverage and the American Reporter-Novelist," *American Literary History* 19.2 (Summer 2007), 459.

33. Ida B. Wells, "A Red Record" (1895), in *Southern Horrors and Other Writings,* ed. Jacqueline Jones Royster (Boston: Bedford Books, 1997), 97. Further references will be cited as RR.

34. According to Michael Hatt, the lynching ritual makes objection irrelevant: "Race, Ritual, and Responsibility: Performativity and the Southern Lynching," in *Performing the Body/Performing the Text,* ed. Amelia Jones and Andrew Stephenson (New York: Routledge, 1999), 80.

35. Wells's diligent citation throughout *A Red Record* distances her from the role of witness. According to Jacqueline Goldsby, *A Red Record* "dissembles a rigorously removed objectivity": *A Spectacular Secret: Lynching in American Life and Literature* (Chicago: University of Chicago Press, 2006), 84. Jean Lutes sees Wells positioning herself

as "interpreter" rather than witness. See *Front-Page Girls: Women Journalists in American Culture and Fiction, 1880–1930* (Ithaca: Cornell University Press, 2006), 59.

36. The Paris, Texas, lynching was the original "spectacle" lynching, an audience-driven drama that collapsed the categories of eyewitness and participant. See Grace Elizabeth Hale, *Making Whiteness: The Culture of Segregation in the South, 1890–1940* (New York: Pantheon, 1998), 207.

37. *Writings II*, 29.

38. See Kenneth Warren on the disavowal of the lynching victim and identification with the perpetrators: "Troubled Black Humanity in *The Souls of Black Folk* and *The Autobiography of an Ex-Coloured Man*," in *The Cambridge Companion to American Realism and Naturalism: Howells to London*, ed. Donald Pizer (New York: Cambridge University Press, 1995), 274.

39. According to Walter White, Johnson's colleague and successor at the helm of the NAACP, lynching was "part of our national folkways," uncannily integrated into the culture: "an uncomfortably large percentage of American citizens can read in their newspapers of the slow roasting alive of a human being in Mississippi and turn, promptly and with little thought, to the comic strip or sporting page." White, *Rope and Faggot: A Biography of Judge Lynch* (New York: Alfred A. Knopf, 1929), viii.

40. See Carrie Tirado Bramen on the Progressive-era use of the picturesque to naturalize urban shocks: *The Uses of Variety: Modern Americanism and the Quest for National Distinctiveness* (Cambridge: Harvard University Press, 2000), chap. 4, "The Urban Picturesque and Americanization."

41. Wells, RR, 98.

42. Levy, *James Weldon Johnson*, 232.

43. Russ Castronovo, *Beautiful Democracy: Aesthetics and Anarchy in a Global Era* (Chicago: University of Chicago Press, 2007), 122.

44. James Weldon Johnson, "Preface to *The Book of American Negro Poetry*" [1922], in *James Weldon Johnson: Selected Writings*, 693. Further references to this essay will be cited as PNP.

45. On form in Johnson's prefaces, see Brent Edwards, "The Seemingly Eclipsed Window of Form: James Weldon Johnson's Prefaces," in *The Jazz Cadence of American Culture*, ed. Robert G. O'Meally (New York: Columbia University Press, 1998), 580–601.

46. James Weldon Johnson, "Preface to *The First Book of Negro Spirituals*" (1925), in Johnson and J. Rosamond Johnson, eds., *The Books of American Negro Spirituals* (New York: Da Capo, 1970), 30, 28.

47. Hortense J. Spillers, "Moving On Down the Line: Variations on the African-American Sermon," in *Black, White, and in Color: Essays on American Literature and Culture* (Chicago: University of Chicago Press, 2003), 263. Spillers also asserts that "the African-American church...sustains a special relationship of *attentiveness* to the literal word that liberates," and that "sermons provide a strategy of identity for persons forced to operate under a foreign code of culture; they offer an equipment not only for literacy, but a ground for hermeneutical play in which the subject gains competence in the interpretation and manipulation of systems of signs and their ground of interrelatedness" (252, 258).

48. Johnson, "Preface," from *God's Trombones: Seven Negro Sermons in Verse* (New York: Viking, 1927), 8. Further references to this edition will be cited as *GT*.

49. Johnson, "Listen, Lord—A Prayer," l. 8 (*GT,* 13).

50. In contrast, Johnson condemned dialect as "an instrument with but two complete stops, humor and pathos" (GT, 7).

51. Johnson, "Preface to *The Second Book of Negro Spirituals*" [1926], in *James Weldon Johnson: Selected Writings,* 732.

52. Johnson, "Preface to *The First Book of Negro Spirituals,*" 28.

53. Johnson, "Preface to *The Second Book of Negro Spirituals,*" 737.

54. The preface to *The Book of American Negro Poetry* (1922) is one of many places in which he points out that African Americans have created "the only things artistic that have yet sprung from American soil and been universally acknowledged as distinctive American products": the folk tales collected as Uncle Remus stories, the spirituals, the cakewalk, and ragtime (PNP, 689).

55. Johnson, "Preface to *The Second Book of Negro Spirituals,*" 737.

56. Johnson, *AIW,* 377.

57. Johnson, "Preface to *The Second Book of Negro Spirituals,*" 738.

58. "Within the past decade there has grown a general recognition that the Negro is a contributor to American life not only of material but of artistic, cultural, and spiritual values; that in the making and shaping of American civilization he is an active force, a giver as well as a receiver, a creator as well as a creature." Johnson, "Preface to the Revised Edition," *The Book of American Negro Poetry* (New York: Harcourt, Brace, 1931), 3.

59. James Weldon Johnson, *Complete Poems,* ed. Sondra Kathryn Wilson (New York: Penguin, 2000), 55.

60. Randolph Bourne, "Trans-National America," in *The Radical Will: Selected Writings, 1911–1918,* ed. Olaf Hansen (Berkeley: University of California Press, 1977), 254.

Chapter 4. Recollection, Reform, and "Broken Time" in Willa Cather

1. Jane Addams, "Immigration: A Field Neglected by the Scholar" (1905), in *Immigration and Americanization: Selected Readings,* ed. Philip Davis (Boston: Ginn, 1920), 11. On the question of "gifts," see Orm Øverland, "The First World War Americanization Movement and Immigrant Resistance to the Melting Pot," in *Multiculturalism and the American Self,* ed. William Boelhower and Alfred Hornung (Heidelberg: C. Winter, 2000), 139–56.

2. Such an ideology, Kallen alleged in Veblenian terms, was complicit with a late nineteenth-century ethos of display: "'Culture' was understood, not as a way of life, but as a decoration of the liver." Horace Kallen, "'Americanization' and the Cultural Prospect," *CD,* 215.

3. *Omaha World-Herald,* 30 October 1921; rpt. in *Willa Cather in Person: Interviews, Speeches, and Letters,* ed. L. Brent Bohlke (Lincoln: University of Nebraska Press, 1986), 147. Further references will be cited as *IP.*

4. *Omaha World-Herald, IP,* 146–47.

5. Henry James, *AS,* 98.

6. Park, *ISS,* 735.

7. See Lisa Lowe on the variable "temporality of assimilation": *Immigrant Acts: On Asian American Cultural Politics* (Durham: Duke University Press, 1996), 6.

8. Mary Antin, *PL,* 3.

9. On Cather's involvement with McClure's autobiography, see Robert Thacker's introduction to the University of Nebraska Press edition of the autobiography: Willa Cather, *The Autobiography of S. S. McClure* (Lincoln: University of Nebraska Press, 1997). Further references to this edition will be cited as *SSM.*

10. For convenience and clarity, I will most often refer to this voice as McClure, but it should be kept in mind that it is, indeed, a "McClure" in quotation marks, Cather's character, at the very least a complex amalgam of McClure's and Cather's contributions.

11. Edward Bok incorporated a comparable feature into his famous melting-pot autobiography, *The Americanization of Edward Bok;* he includes samples from his autograph collection, graphically reproducing the personalized handwritten notes he received from many prominent Americans. Like McClure's interlocutors, Bok's outside contributions are tokens of the past. However, they represent an official national past rather than a personal past; counting among them messages from figures such as Rutherford B. Hayes, Oliver Wendell Holmes, and Henry W. Longfellow, these additions to the narrative buttress the authority of Bok's "Americanization."

12. Edward Bok, *The Americanization of Edward Bok: The Autobiography of a Dutch Boy Fifty Years After* (New York: Scribner's, 1920), 164.

13. See Herbert G. Gutman, "Work, Culture, and Society in Industrializing America, 1815—1919," *American Historical Review* 78 (1973), 531—88.

14. McClure meets his challenge in a way similar to contemporary economic observers, who saw the key to prosperity in stimulating demand, emphasizing that persons, businesses, and households were incomplete and not yet "done." Through McClure's use of "broken time," it becomes clear that the historical anxieties and strategies of the melting pot are fundamentally informed by the market anxieties and strategies of their moment, and that the forms of historical agency proposed by melting-pot thinkers are accordingly implicated in market-based conceptions of agency.

15. Riis, *The Making of an American,* 166.

16. "Publishers' Note," Annie E. S. Beard, *Our Foreign-Born Citizens: What They Have Done for America* (New York: Thomas Y. Crowell, 1922), v.

17. Cahan, *The Rise of David Levinsky,* 530. In a further parallel with the Cather-McClure text (and with Johnson's *Autobiography of an Ex-Coloured Man*), Cahan's text was identified as an authentic autobiography as it appeared in *McClure's.*

18. Willa Cather, *My Ántonia* (1918; New York: Vintage, 1994), 272. Further references will be cited as *MA.*

19. Lippmann, *Drift and Mastery,* 163.

20. Lippmann, 163.

21. On this see Walter Benn Michaels, *Our America.*

22. Horace Kallen, "Democracy *Versus* the Melting-Pot," *CD,* 85.

23. Willa Cather, *The Professor's House* (1925; New York: Vintage, 1990), 219. Further references will be cited as *PH.*

24. Michaels's *Our America,* for example, takes Tom's claim on the Indian past seriously. Guy Reynolds also reads Tom Outland as a "savage": *Willa Cather in Context: Progress, Race, Empire* (London: Macmillan, 1996), 125. See Michaels on the anti-Semitism of Tom's Dreyfus comment.

25. According to Hermione Lee, "in 1899 Cather wrote a stirring tribute to Zola's defense of Dreyfus, speaking of 'the courage of the hand that penned *J'Accuse.*' There is no evidence that she changed her mind." *Willa Cather: A Life Saved Up* (London: Virago, 1989), 251.

26. See Edith Wyschogrod, *An Ethics of Remembering: History, Heterology, and the Nameless Others* (Chicago: University of Chicago Press, 1998).

27. Willa Cather, *The Song of the Lark* (1915; New York: Vintage, 1999), 280. Further references will be cited as *SL*.

28. Elizabeth Shepley Sergeant, *Willa Cather: A Memoir* (1953; Lincoln: Bison–University of Nebraska Press, 1986), 123.

29. See Trachtenberg, *The Incorporation of America,* 144–45, and T. J. Jackson Lears, *No Place of Grace: Antimodernism and the Transformation of American Culture, 1880–1920* (1981; Chicago: University of Chicago Press, 1994), 68–75.

30. Edgar Lee Hewett, "The Art of the Earliest Americans," *El Palacio* 13.1 (1922). Quoted in Molly Mullin, "The Patronage of Difference: Making Indian Art 'Art, Not Ethnology,'" in *The Traffic in Culture: Refiguring Art and Anthropology,* ed. George E. Marcus and Fred R. Myers (Berkeley: University of California Press, 1995), 169.

31. "New Struggle Ahead of Congress on Disposal of Indian Lands," *New York Times,* 21 January 1923: sec. 8, 4. Quoted in Brian Dippie, *The Vanishing American* (Middletown, CT: Wesleyan University Press, 1982), 277.

32. "President Roosevelt's Desire," *American Indian* II (1928): 4. Quoted in Dippie, 250.

33. Mabel Dodge Luhan, *Lorenzo in Taos* (New York: Knopf, 1932), 52.

34. James Harvey Robinson, *The New History: Essays Illustrating the Modern Historical Outlook* (New York: Macmillan, 1912), 134–35. On Dewey's version of this historical philosophy, see *The Influence of Darwinism on Philosophy and Other Essays* (New York: Henry Holt, 1910). For more on the Progressive historians, see Ernst A. Breisach, *American Progressive History: An Experiment in Modernization* (Chicago: University of Chicago Press, 1993); and Richard Hofstadter, *The Progressive Historians: Turner, Beard, Parrington* (New York: Knopf, 1968).

35. Although Tom Outland claims the mesa artifacts for "boys like you and me," he promptly sacrifices the only real community with whom he has shared these artifacts, the very "boy" to whom these words are spoken (*PH,* 219). Tom cares more about this past "than about anything else in the world" (*PH,* 216). Indeed, he heatedly declares that he'd "as soon have sold my own grandmother as [the mummy] Mother Eve—I'd have sold any living woman first" (*PH,* 221). As far as Tom is concerned, what Roddy has done transforms him from custodian of the past into vulgar looter. Roddy, on the other hand, understood his labor as earning him a part of the claim: "I supposed I had some share in the relics we dug up.... But now I see I was working for you like a hired man" (*PH,* 221–22). Roddy's misstep stems from his McClure-like belief that everything can be "realized" on (*PH,* 220). This sense of the fungibility of the past, which echoes a number of first-generation immigrant accounts, represents an important antecedent for the melting-pot historical utilitarianism that Cather's novel later locates in Louie Marsellus.

36. See John Hilgart on appropriations of "the Outland vacuum": "Death Comes for the Aesthete: Commodity Culture and the Artifact in Cather's *The Professor's House,*" *Studies in the Novel* 30.3 (1998), 396.

37. On the troubling historical ethics of collecting and collections see Susan Stewart, *On Longing: Narratives of the Miniature, the Gigantic, the Souvenir, the Collection* (Baltimore: Johns Hopkins University Press, 1984); George Stocking, Jr., ed., *Objects and Others: Essays on Museums and Material Culture* (Madison: University of Wisconsin Press, 1985); and Ivan Karp, *Exhibiting Cultures: The Poetics and Politics of Museum Display* (Washington: Smithsonian, 1991).

38. I am particularly interested in Boas's famous argument against the display practice of grouping items by "type" to demonstrate progression, and for the contextual display of ethnographic items. See Ira Jacknis, "Franz Boas and Exhibits: On the Limitations of the Museum Method of Anthropology," in *Objects and Others,* ed. Stocking, 75–111.

39. Jane Addams, *Twenty Years at Hull-House,* 156.

40. Addams, *Twenty Years at Hull-House,* 157.

41. Robinson, *New History,* 255.

42. Cahan, *Levinsky,* 110.

43. Joseph Wood Krutch, "Second Best" (1925), in *Willa Cather and Her Critics,* ed. James Schroeter (Ithaca: Cornell University Press, 1968), 56; Alfred Kazin, *On Native Grounds* (New York: Reynal & Hitchcock, 1942), 255.

44. Willa Cather, *Not Under Forty* (New York: Alfred A. Knopf, 1936), v.

45. See Christopher S. Nealon, "Affect-Genealogy: Feeling and Affiliation in Willa Cather," *American Literature* 69.1 (March 1997), 5–37.

46. E. G. Stern, *My Mother and I,* 169.

47. See Laura Browder, *Slippery Characters,* on the problematic status of the mother Stern's autobiography proposes to illuminate.

48. Antin, *PL,* 3.

49. Anzia Yezierska, *Bread Givers* (1925; New York: Persea Books, 2003), 297.

50. Antin, *PL,* 3.

51. Willa Cather, *Death Comes for the Archbishop* (1927; New York: Vintage, 1990), 274. Further references will be to this edition and will be cited in the text as *DCA.*

52. Stern, 11.

53. Willa Cather, "(Letter) On *Death Comes for the Archbishop,*" in *Willa Cather On Writing: Critical Studies on Writing as an Art* (Lincoln: University of Nebraska Press, 1988), 9. Further references to this edition will be cited as *OW.*

54. See Bill Brown, *A Sense of Things: The Object Matter of American Literature* (Chicago: University of Chicago Press, 2003).

55. See Ramón Gutiérrez on the mediations of materiality in colonial New Mexico: *When Jesus Came, the Corn Mothers Went Away* (Stanford: Stanford University Press, 1991). Douglas Mao's *Solid Objects* observes a similar communicative materialism in modernist texts: see *Solid Objects: Modernism and the Test of Production* (Princeton: Princeton University Press, 1998). See also Steven Lubar and W. David Kingery, eds., *History from Things: Essays on Material Culture* (Washington: Smithsonian Institution Press, 1993).

56. See Brad Evans, *Before Cultures: The Ethnographic Imagination in American Literature, 1865–1920* (Chicago: University of Chicago Press, 2005), especially the introduction and chap. 2.

57. Rev. W. J. Howlett, *Life of the Right Reverend Joseph P. Machebeuf, D.D.: Pioneer Priest of Ohio, Pioneer Priest of New Mexico, Pioneer Priest of Colorado, Vicar*

Apostolic of Colorado and Utah and First Bishop of Denver (Pueblo, CO: Franklin Press, 1908), 9.

58. On the switched roles of Macheboeuf and Lamy, see Edward A. Bloom and Lillian D. Bloom, "The Genesis of *Death Comes for the Archbishop,*" *American Literature* 26.4 (1955), 479–506. See Scott E. Casper on the coherence, romanticism, and individualism of nineteenth-century American biography: *Constructing American Lives: Biography and Culture in Nineteenth-Century America* (Chapel Hill: University of North Carolina Press, 1999), 322.

59. Cather connected individualism with the erasure of immigrant cultural legacies particularly forcefully in an interview of 1924, railing against the American way of "turning [immigrants] into stupid replicas of smug American citizens." According to her, "passion for Americanizing everything and everybody is a deadly disease with us. We do it the way we build houses. Speed, uniformity, dispatch, nothing else matters." The Americanized immigrant is a cookie-cutter house thrown up where a heritage home once stood (or where a hogan might stand). "Restlessness Such as Ours does not Make for Beauty," interview by Rose C. Feld, *New York Times Book Review,* 21 December 1924: 11, cols. 1–5; *IP,* 71–72.

60. Kallen, "Democracy *Versus* the Melting-Pot," *CD,* 86.

Chapter 5. Gertrude Stein and "Individual Anything"

1. See Michael McKeon, *The Secret History of Domesticity: Public, Private, and the Division of Knowledge* (Baltimore: Johns Hopkins University Press, 2005); Gillian Brown, *Domestic Individualism: Imagining Self in Nineteenth-Century America* (Berkeley: University of California Press, 1990). See also Linda Kerber, "Separate Spheres, Female Worlds, Woman's Place: The Rhetoric of Women's History," *Journal of American History* 75.1 (June 1988), 9–39, and Cathy Davidson, "Preface: No More Separate Spheres!" *American Literature* 70.3 (September 1998), 443–63.

2. On the indirection required of Dewey and Addams in their expression of their labor sympathies, see Robert B. Westbrook, *John Dewey and American Democracy* (Ithaca: Cornell University Press, 1991), 83–113.

3. On the use of economic tropes to imagine selfhood, see Walter Benn Michaels, *The Gold Standard and the Logic of Naturalism* (Berkeley: University of California Press, 1987), esp. 8–9, 22; and James Livingston, *Pragmatism and the Political Economy of Cultural Revolution, 1850–1940,* esp. 158–72, 263–73.

4. Jane Addams, *Democracy and Social Ethics,* 269.

5. Mary Kingsbury Simkhovitch, *The City Worker's World in America* (New York: Macmillan, 1917), 43.

6. C. B. Macpherson, *The Political Theory of Possessive Individualism: Hobbes to Locke* (Oxford: Oxford University Press, 1962), 2–4 and passim.

7. According to *Everybody's Autobiography, The Making of Americans* describes not only "the bottom nature" of every kind of man and woman, but "the way it [the bottom nature] was *mixed up with the other natures* in them." Gertrude Stein, *Everybody's Autobiography* (1937; London: Virago, 1985), 231 (my emphasis); further references are to this edition and will be cited parenthetically as *EA.*

8. Frederick Winslow Taylor, *The Principles of Scientific Management* (1911; New York: Norton, 1967), 73. See also Joel Pfister, *Individuality Incorporated: Indians and the Multicultural Modern* (Durham: Duke University Press, 2004).

9. Robert Park, "Racial Assimilation in Secondary Groups with Particular Reference to the Negro," *American Journal of Sociology* 19.5 (March 1914), 608.

10. According to Seltzer, this logic "makes metaphorics and the market two ways of saying the same thing." Mark Seltzer, *Bodies and Machines* (New York: Routledge, 1992), 51, 84.

11. Jane Addams, *Democracy and Social Ethics,* 5; John Dewey, "Nationalizing Education," 267.

12. Mabel Weeks to GS, April 21, 1907. Yale Collection of American Literature, Beinecke Library, MSS 76, Box 130, Folder 2834.

13. Amy Kaplan argues that "part of the cultural work of domesticity might be to unite men and women in a national domain and to generate notions of the foreign against which the nation can be imagined as home": "Manifest Domesticity," *American Literature* 70.3 (September 1998), 582. However, the signal innovation of the melting pot entails conceiving of the "foreign" primarily in terms of "inside."

14. See Brown, *Domestic Individualism.*

15. Addams, *Democracy and Social Ethics,* 103.

16. Gertrude Stein, *Three Lives* (New York: Vintage, 1936), 23. Further references will be cited as *TL.*

17. Mary Antin, *PL,* 213.

18. Simkhovitch, *The City Worker's World,* 128.

19. According to Michael North, the racial mask represents "convention embodied, the sign of signs": *The Dialect of Modernism,* 63.

20. Drawing on William James's theories of attention, Lisa Ruddick opposes Melanctha's "nonegoistic" wandering to the "selfish" safety of mental conservatism: *Reading Gertrude Stein: Body, Text, Gnosis* (Ithaca: Cornell University Press, 1990), 21.

21. Harriet Scott Chessman, *The Public Is Invited to Dance: Representation, the Body, and Dialogue in Gertrude Stein* (Stanford: Stanford University Press, 1989), 35.

22. Simkhovitch, *The City Worker's World,* 130, 138.

23. Henry James's *American Scene* and Jane Addams's *Democracy and Social Ethics* also imagine the streetcar as a place of unexpected intersections and combination.

24. Jane Addams, *Twenty Years at Hull-House,* 155.

25. Gertrude Stein, *The Making of Americans: Being a History of a Family's Progress* (1925; Normal, IL: Dalkey Archive, 1995), 335. Further references to this edition will be cited as *MAm.*

26. See Barrett Watten on how "socially reflexive subjectivity" is both subject and object of *The Making of Americans:* "An Epic of Subjectivation: *The Making of Americans,*" *Modernism/Modernity* 5.2 (1998), 95.

27. John Dewey, *Democracy and Education,* 291, 292. Further references will be cited as *DE.*

28. Gertrude Stein, "The Gradual Making of *The Making of Americans,*" from *Lectures in America,* in *Writings 1932–1946* (New York: Library of America, 1998), 276. Further references to *Writings 1932–1946* will be cited as *GSW.*

29. Ulla E. Dydo, ed., *A Stein Reader* (Evanston: Northwestern University Press, 1993), 21.

30. Though Stein herself wrote in longhand, leaving the typing of her manuscripts to Alice Toklas, the typing (and eventual type-setting) of her "masterpiece" was never in question for her.

31. On "losing-self sense," see Priscilla Wald's discussion in *Constituting Americans,* 238 and passim.

32. Ruddick, *Reading Gertrude Stein,* 77.

33. On the intertwining of the formal categories of novel and individual, see Nancy Armstrong, *How Novels Think: The Limits of Individualism from 1719–1900* (New York: Columbia University Press, 2005).

34. "Accordingly they escape the structure of meanings built around modern subjectivity, which presupposes the self's separation or cognitive distance from this reified realm of objects." Livingston, *Pragmatism and the Political Economy of Cultural Revolution,* 214.

35. Gertrude Stein, "The Story of a Book" [September 1933], in Robert Bartlett Haas, ed., *How Writing Is Written* (Los Angeles: Black Sparrow Press, 1974), 61. On this turn see Ulla E. Dydo, *Gertrude Stein: The Language That Rises, 1923–1934* (Evanston: Northwestern University Press, 2003), 534–94.

36. In Sara Blair's words, 27, rue de Fleurus is "a distinctly American-yet-metropolitan social form": Sara Blair, "Home Truths: Gertrude Stein, 27 Rue de Fleurus, and the Place of the Avant-Garde," *American Literary History* 12.3 (2000), 420. See also Marianne DeKoven, "'Excellent Not a Hull House': Gertrude Stein, Jane Addams, and Feminist-Modernist Political Culture," in *Rereading Modernism: New Directions in Feminist Criticism,* ed. Lisa Rado (New York: Garland, 1994), 341.

37. Bob Perelman also identifies *Alice B. Toklas* as an attempt at "the domestication of modernist art and writing" (*The Trouble with Genius: Reading Pound, Joyce, Stein, and Zukofsky* [Berkeley: University of California Press, 1994], 45). See also Margot Norris, "The 'Wife' and the 'Genius': Domesticating Modern Art in Stein's *Autobiography of Alice B. Toklas,*" in *Modernism, Gender, and Culture: A Cultural Studies Approach,* ed. Lisa Rado (New York: Garland, 1997), 79–99.

38. Gertrude Stein, *The Autobiography of Alice B. Toklas* (New York: Vintage, 1990), 13; further references will be cited as *ABT.*

39. For convenience, I will refer to the narrator as Toklas, but she should, of course (like Cather's McClure), be understood as "Toklas."

40. Mark Goble, "Cameo Appearances; or, When Gertrude Stein Checks into *Grand Hotel,*" *MLQ: Modern Language Quarterly* 62.2 (2001), 121.

41. Georgia Johnston, "Narratologies of Pleasure: Gertrude Stein's *The Autobiography of Alice B. Toklas.*" *Modern Fiction Studies* 42.3 (1996), 596.

42. For critical engagements with the intertwining of the two women's selves, see Catharine R. Stimpson, "Gertrice/Altrude: Stein, Toklas, and the Paradox of the Happy Marriage," in *Mothering the Mind: Twelve Studies of Writers and Their Silent Partners,* ed. Ruth Perry and Martine Watson Brownley (New York: Holmes and Meier, 1984), 122–39; Leigh Gilmore, "A Signature of Lesbian Autobiography: 'Gertrice/Altrude,'" in *Autobiography and Questions of Gender,* ed. Shirley Neuman (London: Frank Cass, 1991), 56–75; and Sidonie Smith, *Subjectivity, Identity, and the Body: Women's Autobiographical Practices in the Twentieth Century* (Bloomington: Indiana University Press, 1993).

43. Walter Lippmann, *The Phantom Public* (New York: Macmillan, 1925), 51.

44. John Dewey, *The Public and Its Problems* (New York: Henry Holt, 1927), 213.

45. Haas, ed. *Writing,* 69.

46. See Kirk Curnutt, "Inside and Outside: Gertrude Stein on Identity, Celebrity, and Authenticity," *Journal of Modern Literature* 23.2 (1999), 291–308, and Barbara

Will, *Gertrude Stein, Modernism, and the Problem of "Genius"* (Edinburgh: Edinburgh University Press, 2000).

47. See Stein's third and fourth lectures in *Narration* (1935; New York: Greenwood Press, 1969) and her article "American Newspapers" (*New York Herald Tribune,* 23 March 1935).

48. See James Livingston on Dewey's idea of the "thought-speculator," which neatly fits the Stein of the American tour (*Pragmatism and the Political Economy of Cultural Revolution,* 192–95).

49. Lansing Warren, "Gertrude Stein Views Life and Politics," *New York Times* 6 May 1934, SM23.

50. On the thirties incarnations of the liberal ideas at issue in the Steinian melting pot, see Sean McCann, *Gumshoe America: Hard-boiled Crime Fiction and the Rise and Fall of New Deal Liberalism* (Durham: Duke University Press, 2000).

51. Livingston, *Pragmatism and the Political Economy of Cultural Revolution,* 147.

52. Stein, "Money" (*Saturday Evening Post,* 13 June 1936), in Haas, ed., *Writing,* 107.

53. Haas, ed., *Writing,* 107.

54. Stein, "All About Money" (*Saturday Evening Post,* 22 August 1936), in Haas, ed., *Writing,* 110.

55. Michael Szalay, *New Deal Modernism: American Literature and the Invention of the Welfare State* (Durham: Duke University Press, 2000), 89.

56. Walter Lippmann, *Public Opinion* (1922; New York: Free Press, 1997), 186.

57. Stein, "American Crimes and How They Matter," in Haas, ed. *Writing,* 100.

58. Dewey, "The Lost Individual," *Individualism Old and New* (1930; New York: Capricorn Books, 1962), 71–72.

59. Though this late Dewey did show more interest in aesthetic matters, he is nowhere near Stein in his priorities. On art and the late Dewey, see Westbrook, *John Dewey and American Democracy,* 380–87.

Afterword

1. Marjorie Levinson, "What Is New Formalism?" *PMLA* 122.2 (2007), 558–69.

2. Wai Chee Dimock, *Through Other Continents: American Literature Across Deep Time* (Princeton: Princeton University Press, 2006), 23.

✭ SELECTED BIBLIOGRAPHY

Ackerman, Alan. *The Portable Theater: American Literature and the Nineteenth-Century Stage.* Baltimore: Johns Hopkins University Press, 1999.

Adams, Henry. *The Education of Henry Adams.* New York: Penguin, 1995.

Addams, Jane. *Democracy and Social Ethics.* New York: Macmillan, 1907.

——. "Immigration: A Field Neglected by the Scholar." In *Immigration and Americanization: Selected Readings,* edited by Philip Davis, 3–22. Boston: Ginn, 1920.

——. "Respect for Law." *New York Independent* 53 (1901): 18–20.

——. *The Second Twenty Years at Hull-House.* New York: Macmillan, 1930.

——. *Twenty Years at Hull-House.* New York: Macmillan, 1910.

Antin, Mary. *The Promised Land.* New York: Penguin, 1997.

——. *They Who Knock at Our Gates: A Complete Gospel of Immigration.* Boston: Houghton Mifflin, 1914.

Appiah, K. Anthony, and Amy Gutmann. *Color Conscious: The Political Morality of Race.* Princeton: Princeton University Press, 1996.

Armstrong, Nancy. *How Novels Think: The Limits of Individualism from 1719–1900.* New York: Columbia University Press, 2005.

Arnold, Matthew. *Culture and Anarchy.* New Haven: Yale University Press, 1994.

Baudelaire, Charles. *The Painter of Modern Life and Other Essays,* edited and translated by Jonathan Mayne. New York: Phaidon, 1970.

Beard, Annie E. S. *Our Foreign-Born Citizens: What They Have Done for America.* New York: Thomas Y. Crowell, 1922.

Bell, Ian F. A. *Henry James and the Past: Readings into Time.* London: Macmillan, 1991.

Bender, Thomas. *Toward an Urban Vision: Ideas and Institutions in Nineteenth-Century America.* Lexington: University of Kentucky Press, 1975.

Berlant, Lauren. "National Brands/National Body: *Imitation of Life.*" In *The Phantom Public Sphere,* edited by Bruce Robbins, 173–208. Minneapolis: University of Minnesota Press, 1993.

Blair, Sara. *Henry James and the Writing of Race and Nation.* New York: Cambridge University Press, 1996.

——. "Home Truths: Gertrude Stein, 27 Rue de Fleurus, and the Place of the Avant-Garde." *American Literary History* 12 (2000): 417–37.

——. "Modernism and the Politics of Culture." In *The Cambridge Companion to Modernism,* edited by Michael Levenson, 157–74. Cambridge: Cambridge University Press, 1999.

Bloom, Edward A., and Lillian D. Bloom. "The Genesis of *Death Comes for the Archbishop.*" *American Literature* 26 (1955): 479–506.

Boas, Franz. *The Shaping of American Anthropology, 1883–1911: A Franz Boas Reader,* edited by George W. Stocking, Jr. New York: Basic Books, 1974.

Boelhower, William. *Immigrant Autobiography in the United States: Four Versions of the Italian American Self.* Verona: Essedue, 1982.

——. *Through a Glass Darkly: Ethnic Semiosis in American Literature.* New York: Oxford University Press, 1984.

Bohlke, L. Brent, ed. *Willa Cather in Person: Interviews, Speeches, and Letters.* Lincoln: University of Nebraska Press, 1986.

Bok, Edward. *The Americanization of Edward Bok: The Autobiography of a Dutch Boy Fifty Years After.* New York: Scribner's, 1920.

Boone, Joseph Allen. *Libidinal Currents: Sexuality and the Making of Modernism.* Chicago: University of Chicago Press, 1998.

Bourne, Randolph. "Trans-National America." In *The Radical Will: Selected Writings 1911–1918,* edited by Olaf Hansen, 248–64. Berkeley: University of California Press, 1977.

Bramen, Carrie Tirado. "The Urban Picturesque and the Spectacle of Americanization." *American Quarterly* 52 (2000): 444–77.

——. *The Uses of Variety: Modern Americanism and the Quest for National Distinctiveness.* Cambridge: Harvard University Press, 2000.

Breisach, Ernst A. *American Progressive History: An Experiment in Modernization.* Chicago: University of Chicago Press, 1993.

Brodkin, Karen. *How Jews Became White Folks and What That Says about Race in America.* New Brunswick: Rutgers University Press, 1999.

Browder, Laura. *Slippery Characters: Ethnic Impersonators and American Identities.* Chapel Hill: University of North Carolina Press, 2000.

Brown, Bill. *The Material Unconscious: American Amusement, Stephen Crane, and the Economics of Play.* Cambridge: Harvard University Press, 1996.

——. *A Sense of Things: The Object Matter of American Literature.* Chicago: University of Chicago Press, 2003.

Brown, Gillian. *Domestic Individualism: Imagining Self in Nineteenth-Century America.* Berkeley: University of California Press, 1990.

Buelens, Gert. *Henry James and the "Aliens" in Possession of the American Scene.* Amsterdam: Rodopi, 2003.

Cahan, Abraham. *The Rise of David Levinsky.* New York: Penguin, 1993.

——. *Yekl: A Tale of the New York Ghetto.* New York: D. Appleton, 1896.

Casper, Scott E. *Constructing American Lives: Biography and Culture in Nineteenth-Century America.* Chapel Hill: University of North Carolina Press, 1999.

Castle, Terry. "Phantasmagoria: Spectral Technology and the Metaphorics of Modern Reverie." *Critical Inquiry* 15 (1988): 26–61.

Castronovo, Russ. *Beautiful Democracy: Aesthetics and Anarchy in a Global Era.* Chicago: University of Chicago Press, 2007.

Cather, Willa. *Death Comes for the Archbishop.* New York: Vintage, 1990.

——. *My Ántonia.* New York: Vintage, 1994.

——. *Not Under Forty.* New York: Alfred A. Knopf, 1936.

——. *The Professor's House.* New York: Vintage, 1990.

——. *The Song of the Lark.* New York: Vintage, 1999.

——. *Willa Cather On Writing: Critical Studies on Writing as an Art.* Lincoln: University of Nebraska Press, 1988.

Chesnutt, Charles W. *The Marrow of Tradition.* New York: Penguin, 1993.

Chessman, Harriet Scott. *The Public Is Invited to Dance: Representation, the Body, and Dialogue in Gertrude Stein*. Stanford: Stanford University Press, 1989.

Cole, Bob, J. Rosamond Johnson, and James Weldon Johnson. "Under the Bamboo Tree." New York: Jos. W. Stern, 1902.

Cooley, Charles Horton. *Human Nature and the Social Order*. New York: Scribner's, 1902.

Croly, Herbert. *The Promise of American Life*. Indianapolis: Bobbs-Merrill, 1965.

Cruse, Harold. *The Crisis of the Negro Intellectual*. New York: William Morrow, 1967.

Curnutt, Kirk. "Inside and Outside: Gertrude Stein on Identity, Celebrity, and Authenticity." *Journal of Modern Literature* 23 (1999): 291–308.

Davidson, Cathy. "Preface: No More Separate Spheres!" *American Literature* 70 (1998): 443–63.

Deegan, Mary Jo. *Race, Hull-House, and the University of Chicago: A New Conscience Against Ancient Evils*. Westport, CT: Praeger, 2002.

Degler, Carl. *In Search of Human Nature: The Decline and Revival of Darwinism in American Social Thought*. New York: Oxford University Press, 1992.

DeKoven, Marianne. "'Excellent Not a Hull House': Gertrude Stein, Jane Addams, and Feminist-Modernist Political Culture." In *Rereading Modernism: New Directions in Feminist Criticism*, edited by Lisa Rado, 321–43. New York: Garland, 1994.

———. "The Politics of Modernist Form." *New Literary History* 23 (1992): 675–90.

De Man, Paul. "Autobiography as De-facement." *MLN* 94 (1979): 919–30.

Dewey, John. *Democracy and Education: An Introduction to the Philosophy of Education*. New York: Free Press, 1997.

———. *The Essential Dewey, Volume I: Pragmatism, Education, Democracy*, edited by Larry A. Hickman and Thomas M. Alexander. Bloomington: Indiana University Press, 1998.

———. *Individualism Old and New*. New York: Capricorn Books, 1962.

———. *The Public and Its Problems*. New York: Henry Holt, 1927.

Dillon, Elizabeth Maddock. "Fear of Formalism: Kant, Twain, and Cultural Studies in American Literature." *diacritics* 27 (1998): 46–69.

Dimock, Wai Chee. *Residues of Justice: Literature, Law, Philosophy*. Berkeley: University of California Press, 1996.

———. *Through Other Continents: American Literature Across Deep Time*. Princeton: Princeton University Press, 2006.

Dippie, Brian. *The Vanishing American*. Middletown, CT: Wesleyan University Press, 1982.

Douglas, Ann. *Terrible Honesty: Mongrel Manhattan in the 1920s*. New York: Farrar, Straus and Giroux, 1995.

Drachsler, Julius. *Democracy and Assimilation*. New York: Macmillan, 1920.

Du Bois, W. E. B. *Dusk of Dawn: An Essay Toward an Autobiography of a Race Concept*. In *W. E. B. Du Bois: Writings*, edited by Nathan Huggins, 549–802. New York: Library of America, 1986.

———. "The Evolution of the Race Problem." In *W. E. B. Du Bois Speaks: Speeches and Addresses, 1890–1919*, edited by Philip S. Foner, 196–210. New York: Pathfinder, 1970.

———. *The Souls of Black Folk*. New York: Knopf, 1993.

Dydo, Ulla E. *Gertrude Stein: The Language That Rises, 1923–1934*. Evanston: Northwestern University Press, 2003.

Dydo, Ulla E., ed. *A Stein Reader*. Evanston: Northwestern University Press, 1993.

Eakin, Paul John. *Fictions in Autobiography: Studies in the Art of Self-Invention*. Princeton: Princeton University Press, 1985.

Edel, Leon, ed. *Henry James Letters*, vol. I. Cambridge: Belknap Press of Harvard University, 1974.

——. *Henry James Letters*, vol. IV. Cambridge: Harvard University Press, 1984.

Edwards, Brent. "The Seemingly Eclipsed Window of Form: James Weldon Johnson's Prefaces." In *The Jazz Cadence of American Culture,* edited by Robert G. O'Meally, 580–601. New York: Columbia University Press, 1998.

Eisenach, Eldon J. *The Lost Promise of Progressivism*. Lawrence: University Press of Kansas, 1994.

Elliott, Michael. *The Culture Concept: Writing and Difference in the Age of Realism*. Minneapolis: University of Minnesota Press, 2002.

Ellison, Ralph. "The Little Man at Chehaw Station." In *The Collected Essays of Ralph Ellison,* edited by John F. Callahan, 489–519. New York: Modern Library, 1995.

English, Daylanne. *Unnatural Selections: Eugenics in American Modernism and the Harlem Renaissance*. Chapel Hill: University of North Carolina Press, 2004.

Entin, Joseph. *Sensational Modernism: Experimental Fiction and Photography in Thirties America*. Chapel Hill: University of North Carolina Press, 2007.

Esch, Deborah. "A Jamesian About-Face: Notes on 'The Jolly Corner.'" *ELH* 50 (1983): 587–605.

Ethington, Philip J. *The Public City: The Political Construction of Urban Life in San Francisco, 1850–1900*. Cambridge: Cambridge University Press, 1994.

Evans, Brad. *Before Cultures: The Ethnographic Imagination in American Literature, 1865–1920*. Chicago: University of Chicago Press, 2005.

——. "Where Was Boas During the Renaissance in Harlem? Diffusion, Race, and the Culture Paradigm in the History of Anthropology." In *Central Sites, Peripheral Visions: Cultural and Institutional Crossing in the History of Anthropology,* edited by Richard Handler, 69–98. Madison: University of Wisconsin Press, 2006.

Fairchild, Henry Pratt. *Immigration: A World Movement and Its American Significance*. New York: Macmillan, 1913.

——. *The Melting-Pot Mistake*. Boston: Little, Brown, 1926.

Farland, Maria. "Gertrude Stein's Brain Work." *American Literature* 76 (2004): 117–48.

——. "W. E. B. Du Bois, Anthropometric Science, and the Limits of Racial Uplift." *American Quarterly* 58 (2006): 1017–45.

Felski, Rita. "Modernist Studies and Cultural Studies: Reflections on Method." *Modernism/Modernity* 10 (September 2003): 501–17.

Ferguson, Frances. *Solitude and the Sublime: Romanticism and the Aesthetics of Individuation*. New York: Routledge, 1992.

Filene, Peter G. "An Obituary for 'The Progressive Movement'." *American Quarterly* 22 (1970): 20–34.

Frazier, E. Franklin. "Sociological Theory and Race Relations." *American Sociological Review* 12 (1947): 265–71.

Freedman, Jonathan. "Lessons Out of School: T. S. Eliot's Jewish Problem and the Making of Modernism." *Modernism/Modernity* 10 (2003): 419–29.

———. *The Temple of Culture: Assimilation and Anti-Semitism in Literary Anglo-America.* New York: Oxford University Press, 2000.

Fuchs, Laurence. *The American Kaleidoscope: Race, Ethnicity, and the Civic Culture.* Hanover: University Press of New England, 1990.

Gaines, Kevin K. *Uplifting the Race: Black Leadership, Politics, and Culture in the Twentieth Century.* Chapel Hill: University of North Carolina Press, 1996.

Gandal, Keith. *The Virtues of the Vicious: Jacob Riis, Stephen Crane, and the Spectacle of the Slum.* New York: Oxford University Press, 1997.

Gans, Herbert J. "Symbolic Ethnicity: The Future of Ethnic Groups and Cultures in America." In *On the Making of Americans: Essays in Honor of David Riesman,* edited by Herbert J. Gans, Nathan Glazer, Joseph R. Gusfield, and Christopher Jenks, 193–220. Philadelphia: University of Pennsylvania Press, 1979.

Gates, Henry Louis, Jr. "The Trope of a New Negro and the Reconstruction of the Image of the Black." *Representations* 24 (1988): 129–55.

Geismar, Maxwell David. *Henry James and the Jacobites.* Boston: Houghton Mifflin, 1963.

Gerstle, Gary. *American Crucible: Race and Nation in the Twentieth Century.* Princeton: Princeton University Press, 2002.

Gilmore, Leigh. "A Signature of Lesbian Autobiography: 'Gertrice/Altrude.'" In *Autobiography and Questions of Gender,* edited by Shirley Neuman, 56–75. London: Frank Cass, 1991.

Gilroy, Paul. *The Black Atlantic: Modernity and Double Consciousness.* New York: Verso, 1993.

Gleason, Philip. "The Melting Pot: Symbol of Fusion or Confusion?" *American Quarterly* 16 (1964): 20–46.

———. *Speaking of Diversity: Language and Ethnicity in Twentieth-Century America.* Baltimore: Johns Hopkins University Press, 1992.

Gleason, William. *The Leisure Ethic: Work and Play in American Literature, 1840–1940.* Stanford: Stanford University Press, 1999.

Goble, Mark. "Cameo Appearances; or, When Gertrude Stein Checks into *Grand Hotel.*" *MLQ: Modern Language Quarterly* 62 (2001): 117–63.

———. "Delirious Henry James: A Small Boy and New York." *Modern Fiction Studies* 50 (2004): 351–84.

Goellnicht, Donald. "Passing as Autobiography: James Weldon Johnson's *The Autobiography of an Ex-Coloured Man.*" *African American Review* 30 (1996): 17–33.

Goldsby, Jacqueline. *A Spectacular Secret: Lynching in American Life and Literature.* Chicago: University of Chicago Press, 2006.

Gordon, Milton. *Assimilation in American Life.* New York: Oxford University Press, 1964.

Gunning, Tom. "From the Kaleidoscope to the X-Ray: Urban Spectatorship, Poe, Benjamin, and *Traffic in Souls* (1913)." *Wide Angle* 19 (1997): 25–61.

Gutiérrez, Ramón. *When Jesus Came, the Corn Mothers Went Away.* Stanford: Stanford University Press, 1991.

Gutman, Herbert G. "Work, Culture, and Society in Industrializing America, 1815–1919." *American Historical Review* 78 (1973): 531–88.

Haenni, Sabine. "Visual and Theatrical Culture, Tenement Fiction, and the Immigrant Subject in Abraham Cahan's *Yekl." American Literature* 71 (1999): 493–527.

Hale, Dorothy J. *Social Formalism: The Novel in Theory from Henry James to the Present.* Stanford: Stanford University Press, 1998.

Hale, Grace Elizabeth. *Making Whiteness: The Culture of Segregation in the South, 1890–1940.* New York: Pantheon, 1998.

Hamilton, J. Crawford. "Snap Shots in Central Park." *Munsey's Magazine* 6 (1891): 3–10.

Hamington, Maurice. "Public Pragmatism: Jane Addams and Ida B. Wells on Lynching." *Journal of Speculative Philosophy* 19 (2005): 167–74.

Hansen, Jonathan M. *The Lost Promise of Patriotism: Debating American Identity, 1890–1920.* Chicago: University of Chicago Press, 2003.

Harding, Sandra, ed. *The 'Racial' Economy of Science: Toward a Democratic Future.* Bloomington: Indiana University Press, 1993.

Hatt, Michael. "Race, Ritual, and Responsibility: Performativity and the Southern Lynching." In *Performing the Body/ Performing the Text,* edited by Amelia Jones and Andrew Stephenson, 76–88. New York: Routledge, 1999.

Haviland, Beverly. *Henry James's Last Romance: Making Sense of the Past and the American Scene.* New York: Cambridge University Press, 1997.

Hegeman, Susan. *Patterns for America: Modernism and the Concept of Culture.* Princeton: Princeton University Press, 1999.

Heinze, Andrew. *Adapting to Abundance: Jewish Immigrants, Mass Consumption, and the Search for American Identity.* New York: Columbia University Press, 1990.

——. *"Schizophrenia Americana:* Aliens, Alienists and the 'Personality Shift' of Twentieth-Century Culture." *American Quarterly* 55 (2003): 227–56.

Higham, John. *History: Professional Scholarship in America.* Baltimore: Johns Hopkins University Press, 1989.

——. *Send These to Me: Immigrants in Urban America.* Baltimore: Johns Hopkins University Press, 1984.

——. *Strangers in the Land: Patterns of American Nativism, 1860–1925.* New Brunswick, NJ: Rutgers University Press, 1955.

Hilgart, John. "Death Comes for the Aesthete: Commodity Culture and the Artifact in Cather's *The Professor's House." Studies in the Novel* 30 (1998): 377–404.

Historical Statistics of the United States, Colonial Times to 1970. Washington, D.C.: U.S. Bureau of the Census, 1975.

Hofstadter, Richard. *The Progressive Historians: Turner, Beard, Parrington.* New York: Knopf, 1968.

Howells, William Dean. "Autobiography, A New Form of Literature." *Harper's Monthly* 119 (1909): 795–98.

Howlett, W. J. *Life of the Right Reverend Joseph P. Machebeuf, D.D.: Pioneer Priest of Ohio, Pioneer Priest of New Mexico, Pioneer Priest of Colorado, Vicar Apostolic of Colorado and Utah and First Bishop of Denver.* Pueblo, CO: The Franklin Press, 1908.

Hungerford, Amy. *The Holocaust of Texts: Genocide, Literature, and Personification.* Chicago: University of Chicago Press, 2003.

Hutchinson, George. *The Harlem Renaissance in Black and White.* Cambridge: Harvard University Press, 1995.

Ignatiev, Noel. *How the Irish Became White.* New York: Routledge, 1995.

Irving, Katrina. *Immigrant Mothers: Narratives of Race and Maternity, 1890–1925.* Urbana: University of Illinois Press, 2000.

Jacknis, Ira. "Franz Boas and Exhibits: On the Limitations of the Museum Method of Anthropology." In *Objects and Others: Essays on Museums and Material Culture,* edited by George Stocking, Jr., 75–111. Madison: University of Wisconsin Press, 1985.

Jacobson, Matthew. *Barbarian Virtues: The United States Encounters Foreign Peoples at Home and Abroad, 1876–1917.* New York: Hill and Wang, 2000.

——. *Whiteness of a Different Color: European Immigrants and the Alchemy of Race.* Cambridge: Harvard University Press, 1998.

James, Henry. *The American Scene.* New York: Penguin, 1994.

——. "The Art of Fiction." In *Literary Criticism: French Writers, Other European Writers, The Prefaces to the New York Edition,* edited by Leon Edel, 1035–341. New York: Library of America, 1984.

——. *The Art of the Novel: Critical Prefaces.* New York: Scribner, 1934.

——. *Hawthorne.* London: Macmillan, 1879.

——. "The Jolly Corner." In *Eight Tales from the Major Phase,* 314–50. New York: Norton, 1969.

——. *Notes of a Son and Brother.* New York: Scribner's, 1914.

——. "Review of Theodore Roosevelt, *American Ideals and Other Essays Social and Political.*" In *Literary Criticism: Essays on Literature, American Writers, English Writers,* edited by Leon Edel, 663–67. New York: Library of America, 1985.

——. *A Small Boy and Others.* New York: Scribner's, 1913.

——. *The Tragic Muse.* New York: Penguin, 1995.

James, William. *A Pluralistic Universe.* London: Longmans, Green, 1909.

——. *The Varieties of Religious Experience.* New York: Penguin, 1985.

——. *The Will to Believe and Other Essays in Popular Philosophy.* New York: Longmans, Green, 1897.

Johnson, Barbara. "Thresholds of Difference: Structures of Address in Zora Neale Hurston." In *"Race," Writing, and Difference,* edited by Henry Louis Gates, Jr., 317–28. Chicago: University of Chicago Press, 1986.

Johnson, James Weldon. *Along This Way.* New York: Da Capo, 2000.

——. *The Autobiography of an Ex-Coloured Man.* New York: Vintage, 1989.

——. *The Book of American Negro Poetry.* New York: Harcourt, Brace, 1931.

——. *The Books of American Negro Spirituals,* edited by James Weldon Johnson and J. Rosamond Johnson. New York: Da Capo, 1970.

——. *God's Trombones: Seven Negro Sermons in Verse.* New York: Viking, 1927.

——. *James Weldon Johnson: Selected Writings,* edited by Sondra Kathryn Wilson. New York: Library of America, 2004.

——. *The Selected Writings of James Weldon Johnson, Volume I: The New York Age Editorials (1914–1923),* edited by Sondra Kathryn Wilson. New York: Oxford University Press, 1995.

——. *The Selected Writings of James Weldon Johnson, Volume II: Social, Political, and Literary Essays,* edited by Sondra Kathryn Wilson. New York: Oxford University Press, 1995.

Johnston, Georgia. "Narratologies of Pleasure: Gertrude Stein's *The Autobiography of Alice B. Toklas.*" *Modern Fiction Studies* 42 (1996): 590–606.

Jolly, Roslyn. *Henry James: History, Narrative, Fiction.* Oxford: Clarendon Press, 1993.

Jones, Gavin. *Strange Talk: The Politics of Dialect Literature in Gilded Age America.* Berkeley: University of California Press, 1999.

Kadlec, David. *Mosaic Modernism: Anarchism, Pragmatism, Culture.* Baltimore: Johns Hopkins University Press, 2000.

Kallen, Horace. *Culture and Democracy in the United States.* New York: Boni & Liveright, 1924.

Kaplan, Amy. "Manifest Domesticity." *American Literature* 70 (1998): 581–606.

———. *The Social Construction of American Realism.* Chicago: University of Chicago Press, 1988.

Karp, Ivan. *Exhibiting Cultures: The Poetics and Politics of Museum Display.* Washington: Smithsonian, 1991.

Kazal, Russell A. "Revisiting Assimilation: The Rise, Fall, and Reappraisal of a Concept in American Ethnic History." *American Historical Review* 100 (1995): 437–71.

Kazin, Alfred. *On Native Grounds.* New York: Reynal & Hitchcock, 1942.

Kerber, Linda. "Separate Spheres, Female Worlds, Woman's Place: The Rhetoric of Women's History." *Journal of American History* 75 (1988): 9–39.

Kloppenberg, James T. *Uncertain Victory: Social Democracy and Progressivism in European and American Thought, 1870–1920.* New York: Oxford University Press, 1986.

Knapp, Steven. *Literary Interest: The Limits of Anti-Formalism.* Cambridge: Harvard University Press, 1993.

Lal, Barbara Ballis. *The Romance of Culture in an Urban Civilization: Robert Park on Race and Ethnic Relations in Cities.* London: Routledge, 1990.

Larson, Erik. *The Devil in the White City.* New York: Random House, 2003.

Lears, T. J. Jackson. *No Place of Grace: Antimodernism and the Transformation of American Culture, 1880–1920.* Chicago: University of Chicago Press, 1994.

Lee, Hermione. *Willa Cather: A Life Saved Up.* London: Virago, 1989.

Levine, Lawrence W. *Highbrow/Lowbrow: The Emergence of Cultural Hierarchy in America.* Cambridge: Harvard University Press, 1988.

Levinson, Marjorie. "What Is New Formalism?" *PMLA* 122.2 (2007), 558–69.

Levy, Eugene. *James Weldon Johnson: Black Leader, Black Voice.* Chicago: University of Chicago Press, 1973.

Lewis, David Levering. *W. E. B. Du Bois: Biography of a Race.* New York: Henry Holt, 1993.

———. *When Harlem Was in Vogue.* New York: Alfred A. Knopf, 1981.

Lhamon, W. T. *Raising Cain: Blackface Performance from Jim Crow to Hip Hop.* Cambridge: Harvard University Press, 1998.

Lippmann, Walter. *Drift and Mastery: An Attempt to Diagnose the Current Unrest.* Madison: University of Wisconsin Press, 1985.

———. *The Phantom Public.* New York: Macmillan, 1925.

Lissak, Rivka Shpak. *Pluralism and Progressives: Hull House and the New Immigrants, 1890–1919.* Chicago: University of Chicago Press, 1989.

Livingston, James. *Pragmatism and the Political Economy of Cultural Revolution, 1850–1940.* Chapel Hill: University of North Carolina Press, 1994.

———. *Pragmatism, Feminism, and Democracy: Rethinking the Politics of American History.* New York: Routledge, 2001.

Lott, Eric. *Love and Theft: Blackface Minstrelsy and the American Working Class.* New York: Oxford University Press, 1993.

Lowe, Lisa. *Immigrant Acts: On Asian American Cultural Politics.* Durham: Duke University Press, 1996.

Lubar, Steven, and W. David Kingery, eds. *History from Things: Essays on Material Culture.* Washington: Smithsonian Institution Press, 1993.

Luhan, Mabel Dodge. *Lorenzo in Taos.* New York: Knopf, 1932.

Lutes, Jean. *Front-Page Girls: Women Journalists in American Culture and Fiction, 1880–1930.* Ithaca: Cornell University Press, 2006.

———. "Lynching Coverage and the American Reporter-Novelist." *American Literary History* 19 (2007): 456–81.

Macpherson, C. B. *The Political Theory of Possessive Individualism: Hobbes to Locke.* Oxford: Oxford University Press, 1962.

Mao, Douglas. *Solid Objects: Modernism and the Test of Production.* Princeton: Princeton University Press, 1998.

McCann, Sean. *Gumshoe America: Hard-boiled Crime Fiction and the Rise and Fall of New Deal Liberalism.* Durham: Duke University Press, 2000.

McKee, James B. *Sociology and the Race Problem: The Failure of a Perspective.* Urbana: University of Illinois Press, 1993.

McKeon, Michael. *The Secret History of Domesticity: Public, Private, and the Division of Knowledge.* Baltimore: Johns Hopkins University Press, 2005.

McWhirter, David. "'A Provision of Responsibilities': Senses of the Past in Henry James's Fourth Phase." In *Enacting History in Henry James: Narrative, Power, and Ethics,* edited by Gert Buelens, 148–65. Cambridge: Cambridge University Press, 1997.

McWhirter, David, ed. *Henry James's New York Edition: The Construction of Authorship.* Stanford: Stanford University Press, 1995.

McWilliams, Wilson Carey. "Standing at Armageddon: Morality and Religion in Progressive Thought." In *Progressivism and the New Democracy,* edited by Sidney M. Milkis and Jerome M. Mileur, 103–25. Amherst: University of Massachusetts Press, 1999.

Mead, George Herbert. "The Social Self." *Journal of Philosophy, Psychology, and Scientific Methods* 10 (1913): 374–80.

Michaels, Walter Benn. *The Gold Standard and the Logic of Naturalism.* Berkeley: University of California Press, 1987.

———. *Our America: Nativism, Modernism, and Pluralism.* Durham: Duke University Press, 1995.

Michaelsen, Scott. *The Limits of Multiculturalism: Interrogating the Origins of American Anthropology.* Minneapolis: University of Minnesota Press, 1999.

Millgate, Michael. *Testamentary Acts: Browning, Tennyson, James, Hardy.* New York: Oxford University Press, 1992.

Morton, Leah. *I Am a Woman—and a Jew.* New York: J. H. Sears, 1926.

Most, Andrea. *Making Americans: Jews and the Broadway Musical.* Cambridge: Harvard University Press, 2004.

Mullin, Molly. "The Patronage of Difference: Making Indian Art 'Art, Not Ethnology'." In *The Traffic in Culture: Refiguring Art and Anthropology,* edited by George E. Marcus and Fred R. Myers, 166–99. Berkeley: University of California Press, 1995.

Nealon, Christopher. "Affect-Genealogy: Feeling and Affiliation in Willa Cather." *American Literature* 69 (1997): 5–37.

Nicholls, Peter. *Modernisms: A Literary Guide.* Berkeley: University of California Press, 1995.

Norris, Margot. "The 'Wife' and the 'Genius': Domesticating Modern Art in Stein's *Autobiography of Alice B. Toklas.*" In *Modernism, Gender, and Culture: A Cultural Studies Approach,* edited by Lisa Rado, 79–99. New York: Garland, 1997.

North, Michael. *The Dialect of Modernism: Race, Language, and Twentieth-Century Literature.* New York: Oxford University Press, 1994.

Nussbaum, Martha. *Poetic Justice: The Literary Imagination and Public Life.* Boston: Beacon Press, 1995.

Olney, James, ed. *Autobiography: Essays Theoretical and Critical.* Princeton: Princeton University Press, 1980.

Omi, Michael, and Howard Winant. *Racial Formation in the United States: From the 1960s to the 1980s.* New York: Routledge, 1986.

Oster, Judith. "See(k)ing the Self: Mirrors and Mirroring in Bicultural Texts." *MELUS* 23 (1998): 59–83.

Øverland, Orm. "The First World War Americanization Movement and Immigrant Resistance to the Melting Pot." In *Multiculturalism and the American Self,* edited by William Boelhower and Alfred Hornung, 139–56. Heidelberg: C. Winter, 2000.

Panunzio, Constantine. *The Soul of an Immigrant.* New York: Macmillan, 1921.

Parisi, Joseph, and Stephen Young, eds. *Dear Editor: A History of Poetry in Letters: The First Fifty Years, 1912–1962.* New York: W. W. Norton, 2002.

Park, Robert. "Racial Assimilation in Secondary Groups with Particular Reference to the Negro." *American Journal of Sociology* 19 (1914): 606–23.

Park, Robert E., and Ernest W. Burgess. *Introduction to the Science of Sociology,* 2nd ed. Chicago: University of Chicago Press, 1924.

Park, Robert E., and Herbert A. Miller. *Old World Traits Transplanted.* New York: Harper & Bros., 1921.

Perelman, Bob. *The Trouble with Genius: Reading Pound, Joyce, Stein, and Zukofsky.* Berkeley: University of California Press, 1994.

Pfister, Joel. *Individuality Incorporated: Indians and the Multicultural Modern.* Durham: Duke University Press, 2004.

Pittenger, Mark. "A World of Difference: Constructing the 'Underclass' in Progressive America." *American Quarterly* 49 (1997): 26–65.

Poole, Ernest. *The Voice of the Street.* New York: A. S. Barnes, 1906.

Posnock, Ross. *Color and Culture: Black Writers and the Making of the Modern Intellectual.* Cambridge: Harvard University Press, 1998.

———. *The Trial of Curiosity: Henry James, William James, and the Challenge of Modernity.* New York: Oxford University Press, 1991.

Pupin, Michael. *From Immigrant to Inventor.* New York: Scribner's, 1924.

Ravage, Marcus Eli. *The Making of an American.* New York: Harper & Bros., 1917.

Reynolds, Guy. *Willa Cather in Context: Progress, Race, Empire.* London: Macmillan, 1996.

Richards, I. A. *Science and Poetry.* New York: W. W. Norton, 1962.

Riis, Jacob A. *How the Other Half Lives.* New York: Scribner, 1917.

———. *The Making of an American.* New York: Macmillan, 1901.

Rivkin, Julie. *False Positions: The Representational Logics of Henry James's Fiction.* Stanford: Stanford University Press, 1996.

Robinson, James Harvey. *The New History: Essays Illustrating the Modern Historical Outlook.* New York: Macmillan, 1912.

Rodgers, Daniel T. "In Search of Progressivism." *Reviews in American History* 10 (1982): 113–32.

Roediger, David. *The Wages of Whiteness: Race and the Making of the American Working Class.* London: Verso, 1991.

Rogin, Michael. *Blackface, White Noise: Jewish Immigrants in the Hollywood Melting Pot.* Berkeley: University of California Press, 1996.

Rosenzweig, Roy, and Elizabeth Blackmar. *The Park and the People: A History of Central Park.* Ithaca: Cornell University Press, 1992.

Ross, Dorothy. *The Origins of American Social Science.* Cambridge: Cambridge University Press, 1992.

Rowe, John Carlos. *The Other Henry James.* Durham: Duke University Press, 1998.

Ruddick, Lisa. *Reading Gertrude Stein: Body, Text, Gnosis.* Ithaca: Cornell University Press, 1990.

Schroeter, James, ed. *Willa Cather and Her Critics.* Ithaca: Cornell University Press, 1968.

Scudder, Vida. *A Listener in Babel: Being a Series of Imaginary Conversations Held at the Close of the Last Century and Reported.* Boston: Houghton Mifflin, 1903.

Seigfried, Charlene Haddock. *William James's Radical Reconstruction of Philosophy.* Albany: State University of New York Press, 1990.

Seltzer, Mark. *Bodies and Machines.* New York: Routledge, 1992.

———. *Henry James and the Art of Power.* Ithaca: Cornell University Press, 1984.

Sergeant, Elizabeth Shepley. *Willa Cather: A Memoir.* Lincoln: Bison–University of Nebraska Press, 1986.

Simkhovitch, Mary Kingsbury. *The City Worker's World in America.* New York: Macmillan, 1917.

Simons, Sarah E. "Social Assimilation. I." *American Journal of Sociology* 6 (1901): 790–822.

Singal, Daniel Joseph. "Towards a Definition of American Modernism." *American Quarterly* 39 (1987): 7–26.

Slosson, Edwin E. Introduction to *The Life Stories of Undistinguished Americans as Told By Themselves,* edited by Hamilton Holt, 1–5. New York: Routledge, 1999.

Smith, Rogers. *Civic Ideals: Conflicting Visions of Citizenship in U.S. History.* New Haven: Yale University Press, 1997.

Smith, Sidonie. *Subjectivity, Identity, and the Body: Women's Autobiographical Practices in the Twentieth Century.* Bloomington: Indiana University Press, 1993.

Smith-Rosenberg, Carroll. "Domesticating Virtue: Coquettes and Revolutionaries in Young America." In *Literature and the Body: Essays on Populations and Persons: Selected Papers from the English Institute,* edited by Elaine Scarry, 160–84. Baltimore: Johns Hopkins University Press, 1988.

Sollors, Werner. *Beyond Ethnicity: Consent and Descent in American Culture.* New York: Oxford University Press, 1986.

———. "A Critique of Pure Pluralism." In *Reconstructing American Literary History,* edited by Sacvan Bercovitch, 250–79. Cambridge: Harvard University Press, 1986.

——. "Ethnic Modernism." In *The Cambridge History of American Literature,* Vol. 6, edited by Sacvan Bercovitch, 353–556. Cambridge: Cambridge University Press, 2002.

——. *Ethnic Modernism.* Cambridge: Harvard University Press, 2008.

——. *The Invention of Ethnicity.* New York: Oxford University Press, 1986.

——. *Neither White Nor Black Yet Both.* New York: Oxford University Press, 1997.

Spillers, Hortense J. "Moving on Down the Line: Variations on the African-American Sermon." In *Black, White, and in Color: Essays on American Literature and Culture,* 251–76. Chicago: University of Chicago Press, 2003.

Stansell, Christine. *American Moderns: Bohemian New York and the Creation of a New Century.* New York: Henry Holt, 2000.

Stein, Gertrude. *The Autobiography of Alice B. Toklas.* New York: Vintage, 1990.

——. *Everybody's Autobiography.* London: Virago, 1985.

——. *How Writing Is Written,* edited by Robert Bartlett Haas. Los Angeles: Black Sparrow Press, 1974.

——. *The Making of Americans: Being a History of a Family's Progress.* Normal, IL: Dalkey Archive, 1995.

——. *Narration.* New York: Greenwood Press, 1969.

——. *A Stein Reader,* edited by Ulla E. Dydo. Evanston: Northwestern University Press, 1993.

——. *Three Lives.* New York: Vintage, 1936.

——. *Writings 1932–1946,* edited by Catharine Stimpson. New York: Library of America, 1998.

Stepto, Robert. *From Behind the Veil: A Study of Afro-American Narrative.* Urbana: University of Illinois Press, 1979.

Stern, E. G. *My Mother and I.* New York: Macmillan, 1917.

Stewart, Susan. *On Longing: Narratives of the Miniature, the Gigantic, the Souvenir, the Collection.* Baltimore: Johns Hopkins University Press, 1984.

Stimpson, Catharine R. "Gertrice/Altrude: Stein, Toklas, and the Paradox of the Happy Marriage." In *Mothering the Mind: Twelve Studies of Writers and Their Silent Partners,* edited by Ruth Perry and Martine Watson Brownley, 122–39. New York: Holmes and Meier, 1984.

Stocking, George, Jr., ed. *Objects and Others: Essays on Museums and Material Culture.* Madison: University of Wisconsin Press, 1985.

Stocking, George W., Jr. *Race, Culture, and Evolution: Essays in the History of Anthropology.* Chicago: University of Chicago Press, 1968.

Sundquist, Eric J. *The Hammers of Creation: Folk Culture in Modern African-American Fiction.* Athens: University of Georgia Press, 1992.

——. "In the Lion's Mouth." *American Literary History* 15 (2003): 35–38.

——. *To Wake the Nations: Race in the Making of American Literature.* Cambridge: The Belknap Press of Harvard University Press, 1993.

Szalay, Michael. *New Deal Modernism: American Literature and the Invention of the Welfare State.* Durham: Duke University Press, 2000.

Taylor, Frederick Winslow. *The Principles of Scientific Management.* New York: Norton, 1967.

Tintner, Adeline. "Autobiography as Fiction: The 'Usurping Consciousness' as Hero of Henry James's Memoirs." *Twentieth Century Literature* 23 (1977): 239–60.

Trachtenberg, Alan. *The Incorporation of America: Culture and Society in the Gilded Age.* New York: Hill and Wang, 1982.

Tuttle, William M., Jr. "W. E. B. DuBois' Confrontation with White Liberalism during the Progressive Era: A Phylon Document." *Phylon* 35 (1974): 241–58.

Urgo, Joseph. *Willa Cather and the Myth of American Migration.* Urbana: University of Illinois Press, 1995.

Wagner-Martin, Linda. "The Hemingway-Stein Story." In *Ernest Hemingway: Seven Decades of Criticism,* edited by Linda Wagner-Martin, 389–401. East Lansing: Michigan State University Press, 1998.

Wald, Lillian D. *The House on Henry Street.* New York: Dover, 1971.

Wald, Priscilla. *Constituting Americans: Cultural Anxiety and Narrative Form.* Durham: Duke University Press, 1995.

Warren, Kenneth. *Black and White Strangers: Race and American Literary Realism.* Chicago: University of Chicago Press, 1993.

———. "Troubled Black Humanity in *The Souls of Black Folk* and *The Autobiography of an Ex-Coloured Man.*" In *The Cambridge Companion to American Realism and Naturalism: Howells to London,* edited by Donald Pizer, 163–77. New York: Cambridge University Press, 1995.

Warren, Lansing. "Gertrude Stein Views Life and Politics." *New York Times,* 6 May 1934, SM23.

Waters, Mary C. *Ethnic Options: Choosing Identities in America.* Berkeley: University of California Press, 1990.

Watten, Barrett. "An Epic of Subjectivation: *The Making of Americans,*" *Modernism/ Modernity* 5 (1998): 95–121.

Weinstein, Cindy. *Family, Kinship, and Sympathy in Nineteenth-Century American Literature.* New York: Cambridge University Press, 2004.

Wells, Ida B. "Lynching and the Excuse for It." *New York Independent* 53 (1901): 1133–6.

———. "A Red Record." In *Southern Horrors and Other Writings,* edited by Jacqueline Jones Royster, 73–157. Boston: Bedford Books, 1997.

Westbrook, Robert B. *John Dewey and American Democracy.* Ithaca: Cornell University Press, 1991.

White, Morton. *Social Thought in America: The Revolt Against Formalism.* New York: Viking, 1949.

White, Walter. *Rope and Faggot: A Biography of Judge Lynch.* New York: Alfred A. Knopf, 1929.

Wiegman, Robyn. *American Anatomies: Theorizing Race and Gender.* Durham: Duke University Press, 1995.

———. "The Anatomy of Lynching." *Journal of the History of Sexuality* 3 (1993): 445–67.

Will, Barbara. *Gertrude Stein, Modernism, and the Problem of "Genius."* Edinburgh: Edinburgh University Press, 2000.

Wirth-Nesher, Hana. *Call It English: The Languages of Jewish-American Literature.* Princeton: Princeton University Press, 2006.

Wolfson, Susan. *Formal Charges: The Shaping of Poetry in British Romanticism.* Stanford: Stanford University Press, 1997.

Wyschogrod, Edith. *An Ethics of Remembering: History, Heterology, and the Nameless Others.* Chicago: University of Chicago Press, 1998.

Yezierska, Anzia. *Bread Givers.* New York: Persea Books, 2003.

Zangwill, Israel. *The Melting-Pot.* New York: Macmillan, 1920.

Zeidel, Robert F. *Immigrants, Progressives, and Exclusion Politics: The Dillingham Commission, 1900–1927.* DeKalb: Northern Illinois University Press, 2004.

✒ INDEX

Note: Page numbers in *italics* indicate figures.